Animation
Under the Swastika

It is the unique German mental and emotional world as it is expressed in medieval puppet plays and death dances, in the fairy tales by the Brothers Grimm, by Musaeus and Hauff, in the spooky tales by E.T.A. Hoffmann, the fantasies of Munchhausen etc., that should perform as the source of ideas for German animation films. [...] The German artist should be able to set against American style something totally equal, even superior and originally German with a little support. Certainly the idiosyncrasy of works inspired by the true German spirit should be successful beyond our borders in practice and for sentimental value and would mean important promotion of our culture.

Der Zeichen- und Trickfilm: Neue Ausdrucksmöglichkeiten für die künstlerische Kinematographie (Berlin, March 14, 1935)

Animation Under the Swastika

A History of Trickfilm in Nazi Germany, 1933–1945

Rolf Giesen and J. P. Storm

McFarland & Company, Inc., Publishers
Jefferson, North Carolina, and London

Also of Interest

Special Effects Artists: A Worldwide Biographical Dictionary of the Pre–Digital Era with a Filmography, by Rolf Giesen (McFarland, 2008)

Nazi Propaganda Films: A History and Filmography, by Rolf Giesen (McFarland 2003; paperback 2008)

Photographs courtesy of the J.P. Storm collection unless otherwise indicated

Library of Congress Cataloguing-in-Publication Data

Giesen, Rolf.
Animation under the swastika : a history of trickfilm in Nazi Germany, 1933–1945 / Rolf Giesen and J.P. Storm.
p. cm.
Includes bibliographical references and index.

ISBN 978-0-7864-4640-7
softcover : acid free paper ∞

1. Animated films — Germany — History and criticism. 2. National socialism and motion pictures. I. Storm, J.P. II. Title.
NC1766.G3G54 2012
791.43'34094309043 — dc23 2012021541

British Library cataloguing data are available

Front cover: Deutsche Zeichenfilm G.m.b.H. (DZF) 1941, artist unknown (collection of J.P. Storm); cover design by David K. Landis (Shake It Loose Graphics)

Manufactured in the United States of America

McFarland & Company, Inc., Publishers
Box 611, Jefferson, North Carolina 28640
www.mcfarlandpub.com

Acknowledgments

For information, interviews and notes the authors wish to thank Ferdinand Diehl, Peter A. Hagemann, Gerhard Huttula, Ernst Joachim Schienke, Herbert K. Schulz, H[ugo] O[tto] Schulze, Heinz Wolfgang Tischmeyer, Dr. William Moritz, who have all passed away; Dr. Günther Agde, André Eckardt, Elfriede Fischinger, Dr. Ralf Forster, Jeanpaul Goergen (*CineGraph Babelsberg*), Monika Gruss, Werner Hierl, Antonín Horák, Daniel Kothenschulte, Sébastien Roffat, Ulrich Stoll, Christel Strobel, Stefan Thies and Peter Völker.

J. P. Storm conducted interviews with:

Horst Alisch	trainee, DZF	June 17, 1988, in Berlin
Ingeburg Ammon	DZF	February 18, 1989, in Berlin
Irene Arnold	DZF	March 11, 1989, in Göttingen
Werner Bernhardy	Ufa	May 22, 1997, in Berlin
Gerhard Fieber	Ufa/DZF	July 25, 1988/March 10, 1996, in Schlangenbad
Eveline Fischer	DZF	March 11, 1989, in Göttingen
Bernhard Friebel	trainee, DZF	February 2, 1990, in Berlin
Anneliese Gerndt	trainee, DZF	May 14, 1990, in Berlin
Ludwig G'schrey	Fischerkoesen	November 24, 1989, in Berlin
Hans Held	Bavaria	May 12, 1988, in Wessobrunn-Haid
Dr. Werner Kruse	Kruse-Film, Ufa, DZF	August 9, 1988, in Berlin
Horst von Möllendorff	DZF/Fischerkoesen	July 30, 1988, in Berlin
Erika Müller	trainee, DZF	April 23, 1990, in Berlin
Milly Pfützner	DZF	February 5, 1990, in Berlin
Helmuth Plagge	Fischerkoesen	May 22, 1990, in Babelsberg
Günter Schilling	trainee, DZF	May 12, 1988, in Percha
Inge Schittat	DZF	June 4, 1997, in Berlin
Christel Schukat	Fischerkoesen	May 2, 1996, in Bonn
Edgar Schulze	trainee, DZF	May 12, 1990, in Berlin
Helga Seifert	DZF	May 4, 1988, in Berlin
Stephanie Steuer	Ufa/Tobis/DZF	September 22, 1988/March 31, 1989, in Berlin
Anna-Luise Subatzus	DZF	March 11, 1989, in Göttingen

Alfred Thamm	Kruse-Film	June 2, 1997, in Berlin
Eveline Vogel	DZF	February 12, 1990, in Berlin
Sigrid Vogt	trainee, DZF	January 11, 1989, in Berlin
Kurt Weber	DZF	February 3, 1989, in Berlin

All interviewees, some of whom have passed away in the meantime, gave permission to quote them in any kind of publication. In some cases we asked the heirs to renew permission. In spring 2011 we obtained permission from Dr. Hans Fischerkoesen, son of Hans Fischerkoesen; Erika Held, widow of Hans Held; Thomas Stordel, grandson of Kurt Stordel. We appreciate their helpfulness.

More material and information was supplied during the conference, Der deutsche Zeichentrickfilm vor 1945, organized by Deutsche Kinemathek Berlin and hosted by Rolf Giesen in June 2003. Thanks to participants Gerhard Fieber, who generously compiled a paper on the history of Deutsche Zeichenfilm G.m.b.H., and the late Heinz Kaskeline, son of Wolfgang Kaskeline.

The following archives, libraries and institutions helped with documents: Bundesarchiv-Filmarchiv [Federal Archive/Film Archive] Berlin and Koblenz, Berlin Document Center, Staatsbibliothek Berlin, Bayerische Staatsbibliothek Munich, Deutsches Institut für Zeitgeschichte Munich, Deutsches Institut für Filmkunde Frankfurt am Main, Nederlands Instituut voor Animatiefilm (NIAf), Tilburg, Rolf Giesen Collection/ Deutsche Kinemathek [German Cinematheque] Berlin.

Stills depict original artwork from various productions that has been purchased and collected by J. P. Storm, Essen, Germany. The publication of some other stills (Fischerkoesen, Held, Stordel) is made possible with the kind permission of the respective estates. Gerhard Neumann and Gisela Erika Neumann, two of Karl Neumann's children, provided rare stills.

Our grateful thanks are due to Mike Hankin for proofreading and editing tips. Special thanks to Verena from J. P. Storm and to Anna from Rolf Giesen.

Table of Contents

Preface

Recently this author (RG) talked to Israeli filmmaker Ari Folman about his highly personal animation documentary, *Waltz with Bashir*, screened at the Cannes Film Festival in 2008. It retold Folman's traumatic experiences surrounding the massacre of Palestinian refugees during the first Lebanon war in the early 1980s. Together we pondered why there was no personal animation entry dealing with the Third Reich and World War II by a German filmmaker. Oddly enough, the only noteworthy, emotionally moving and still highly impressive animated anti–Nazi cartoon was produced by an American in 1943: No, it's not *Der Fuehrer's Face* but another by Disney, *Education for Death: The Making of a Nazi* from a book by Gregor Ziemer. Folman looked me straight in the face and asked: "Have you ever seen *any* film made by a German that deals with the Nazi era in a personal way, truly describing the sentiments of the filmmaker, his feelings and emotions and not only his intellectual excuse?"

Hitler and Goebbels were cartoon aficionados. There is no doubt about that. Hitler was no philanderer as Reinhard Spitzy, a former National Socialist functionary and diplomat, told TV interviewers.[1] He and Goebbels loved animation and what was left of German animation after World War II seems still under their spell, as are so many things in Germany. They tried hard to establish a cartoon industry to rival Disney and competed with American producers in a love-hate relationship, studying their films behind locked doors. All that remained of their ambitious dreams were a few nice, not overly ambitious cartoon shorts, advertising and puppet films with no propaganda value at all but which illustrate the phrase Hannah Arendt coined in connection with the Eichmann trial: "banality of evil."[2] Of course, there were ideas. Even Nazis have them. Grand ideas. Megalomaniac ideas. Karl Neumann, one of Goebbels' cohorts and head of Deutsche Zeichenfilm G.m.b.H., in all seriousness suggested the transformation of Crimea, with most of it occupied, into the biggest cartoon factory in the world. The tyrants didn't realize that one cannot decree art. There was no freedom in Nazi Germany, no freedom of art and no freedom of will. And Nazi bureaucracy by no means was creative. It was destructive until self-destruction.

Nevertheless, after the war, some critics feared that fairy tale adaptations might not be as harmless as people thought. They feared the pagan violence and cruelty of, for example, the Grimm brothers' tales. Could a story such as that of two kids, Hansel and Gretel, who burnt an old witch, still be told after having heard about the gas chambers and furnaces of Auschwitz? Were these fairy tales constitutive to the German national identity as well as Nazi ideology? This is why after the war German film producers preferred to adapt rather tame versions of Grimm's tales *Kinder- und Hausmärchen.*

In more than 25 years of research, my associate, J. P. Storm, has amassed every kind of document and met many eyewitnesses to Nazi Germany's cartoon dream, some of whom have passed away since. Storm and I had already worked together, in 1986, compiling a wonderful exhibition on the history of animation in Berlin and Frankfurt am Main, and now decide it is time to finally publish this account of a little bourgeois' presumption that failed in establishing a cartoon industry, as well as establishing the Thousand-Year Reich.

Rolf Giesen

1

Optical Lyric and Shadow Plays: The Early History of German Animation

In 1910 veteran cinematographer Friedrich Konrad Guido Seeber (1879–1940), son of a photographer, created what is regarded the first animation ever done in Germany on film. For a 3-minute short, *Der Streichholzkünstler* (*The Match Artist*), Seeber, in a small notebook, prepared an exact storyboard for every scene involving animated matches that would change into various forms and faces, finally building a windmill and burning themselves.

Some years later Seeber, Germany's premier trickfilm technician, became the favorite cameraman of another visionary, actor Paul Wegener (1874–1948), the original *Student of Prague* and *The Golem*. A major force in German silent film, Wegener had a fascination with the romantic and fairy tales that helped shape the creative destiny of his country's fledgling movie industry. Wegener was also one of the earliest advocates of a synthetic cinema using all possible camera effects and animation not as novelty or gimmick but as art. In a 1915 lecture held on Easter Sunday at the vocal arts school in Berlin, Wegener spoke prophetically of his dream to engender an absolutely artificial, animated movie and foresaw what Walt Disney later tried to accomplish with his *Fantasia* project in the 1940s:

> You have all seen films in which suddenly a line appears, curves and changes its form. Out of it grow faces and the line disappears. To me the impression seems highly remarkable. But such things are always shown as an intermezzo and nobody has ever thought of the colossal possibilities of this technique. I think the film as art should be based—as in the case of music—on tones, on rhythm. In these changeable planes, events unreel which are partly identified with natural pattern, yet partly beyond real lines and forms. Imagine one of [Arnold] Böcklin's sea paintings with all the fabulous tritons and nereids. And imagine an artist duplicating this work in hundreds of copies but with each copy having small displacements so that all copies revealed in succession would result in continuous movement. Suddenly we would see before our very eyes a world of pure fantasy come to life. Such effects can also be achieved with specially-constructed little models animated like marionettes.... We are entering a new pictorial fantasy world as we would enter a magic forest. We are setting foot in the field of pure kinetics—or optical lyric as I call it. This field will perhaps be of major importance and will open new beautiful sights. This eventually is the

> final objective of each art, and so cinema would gain an autonomous aesthetic domain for itself. A movie could be created which would become an experience of art — an optical vision, a great symphonic fantasy! That it will happen one day, I am sure — and beyond that, I am certain, later generations will look upon our early efforts as upon childish stuttering.

In the audience was a 15-year-old admirer of Wegener, Lotte Reiniger (1899–1981), who was determined to measure up to this great man. As a girl her enthusiasm for Shakespeare led her construct a primitive shadow theater to perform his classic plays. Wegener became aware of Lotte's ability to cut out silhouettes of actors and actresses in their characteristic poses and asked her to create the title silhouettes and some model animation of rats for his 1918 film version of *Der Rattenfänger* (*The Pied Piper of Hamelin*). One year later Wegener introduced her to a studio for experimental films where she did her first animated silhouette film, *Das Ornament des verliebten Herzens* (*The Ornament of the Heart in Love*), and thus animated on film what had begun in China in the year 1000 A.D. as shadow play. In 1923, with half a dozen collaborators, she started the most ambitious project of her life, one of the first feature-length animated films in history, the silhouette production *Die Abenteuer des Prinzen Achmed* (*The Adventures of Prince Achmed*). An adaptation of the Thousand and One Nights and Chinese sources, a hero's brave battle against an evil sorcerer and the demons from the mysterious kingdom of Wak Wak, it was premiered in September 1926 at the Gloria Palace in Berlin.

2

The March of the Cigarettes

Except for *Prinz Achmed,* however, animation in Germany was reduced to experimental shorts, made by artists like Hans Richter (1888–1976) or Swedish-born Dada artist Viking Eggeling (1880–1925), which, when the filmmakers were lucky, were shown and financed as advertising films. One who saw the enormous possibilities of animated cartoons in advertising was Julius Pinschewer (1883–1961). Pinschewer produced animated commercials from 1912 until 1933, when he left Germany. He even saw that his idea of producing advertising films was patented: "In 1910, when for the first time I attended a cinema, the hundreds of eyes fixed to the screen gave me the idea to use film for promotion."[1] At one time or another, most German animators worked for him. Besides Lotte Reiniger there were Hermann Abeking, Harry Jäger, Hans Zoozmann and Rudi Klemm who animated the silhouettes for the first German sound cartoon, *Die chinesische Nachtigall* (*The Chinese Nightingale*) from the fairy tale by Hans Christian Andersen in 1929.

Even the abstract animation done by Oskar Fischinger (1900–1967) ended as advertisement for tobacco manufacturers, in order to earn bread and butter, like the marching and dancing cigarettes from *Muratti greift ein* (1934). Fischinger's biographer William Moritz called it a miracle of clever animation: "After numerous tests with drawn cigarettes (some showing cigarettes parachuting down on to live-action Wilhelm Straße and walking through the Brandenburg Gate) and actual tobacco cigarettes, Oskar opted for a laborious process of creating small wooden sticks the same size and oval shape as Muratti cigarettes, covering them with genuine Muratti cigarette paper, then fixing a pin into the bottom of each. [...] The 'stage' was a meter-diameter table on ball-bearings, so that it could be moved small calibrated increments to give the impression that the cigarettes would be walking past the background, or that the camera was moving past the scene on a dolly. The glass top of the round table was covered with a layer of kaolin, then sprinkled with sawdust dyed to resemble tobacco. Each 'cigarette' stood up by having its pin stuck down into the kaolin (the sawdust obscured the pinholes), and had to be pulled up and re-inserted for each new frame's exposure — and in many scenes dozens of individual cigarettes are moving at the same time."[2] Like *Komposition in Blau (Composition in Blue,* 1934–35), *Muratti greift ein* was produced in the beautiful Gasparcolor process.[3]

The first to do a commercial with animated cigarettes, however, was Hungarian George Pál (born Gyula György [Pál] Marczincsák, 1908–1980):

> Having graduated from the Technical High School in Budapest, Georg Pál one day happened to stray into a film laboratory, where he learned the technique of trick filming. Confident of his ability to succeed in this field, he later formed a concern of his own and produced advertising films for home and foreign firms. To increase his chances he transferred to Germany and obtained in Berlin a situation as trick film designer, and was eventually engaged by the UFA [Universum Film Aktiengesellschaft] as Chief Designer. In eighteen months he produced here 23 advertising films and also worked during this period for the Scherl Verlag, who published his Habakuk series.[4]

UFA wanted him to rival the stop-motion animation made at Pinschewer's studio. In March 1930 Pinschewer-Film A.-G. had released a puppet advertising film for Nestlé's Milk Chocolate, *Kirmes in Hollywood (Ein Puppenspiel):* Puppet duplicates of actors Emil Jannings and Buster Keaton face each other in a boxing match. Buster wins thanks to delicious Nestlé chocolate and receives from Miss Arabella's hands the prize money of $1,000. Hedwig and Gerda Otto, mother and daughter, had done this short. They were experts in puppet making and animating. Pinschewer had already secured their services to film two other stop-motion shorts, *Im Filmatelier* (1927) and *Das Wetterhäuschen* (1929).[5]

On October 15, 1931, joined by Paul Wittke Jr., a Berlin businessman, Pál founded Trickfilm-Studio G.m.b.H. Pál & Wittke. After a while he completely switched from 2D to 3D which became the basic principle of his later *Puppetoons* replacement series, produced in Eindhoven, Netherlands (for Philips Radio) and Hollywood, U.S.A. (for Paramount release). H.O. Schulze, who was Pál's cinematographer, recalls:

> I became acquainted with George Pál at Ufa Werbefilm where I was responsible for model animation photography and for the photographic quality of the cartoons. In 1932, when he decided to leave Ufa and establish his own company, Pál asked if I was interested in joining him. He told me that he had in mind something really unusual and that he wanted to equip his new studio in a very up-to-date manner. Always interested in experiments, I accepted. Our first commission was an advertising film for Oberst Cigarettes. Pál didn't want to have it drawn frame by frame in the common cartoon fashion, but to do it instead with dimensional animation. A blade of tobacco would fold up by itself, glide into a paper husk, stand up, get legs, and a head and so on. Then the twenty cigarettes from one package would form a squadron, with an *oberst* (colonel) commanding in front, and would march through a futuristic setting which consisted of cigarette packages. The main street of our set was about thirty feet long and ran the whole length of the studio. The cigarettes for each animation step were mounted on boards. All in all, we had approximately sixteen or eighteen boards with squadrons of cigarettes in various walking positions to complete one single walking step which, repeatedly used, resulted in a walking cycle.[6]

When the Nazis came to power Pál left Germany and eventually settled in Eindhoven where he set up Palstudio and worked for Philips Radio. With the outbreak of World War II and Hitler invading the Netherlands as well as the rest of Western Europe, George Pál became a famed puppet producer, branching out into science fiction and fantasy, in Hollywood. Only once did he return to Germany, to do location shots (in Rothenburg ob der Tauber and Dinkelsbühl, near Munich) for Cinerama's *The Wonderful World of the Brothers Grimm* in 1962.

Pál and Fischinger, however, were not the only ones who were interested in model or three-dimensional animation. There was a trend towards puppet animation in those years. In a special screening on February 17, 1930, the *Marmorhaus*, a leading Berlin cinema that belonged to Ufa's chain of film theaters, presented, besides some Mickey Mouse and Silly Symphonies cartoons, a silent puppet film by Ladislas Starevich which was made in 1928 and helped to create a wave: *Zinnsoldaten*. One reviewer compared this short with the imaginative fantasy tales by E.T.A. Hoffmann.[7]

Alexander Gumitsch, a Berlin animator, announced his Plastic Trickfilm process and made *Spuk im Äther*:

> A new course [in animation] has been taken by the Plastic Trickfilm invented by Alexander Gumitsch. One recently could see his convincing tests in the screening room of a film laboratory. Alexander Gumitsch, a sculptor by profession (as puppet filmmaker Starevich), a disciple of Ignatz Taschner, moulds his baroque stylized characters, humans and animals, from clay which he can manipulate into the same funny effects as Walt Disney does with his Mickey Mouse. We saw intriguingly funny excerpts from a short film by Alexander Gumitsch, *Spuk im Äther*, dancing penguins at South Pole, a cat's duet on the roofs of New York, a boxing match between to champions et al.[8]

Another German puppet film pioneer was Alexander von Gontscharoff-Mussalewsky, who on July 28, 1931, applied for a patent for plastic characters for trickfilms which was granted (patent no. 603339) on September 13, 1934. In early 1933, Gontscharoff in his studio in Berlin Dahlem finished a cliché-ridden puppet film for Terra-Film A.-G. featuring the usual racial stereotypes by starring a "stupid Negro," Jim, and his donkey, Plim, in *Hilfe ein Löwe.*

In April 1934, backed by Zeiss Ikon A.-G. in Dresden, Richard Groschopp, who began as a film amateur before he entered professional ranks, presented a puppet film in 9.5 mm format, *Die wundersamen Abenteuer des kleinen Mutz* (a boy's rocket flight to Planet X). It won the silver medal at the 1935 International Amateur Film Festival in London. In 1934 Groschopp animated another short, titled *Eine kleine Königstragödie*, that used chess pieces. It was so impressive that Dresden producer Fritz Boehner (Boehner Film) asked him to redo it on 35mm. It was released by Tobis as a supplement short to Veit Harlan's propaganda film *Der Herrscher* (The Ruler, 1937), starring Emil Jannings and extoling the leadership principle.

Highly popular in Germany, as everywhere in the world, were Willis H. O'Brien's stop-motion dinosaurs and monsters from *The Lost World* (1925) and *King Kong* (1933), which in fact became one of Hitler's favorite movies. Concurrently, Major Hans Ewald of Ewald-Film in Berlin had created a plastilene dinosaur short, *Aus der Urzeit der Erde,* as early as 1925.

In Soviet Russia (1934–35), animation and fantasy film pioneer Aleksandr Ptushko combined puppets and people in *Novyj Gulliver* (*New Gulliver*).

America's competition, however, was pretty tough for the Germans as cinema audiences preferred 2D animation back then. Enviously filmmakers in Europe looked on Walt Disney's international success.

In 1931 SPD, the Social Democratic Party of Germany, released a campaign short by Karl Holtz and Alois Floroth with the visionary title *Ins Dritte Reich!* (*Into the Third Reich!*), technically and aesthetically low-standard cut-out animation. Content-wise it was a clear challenge to the Nazi Party, which had become a serious force in the Reich and promptly forbade this short after coming to power in January 1933. But the Nazis themselves did not do what would have seemed natural: use animation mainly for propaganda. Their interest in animation was to compete with Disney cartoons — and a Disney cartoon had to be nice. Predominantly.

3

Tilo Voss *and the Development of German Sound Cartoons*

A successful evolution of animated subjects often depends on the standard of comic book publishing. Unlike in America there never was much in Germany, neither before nor after the war. One of the few exceptions was a bimonthly children's magazine titled *Dideldum* that had been published since 1929. The cartoonist behind the magazine was Otto Waffenschmied (born on June 16, 1901, in Vienna as Otto Wawrzycke, he legally changed his surname to Waffenschmied in 1918). Waffenschmied had a joint venture with Karstadt department stores as the youth loved his cartoons *Muck, Puck und Adelheid* as well as *Max und Miki als Weltenbummler* (*Max and Miki as Globetrotters*).

It seemed natural to involve Waffenschmied in some sort of film production. In the mid–1930s Tolirag, Doering, Boehner and many small companies mainly produced animated advertising films. Between July 1935 and June 1936 they released 570 commercials (60,044 meters), 404 of these sound films. Additionally there were 220 advertising films in 16mm. The biggest and most prestigious manufacturer was Universum Film Aktiengesellschaft (Ufa).

In October 1934 Ufa commissioned Waffenschmied to develop a new animated cartoon character. After some research Waffenschmied came up with an old German fairy-tale sylvan elf, Tilo Voss, whom he thought would fit the purpose. On November 30, 1934, Waffenschmied was able to screen a test film for the Ufa board of directors. On December 7, 1934, the board of directors discussed the topic of cartoon fairy-tales which would make use of Ufa's new color film stock:

> Herr Lehmann reported on the planned production of fairy-tale films based on the ideas of Herr Waffenschmied as follows:
>
> The production of a color fairy-tale film of c. 250 meters will cost RM 20,000. Enclosed in this sum are the net costs plus production costs of Ufa-Werbefilm, additionally an extra allowance for the heads of trickfilm studios mainly involved in the production, Huth and von Tresckow. Not enclosed is the compensation for ideas and cooperation of Herr Waffenschmied.
>
> A reduction in production costs will be possible if instead of one three films will be projected immediately which would mean a reduction of c. RM 3,000,- per film.
>
> As these fairy-tale films are an attempt to produce novel supplement features, notwithstanding the saving in production costs, only one film should be tackled in the beginning.
>
> Basically it has been decided that Herr Waffenschmied shall discuss his ideas with the

scenario department of Ufa and that the trickfilm unit will receive complete, finished screenplays which will be adapted by Mr. Huth for the special needs of trickfilm directing. The completion of the animated drawings based on the artwork provided by Herr Waffenschmied will be committed to artists' unit von Tresckow which is to release temporarily from advertising film assignments to finish the first fairy-tale film. Hereby exact data will be compiled for a precise estimate of cost. The production is to be promoted so that the first film will be available for distribution program 1935/36.

[In charge Mssrs. Correll, Lehmann, Meydam]

A few months later, on March 12, 1935, the board of directors had serious doubts about the topic to be used in a trickfilm. The advertising film department was asked to revise the story if not to disband the project completely.

On April 10, 1935, a revised script was submitted and the Ufa board of directors gave the green light provided the project would not exceed RM 20,000. Two weeks later, on April 24, 1935, production was stopped again as the movie now would have a length of 300 meters and therefore would cost RM 32,000.

On May 7, 1935, Ufa production chief Ernst Hugo Correll reported to the board of directors

that Waffenschmied's first draft didn't have enough gags. For this reason the manuscript had to be changed to American slapstick. In the new version it is suitable.

The production costs can be reduced, excluding the fee for Herr Waffenschmied, to RM 26,000.

But as the production of color prints would increase the costs for the film considerably the production of the Waffenschmied film shall be terminated nevertheless.

Herr Dr. von Boehmer is asked to check if there is a legal or moral obligation to reimburse Herr Waffenschmied for the work. Mssrs. Correll, Meydam and Lehmann are authorized to negotiate the compensation with Herr Waffenschmied.

A few weeks later, on May 21, 1935, the Ufa board of directors once more had changed its mind and this time accepted a budget of RM 27,000 but when Waffenschmied asked for another RM 2,000 above his regular fee of RM 3,000 Ufa gave up conclusively and cancelled the project.

In September 1935 the whole project had been terminated.

A record of the meeting of Ufa board of directors on September 6, 1935, says:

Herr Lehmann reports about the differences between Ufa and Waffenschmied re: color short film "Tilo Voss." According to the present suggestions made by Waffen-

Tilo Voss project (1935): advertisement.

schmied who contractually has to be involved in production the film would be twice as long and cost three to four times above the approved budget. Ufa has agreed to terminate Waffenschmied's contract if Waffenschmied compensates Ufa for the previous costs of RM 14,000.

[In Charge Mssrs. Grieving, Lehmann]

On February 2, 1937, Ultra Film Berlin made Ufa an offer to produce a color cartoon titled *Die drei getreuen Häschen* (*The Three Faithful Bunnies*). As Ufa initially showed some interest Ultra-Film agreed instead of using Gasparcolor to produce in Ufa Color. However, Ufa remained skeptical and asked Ultra Film to submit a sequence list and one frame detailing each sequence tentatively. Generalmusikdirektor Dr. Julius Kopsch was asked to create a score. He seemed to dislike bunnies and instead preferred dachshunds. One board member came up with a wire fox terrier. On April 6, 1937 the bunny picture was stopped.

Still searching for suitable cartoons on August 9, 1937, Ernst Hugo Correll reported to the board of directors that *Société française des films en couleur*, a Paris company, which was financed by a certain Fabry, would produce animated cartoons along the lines of Walt Disney's Mickey Mouse:

The participating artists are Aryan.

Fabry is prepared to resign and handle the financial transactions.

The company is willing to produce such films on commission for us. They ask for ffrs 450,000,- per film of 300 meters length.

The company is inclined to grant us an option on purchase of the first of these films.

The rights for distribution abroad would be granted to us as well.

The Board takes note of this matter, a final decision should be made after screening films.

On August 20, 1937, the protocol stated that the board of directors had viewed two color films of Fabry production: *Rubens et son temps* and *Jour et Nuit*. It was stated that the company had acquired the rights to Jules Verne's works and intended to produce a series of three Verne pictures, but nothing came out of it.

Ufa got stuck in the attempt to rival Disney's Silly Symphonies. And then came Snow White.

4

How Walt Disney Became Walter Distler: Snow White *for Greater Germany*

Until 1939 most American distributors still had subsidiaries in Germany. In this time more than 250 features and countless shorts were sold to the Third Reich. On long evenings he spent in his Berghof resort Adolf Hitler screened many U.S. movies, including *King Kong*, and films of Fred Astaire, Laurel & Hardy (*Swiss Miss*), and others.

Due to the economic crisis in 1932, 6,000 of 19,000 cinemas in the United States had to be closed, so the American film industry had to rely on export even more to make up for losses. At this time German film distributors had released more than 100 short subjects produced by Disney, starting with *Oswald the Lucky Rabbit*, which was originally made available by Universal's German outfit Matador Filmverleih. Additionally there were *Betty Boop* and *Popeye* cartoons distributed by the German branch of Paramount Pictures.

In the period 1933–34 Germany registered 245 million cinema visits, a number that would triple until 1940. In early 1933 Arthur W. Kelly, vice president of United Artists Corporation, visited several European countries, among them Germany. A few days after Hitler's final rise to power, on February 1, Kelly held a press conference and said that the American film industry couldn't ignore the fact of a hundred million German speakers in Western Europe. Kelly therefore was inviting partners to join him in coproduction. He arranged a special screening of Disney color cartoons in Berlin's Paramount offices. Although Ufa was not interested in coproduction, the concern liked Disney's Technicolor *Silly Symphonies*. On October 13, 1933, the Ufa board of directors approved the purchase of five color Sillys and five black-and-white Mickeys which also would be released as compilation program in Berlin's renowned Marmorhaus theatre.

In 1935 Walt Disney himself, accompanied by his brother Roy, visited Germany for the first time, after negotiating in London and being honored in Paris for introducing through Mickey Mouse an international symbol for goodwill. They drove to Munich where another anthology of Disney shorts (*Die lustige Palette — Im Reiche der Micky Maus*) was screened. Apparently they attended a convention of the Reichsfilmkammer and then, according to a German animator, were flown to Berlin to meet with representatives of the government. Nobody knows exactly whom Disney met in Berlin: Dr. Goebbels, the minister of enlightenment and propaganda? Hitler himself? No document survives. All is speculation. Goebbels didn't mention any meeting in his diary, so it is not likely that they met him or the Führer himself.[1]

There is no speculation about the fact that Hitler loved Mickey Mouse, as indicated in the diary of Dr. Goebbels, Wednesday, 20 December 1937: "As a Christmas present I gave the Führer 30 top movies of the past four years and 18 Mickey Mouse films. He is pleased to no end. Glad to have that treasure which hopefully will give him joy and relaxation." One document about submitting Disney shorts to the Führer reads[2]:

> Reichsministerium
> für Volksaufklärung und Propaganda
>
> Berlin W 8, 27 July 1937
> Wilhelmplatz 8–9
> Phone: A 1 Jäger 0014
>
> To
> Adjutant of the Führer
> ------------
>
> By order of Herr Obergruppenführer [Lt. General Wilhelm] Brückner, we herewith deliver film prints for your archive
>
> 1. Italian movie *Mario* (Italian original with no German subtitles)
> 2. Five Mickey Mouse films: *Romeo und Julia, Käsepiraten, Feuer und Traumland, Das grosse Rennen, Jägerlatein*
>
> Invoices over RM 501.50 and RM 199.64 are attached. May we ask you for immediate payment on behalf of Deutsch-Italienische Film-Union GmbH. resp. Deutsche Fox-Film A.G.
>
> Heil Hitler!
> Signed,
> Seeger

Of course the Nazi film industry had high expectations to present Disney's most Teutonic entry, his first feature-length production, *Snow White and the Seven Dwarfs*, released in the United States in December 1937. The film's budget was $1.2 million, not really that expensive for a Technicolor feature at that time but still a high financial risk for Disney, who up till then had produced only short films, Mickey Mouse and Silly Symphonies. To make a decent profit or just to break even, Disney and other American producers badly needed the European market, including Germany.

The vast majority of German reviewers reported enthusiastically about Disney's successful release:

> On Christmas Eve the first feature-length fairy tale color cartoon, *Snow White and the Seven Dwarfs*, was premiered in Hollywood. It was a premiere event Hollywood hasn't seen for years. The most famous directors and actors attended the screening which took place in Hollywood's noble cinema Cathay Circus. The surroundings of the cinema were changed into a fairy tale kingdom with elves and gnomes which attracted many curious onlookers. During the screening and at the end the movie was met with great enthusiasm by the patrons.
>
> The film runs approximately one and a half hours at a cost of 3,000,000 Mark. 570 artists have worked on it since 1934. [...]
>
> The brilliant success, however, compensated for the high costs. The movie promises to become a global box-office success.[3]

No other American movie received that much attention in the National Socialist press. In 1938, 50 new U.S. movies were passed by the German censors. *Snow White*, however, was the last U.S. production that met with sympathy from many leading Nazi officials.

On February 5, 1938, the Führer himself ordered his adjutant to get him a print of Disney's hottest release for his private cinema on the Obersalzberg. Three weeks later Hitler was able to screen and view it. Without any doubt, it became one of the most cherished movie treasures of his film collection.[4]

However, certain columnists of German trade papers remained skeptical considering the high costs:

> We already have pointed out that the immensely blown-up coverage of the Walt Disney picture *Snow White and the Seven Dwarfs* represents extremely dangerous premature praise. Apart from that it is questionable if this picture will be released in Germany at all; apart from the fact that the costs of this movie amount to the whole annual production budget of a medium-sized German film company; apart from the fact that the number of contributors on this picture equals approximately the whole staff of Ufa Neubabelsberg; apart finally from the fact that Disney thanks to global release chances can work unrestrictedly while German animation artists Lotte Reiniger and Fischinger have left Germany and went abroad for lack of opportunity in Germany—who will guarantee that in this picture the greatest goods of German fairy tales have been preserved faithfully and were not changed into a drawn American revue? This doubt seems likely for one learns from England that the picture was passed by the Board of Censors into A category, i.e. juveniles under age 16 only allowed with parental guide. According to the judgment of the English censor the film contains several passages which are not suitable for children. And this in a Snow White film!!![5]

Nevertheless, the Ministry of Enlightenment and Propaganda, headed by Germany's no. 1 Disney fan, Dr. Goebbels, gave order to acquire *Snow White* for the Reich. Immediately, two German distribution companies set out and tried their luck.

> Protocol Board Meeting of UFA on April 1, 1938
> TOPIC 1)
> Walt Disney Color Film,
> *Snow White*
> The board had a screening of the fairy tale picture *Snow White* made in the Technicolor process by the Walt Disney Company. Mr. Meydam is authorized to conduct negotiations to acquire the German license of said picture and is asked to report to the board conditions for taking of decisions.
> Memo.
> Re: Meeting at Office Dr. Winkler in presence of Mr. Herbell, Klotzsch, Schweikart, Marthens, Raether, Dr. Winkler (handwritten note: on April 4 in Berlin)
> *Snow White* picture is interesting. We should report continuously.
> Signed, Klotzsch.

Ernst Walter Herbell and Fritz Klotzsch were production heads of Bavaria Filmkunst G.m.b.H., newly founded on February 11, 1938, in Munich, which now occupied the former Emelka Studios in Geiselgasteig and owned a distribution arm that included former Bayerische Film- und Verleihgesellschaft. Both companies, UFA as well as Bayerische, already had some experience in releasing Disney shorts. The negotiations on behalf of Bavaria Filmkunst were conducted by an authorized representative, Dr. iur. (Doctor of Civil Law) Hellmuth Keil, who had the power of procuration.

The office of Dr. Max Winkler apparently had given the green light to go ahead. Dr. h.c. (honoris causa) Max Winkler was a kind of éminence grise of press and film. For a short time in 1918 he had been mayor of Graudenz, which made him a mayor retired by title through all the time he served Dr. Goebbels and Nazi Germany. Since 1920 he successfully had acted as trustee on behalf of all German governments. As a "master of tactical dodges and evasions" he had found influential patrons among Hitler's and Göring's circles before both men came to power. In early March 1933, he got to know his new superior, Dr. Joseph Goebbels. Goebbels found warm words of welcome for Winkler: "You don't know how much I am going to appreciate your services and how intimately we know you."

In mid–1937 Goebbels promoted Winkler and made him Reichsbeauftragter in charge of the German film industry. This title included proxies that nobody else had. His decisions were, of course, always approved by Goebbels. So Winkler was the central link between German film boards and the Nazi administration. It was him who not only brought German press into line but also arranged and contrived the Gleichschaltung of Germany's leading film companies under the Reich's control in 1937.

Disney's American distributor, RKO Radio Pictures, had exported its last pictures to Germany in 1935. After that they closed their Berlin branch located on Friedrichstrasse 225 as it didn't seem profitable anymore. For this reason, Bavaria Filmkunst needed an experienced mediator. Although these mediators only had smaller film productions they had good business connections to domestic and foreign partners. Bayerische Film- und Verleihgesellschaft had acquired its Disney short program with the assistance of such a mediator. This practice saved large companies lots of business correspondence and sometimes the big ones hoped, a smaller company would exact lower fees.

To acquire *Snow White*, Bavaria commissioned the Berlin-based company Otzoup-Film, which had a good relationship with film companies in Spain and South America. For good measure, it additionally involved another Berlin-based company, Deka Film G.m.b.H. (Deutsche Kampffilm, Fasanenstrasse 74) to represent their interests for this animated feature.

On April 26, 1938, Dr. Winkler received a letter from Bavaria Company:

> Re: Walt Disney Picture of RKO., New York, *Snow White*.
>
> Dear Dr. Winkler!
>
> We would like to inform you that we are in negotiations for the distribution rights of above mentioned picture, which was notably in U.S.A. a big box-office success. In agreement with the distribution head of our distribution company, Mr. [Gustav] Berloger, we think that the acquisition of this picture would prove very lucky for us resp. our distribution company even more as we would release it in the first period, at a time when our first production program hasn't been finished. This would give us not only outwardly a good name card but also considerable box-office revenues. Mr. Berloger considers the financial chances of this film as very promising.
>
> Deka-Film GmbH., Berlin, already has direct ties with RKO., New York, which has acquired the picture for release in America and abroad. The negotiations are more interesting insofar as Deka possibly through the manager's, Baron von Hirschfeld, personal American relationship, can conduct the deal in a way that we might carry out the whole transaction in Reichsmark currency between German companies. This isn't sure yet but the negotiations are carried on that way. As Mr. Berloger who, by the way, has already seen the film told

us Tobis-Filmkunst GmbH. resp. Tobis Filmverleih GmbH. don't show interest in the picture in favour for us, rightfully realizing that Tobis has more movies than our company which was founded recently.

The negotiations with Deka have come to a standstill as Deka at your request for precise conditions hasn't received an answer for some time. According to informations we have received the reason should be that Ufa has started to negotiate directly about the picture with RKO., especially their Paris branch which handles European business for RKO.

It might be likely that we will intend ourselves in next time to go to Paris in the company of a gentleman of Deka to conduct straight negotiations with RKO. However, to conduct negotiations with RKO., we don't consider it useful if two companies — Ufa and us — will compete in front of RKO. because that would mean that conditions for German distribution might become worse on the part of RKO. Regarding that our company is the youngest among the existent film corporates and currently is not sufficiently supplied with film material we might imagine that you, dear Dr. Winkler, might work so that our company will receive a favorite position in the negotiations with RKO. Ufa is sufficiently supplied with film material from their actual business and would participate in the above mentioned picture provided we would distribute it because the picture would be screened in Ufa cinemas as well so that Ufa will have a share in the box-office receipts.

We would be very grateful, dear Dr. Winkler, if you would consider the question if in this case there shouldn't be a condition for Ufa that it would be wiser to refrain from negotiations in our favour in order to strengthen, as explained, the distribution situation of our company and reduce any grants that otherwise might be expected.

On May 3, 1938, the proxy of Bavaria Filmkunst, Dr. Hellmuth Keil, noticed regarding *Snow White*: "Deka continues negotiations. We try to get a print to Munich for State Minister Wagner and our cultural committee."

Although Bavarian state minister Adolf Wagner expressed sympathy for the newly founded Bavaria Filmkunst Filmverleih G.m.b.H. and suggested that *Snow White* would be the most ideal opening picture, the negotiations of the mediators continued slowly. With Bavaria Filmverleih head Gustav Berloger, this company at least had a man on board who had some experience in releasing and promoting Disney short animation.

Memo by Dr. Keil, May 17, 1938
Re: Deka-Film
Snow White negotiations

The Reich Economics Ministry reportedly hasn't decided about a foreign currency plan, especially the export of certain machines etc., to America to secure funding for the acquisition of this picture. Mr. Winkler shall decide after the decision of the Reich Economics Ministry.

Protocol Board Meeting of UFA on May 17, 1938
TOPIC 8)
American color picture
Snow White

This picture was offered to us for a price of $ 50,000. Further negotiations have been broken off because the American company refused to send print for internal viewing before Ufa would sign. It was decided to ask again for shipping a print. For the rest negotiations shall continue provided no foreign currencies would be required and in consideration that an asking price of RM 100,000 under no circumstances can be granted.

Protocol Board Meeting of UFA on June 3, 1938
TOPIC 11.)
Snow White
for Germany
UFA is willing to pay as license fee for the German distribution territory including Austria for American picture *Snow White* up to RM 150,000.

As already known, Bavaria Filmkunst G.m.b.H. needed the support of mediators to conduct their *Snow White* negotiations while UFA talked face to face with Disney's distributor, RKO. After the union (Anschluss) with Austria, the so-called Greater German Reich (Grossdeutschland), if only briefly, had an RKO branch located in Vienna. Ufa's feelers to RKO, however, didn't work successfully yet.

On the other hand, Bavaria Filmkunst booked its first financial request for an animation picture.

Memo by Dr. Keil June 10, 1938
Re: Deka-Film — Walt Disney picture
Snow White

During my absence on Tuesday and Wednesday of this week in Berlin I have discussed Deka's letter dated June 2, 1938, at great length with Mr. Berloger of the distribution company. Mr. Berloger thinks that we will need for the release of said picture, including reserves, a total of 120 prints. Incidentally, Mr. Berloger told me that his estimation for box-office receipts of this picture would be RM 1.3 million but had to admit that his estimation would be the lowest (one that his assistant had made up totaled RM 3 million). According to his distribution estimate Berloger assumes now too that expenditure of RM 1 million including prints, pre-release and premiere promotion as well as costs (until now not included) for shipping and customs, furthermore seals and contract costs would be way too high. Considering such a sum Mr. Berloger considers the business as not interesting. The limit to which one could go according to Berloger would be about RM 700.000. That means practically that we would need the required dollar sum in official currency.

I informed Mr. Berloger also about the content of Ufa's letter. Mr. Berloger thinks that we must succeed with Dr. Winkler in getting Ufa withdrawn from negotiations for then we could reach better conditions for ourselves. (This opinion contradicts the remarks of Deka-Film GmbH which points out that they already got better conditions than Ufa ever talked about with RKO).

On Wednesday a brief meeting re: above mentioned picture took place with Deka. I explained to Deka-Film that we cannot make a general statement re: letter, inasmuch, as Deka stressed that they couldn't give us definitive proposals before June 15. I therefore suggested first of all to have the final conditions announced by Deka so that we can prepare our statement. I indicated at least that an asking price of RM 1 million for above mentioned film would seem extremely high and that we would have no great hope to close a deal on that basis. I have made it clear that it would be recommendable for Deka to proceed as intended and acquire the required dollar sum to official currency. We agreed that Deka will let us know when definitive conditions are fixed. During the meeting with Deka I attached great importance to the fact that all expenses for the preparation of above mentioned deal of course will not touch us and in case that deal cannot be closed have to be covered by Deka.

Naturally for the German Ministry of Finance, an export of foreign currency totaling Reichsmark 1 million for an American cartoon feature would have been an incalculable risk, as at this point the average production costs of German features were far lower. Nevertheless, the Ministry of Enlightenment and Propaganda was still willing to grant the expenditure especially for this film.

Deka-Film GmbH. June 10, 1938
Re: *Snow White* picture.

We acknowledge receipt of your letter dated June 2 re: a brief meeting that took place on Wednesday with our Dr. Keil in Berlin. As we have stressed we are not capable — as you will not have expected — to give a statement to your comments as far as we don't know your definitive proposal and the conditions for our taking over above mentioned picture. Therefore we would ask you to open these as soon as possible so that we can proceed in negotiations. It is superfluous of course to point out that conditions especially regarding the currency to which dollar sums have to be acquired should be kept as low as possible so that the deal still will be interesting to us.

We are still looking forward to receiving a print of this film as per advice for an internal screening for State Minister Wagner and finally notice with satisfaction that for above mentioned picture you only negotiate with our company and will do so in the future.

The same day Bavaria Filmkunst G.m.b.H. (signed Klotzsch and Dr. Keil) approached again Mayor ret. Dr. Max Winkler:

Regarding further development of the deal one has to say that Deka-Film GmbH. has signed a pre-contract with RKO. and in this has reached by far better conditions than Ufa for above mentioned picture shall have debated. As Deka let us know Ufa shall not have negotiated about above mentioned picture in the past time. This statement is contradicted by above cited letter of Ufa.

According to previous reports by Deka-Film GmbH. we cannot definitely overlook if the conditions Deka will provide us would lead to closing the deal. At least it seems more opportune to us if only one German company would negotiate with RKO., Paris as we have mentioned in our letter of April 4, 1938. Since we furthermore, as we have explained to you, would be capable if at all to close the deal in a way that we have to pay only in Reichsmark we believe that our company will provide conditions which would be best for the German Reich regarding savings of foreign currency.

Therefore we ask you, in order to provide further support for our negotiations, to let Ufa know that they should abstain, withdraw from all further negotiations re: above mentioned picture.

That very day Bavaria addressed a letter also to Ufa-Filmverleih G.m.b.H.:

We regret we feel obliged not to respond to your request to abandon our activities re: above mentioned picture and cannot acknowledge this to you. We have already negotiated about the above mentioned picture through Deka-Film GmbH. for a long period, longer in fact than you estimate in your letter dated June 1 your own negotiations. The said company has already signed pre-contracts [letter of intent] with RKO.

Therefore we are surprised to hear from you that apparently negotiations between yourself and RKO. have been restarted. We only can explain this by the fact that RKO. are going to try to get better conditions.

In the interest of the whole German film industry and hence German Reich, we regard it inopportune if (at all) two German companies simultaneously negotiate with RKO., because this surely will have a negative effect on the conditions provided by RKO. Therefore we don't consider it right when previously terminated negotiations between yourself and RKO. are restarted. This would only lead to an interference of negotiations conducted on behalf of us by Deka-Film GmbH. This, however, cannot be in your interest inasmuch Deka-Film GmbH. tries to conduct the deal according to conditions on far easier terms than any other German company might get with the business manager of Deka-Film GmbH. Finally, we ask your permission to point out that, as newly founded company, we have to attach the greatest importance to above mentioned picture because with the release of this picture we could reach a reduction of expenses for the distribution company.

As you would participate in the picture's release through your company's movie theatres even if we would distribute it we are convinced that we can count on your understanding considering the above explained situation and would like to ask you to issue a statement that you will not continue negotiations with RKO.

Letter to:

Mayor ret.

Dr. Max Winkler June 28, 1938

Re: Movie *Snow White*

Dear Doctor Winkler!

Re: our correspondence we indulge ourselves in telling you that Deka-Film GmbH. negotiates about above mentioned picture with RKO. for a price of 150,000,- American dollar. This sum includes:

The license fee for Greater Germany (old Reich territory and Austria, Free City of Danzig, Memel territory, German ships on the high seas outside of three-miles zone.)

100–120 Technicolor color prints for 500 Dollars each in German language, free from New York harbor. (It is stated that the number of prints might be increased to maybe 120 without affecting the asking price of 150,000 $.)

The costs for dubbing as far as they originate from foreign country.

The production of a German sound and film negative as far as this is provided in Hollywood.

Free shipping of a foreign-language color print for censorship which has to be returned after passing board of censors.

Free shipping of a black and white print for dubbing in Germany. This print, too, will be returned after finishing work.

10 trailers for promotional campaign which show behind-the-scenes shots of work on *Snow White* picture.

4 sets of lobby cards.

The still negatives and slides.

The musical score and the music rights to Germany.

American pressbooks.

14-day free stay in Hollywood incl. trip from New York to Hollywood and back for a gentleman of Deka-Film GmbH to supervise the work and accept prints.

The payment of above mentioned sum shall be conducted in certain instalments (first instalment by signing of contracts, final instalment with shipping of last print included in contract). Payments in dollar to be made by Deka-Film GmbH would be guaranteed to

RKO by the uncle of Baron Hirschberg [*sic* Baron von Hirschfeld], business manager and head of Deka-Film GmbH, Mister Eberhard Faber, New York.

As according to our current agreements the complete dollar transaction shall not touch our company and our own payment to Deka-Film GmbH. shall be limited to Reichsmark.

Regarding the construction of business, in order to avoid payment in foreign currency by our company, Deka-Film GmbH. informs us by letter as follows:

> "We cannot tell for sure at this moment how we are going to pay the asking price in American dollars. In any case, we are capable of offering to RKO. the guarantee of the owner of an American industry company. As we have already told you, a German group has offered us an account in foreign currency totaling the asking price. We still need to negotiate abroad to clear the deposit. There are additional negotiations with American banking house Brown Harriman & Co., Limited, London, for an additional export deal as well. We therefore ask you to tell Office Dr. Winkler that we have agreed with Dr. Wieder that he will render — as far as our negotiations for clearing foreign currency are successful — an opinion about foreign currency for the Office Dr. Winkler. Alas, we are at this point not capable to provide more information for the information of Office Dr. Winkler. [...]"

Signed, Heil Hitler!
Bavaria Filmkunst G.m.b.H.
Klotzsch ppa Dr. Keil

On June 29, 1938, Klotzsch and Dr. Keil wrote a letter to Deka-Film GmbH.:

> To our utmost regret we haven't heard more details in this matter. We do not want to neglect to let you know that we are of the opinion that Ufa will come out triumphant in the race for this picture. On the other hand, we think that such triumph for Ufa is not absolutely necessary; for it remains questionable if Ufa will be able to close a better deal re: question of foreign currency. To our estimate it now is important to tell Office Dr. Winkler very soon some positive about the whole construction of the deal and make Office decide that only one company, that is you, will conduct negotiations with RKO. and hence acquire picture for ourselves. Such a decision will only be taken if Dr. Winkler can be convinced that re: foreign currency bigger advantage will be on our side.
>
> We ourselves cannot actively interfere in the deal, however want make clear seriousness of the situation to avoid useless expenditures on your behalf and then turn out to be the loser. We are highly interested in obtaining this picture and we do not want to miss any opportunity to point out the urgency in this matter.

The deal seemed to fail for Bavaria. The members of the Bavaria board saw their hope dashed.

The most important film event of this summer was La Biennale di Venezia, the Venice Film Festival. RKO was going to screen two new Disney shorts, *Farmyard Symphony* and *Brave Little Tailor* (Mickey Mouse in another adaptation of the Brothers Grimm) as well as, of course, the feature-length *Snow White and the Seven Dwarfs*. Eventually the heads of the German film industry could view *Snow White* themselves. Some enthused over the picture; others remained skeptical, as we know from a few reviews in German trade papers:

> In these days the Walt Disney cartoon feature, *Snow White and the Seven Dwarfs*, which was expected with bated breath was screened here. For many months it now runs successfully in the capitals of the world. The film will not get to Germany and one has to say that in spite of many exceptional ideas not all too much is lost for the German audience.[6]

The evening performance was characterized by the long expected feature-length cartoon *Snow White and the Seven Dwarfs* (Schneewittchen und die sieben Zwerge) which got preliminary laurels as something outstanding and which (besides *The Adventures of Tom Sawyer*) counts for the Americans' prize possession. One has to admit that Walt Disney and his employees have achieved something amazing technically as well as artistically.

The German fairy tale by the Brothers Grimm provided an original source out of which much could be formed for it is inexhaustible. It is anyone's guess why and if at all our old fairy tales should be used to create color cartoons which exclusively and only are reserved for a humourous approach and in some countries even are not allowed for juveniles because they might frighten the young minds too much like the horror scenes in this movie do.

Without any doubt Disney accomplished really magnificent film parts which are stylistically and visually not only beautiful but also stuck in the memory because they are unique. Such as Snow White's flight through the cave where she is pursued and hunted by some beast, the image of dwarves working underground, the rescue of Snow White (with her body laid out) by the handsome, brave prince, the transformation of the evil stepmother into a witch just to mention a few parts which in the long work attracted special attention.

After all what one has read and heard about this film a certain disappointment had to follow. Despite plot, colors and clean, technical and artistic effort by Walt Disney's artists the movie could not hold cause of its length live and awake the interest until the final frame with unchanged intensity. At least the work booked a relatively big success for itself which, however, shouldn't seduce to make more feature-length films along the same lines but to keep the Mickey Mouse and other cartoons as supplementary. It would be better.[7]

At the Lido in Venice, German films were awarded two cups, four medals and two short-film prizes. In recognition of its outstanding technical and artistic achievement, Disney's *Snow White* received the great Art Prize of the festival sponsored by the Partito Nazionale Fascista.

Bavaria wouldn't give up the competition. On September 1, 1938, Dr. Keil noted:

Yesterday I have phoned Mr. Otzoup re: above mentioned movie. He told me that he would work on a new combination after which a South-American industrialist would obtain the picture from the Americans effectively in dollar. The film would then be transferred to us by Hispano against payment in Reichsmark to Hispano's account. According to Mr. Otzoup foreign currency is not necessary in order to sign the deal because South-American industrialist would pay Hispano the amount of money that will flow back in Reichsmark for the production of movies in Spanish language.

But there are still problems because for the worldwide success of the movie the Americans would have raised the price and would currently ask for 200,000 dollar.

The industrialist concerned would be in Berlin around September 10 or 15 and afterwards would conduct negotiations with the American sales organization in Paris. Mr. Otzoup will notify us in due course and pointed out that the only condition he would name in negotiations would be that the film Snow White would be allocated to Bavaria.

A second memo followed the next day:

Re: phone call conducted today in another matter I have asked Mr. Kienzl about the proceedings in the case Snow White on the part of Deka. Mr. Kienzl explained to me that Mr. Merten from Cautio hasn't permitted the combination, as stated at that time, with an ancillary export deal on the part of Deka because basically they didn't wish such a construction. A similar notice Ufa has received from the Office of Dr. Winkler.

> Mr. Kienzl mentioned by the way that he still would try this way or another to get us the movie, explained however explicitly that we as a matter of fact would be free to accept the picture from another party. I have expressed that this would have been our opinion anyhow.

Between December 15, 1938, and January 18, 1939, Dr. Keil repeatedly visited the offices of Otzoup-Film in Berlin's Kaiserallee 55. The Ministry of Enlightenment and Propaganda, however, intervened and prohibited Otzoup all further activities in this matter because the officials of the Third Reich considered only Ufa strong enough to bid for *Snow White*. After all, Bavaria was out.

On the other hand, the ministry was forced to operate more and more against American films and criticize the activities of the Anti-Nazi League which had been founded in a wave of Hollywood films with expressly anti–German tendency. On January 17, 1939, Ufa board member Max Witt announced there would be a direction by now that American movies should not be screened in premieres and first run cinemas.

Without any doubt the Ministry and German film experts regarded *Snow White* as a film of high artistic calibre and a movie for which an exemption clause should be possible.

> Board meeting of UFA on January 20, 1939
> TOPIC 5)
> *Snow White*
> Mr. Meydam reports on the submission about the offer resp. the acquisition of German distribution rights of the American color movie *Snow White* on January 19, 1939.
> The German release rights are for the time being reserved for Ufa by Office Dr. Winkler.
> Licensee is Mr. Schmeling.
> The board authorizes Mr. Meydam to continue negotiations resp. the takeover of the movie for German distribution.
> The board agrees to accounting on the basis 50:50.
> The guarantee will be between RM 300.000 and RM 500.000 to be paid in Reichsmark. Included in the guarantee is the shipping of 100 prints, the costs will total about RM 75,000 inclusive.

The Mr. Schmeling mentioned in the protocol was nobody else than German boxing champion Max Schmeling, who acted as licensee on behalf of RKO for *Snow White*. How did this come about? On August 19, 1936, Schmeling had his bout against Joe Louis in the New York Yankees stadium. RKO had offered him the exclusive screen rights for the match that was expected to last only a few minutes. But when this fight entered the annals of boxing history as "The Fight of the Century," RKO lost millions and sadly realized its mistake. All attempts by RKO to reacquire the world rights to the picture failed, however. The movie was successfully launched in German cinemas under the title *Max Schmelings Sieg, ein deutscher Sieg* (*Max Schmeling's Victory, a German Victory*). In late June 1938, Max Schmeling had a rematch against Joe Louis. This time RKO obtained all rights but Schmeling was k.o.'d after only two minutes. As Schmeling was not only an internationally renowned boxing champ but also a smart businessman he agreed to act on behalf of RKO as salesman for *Snow White* to the German Reich.

> Protocol Board meeting of UFA on January 24, 1939
> TOPIC 5)

Walt Disney color picture

Mr. Zimmermann reports that further negotiations about obtaining picture *Snow White* for German distribution have resulted that licensee Schmeling asks for his shares 60% of gross revenues deducting the usual costs, with a guarantee sum of RM 500,000. Included in the guarantee, however, are 100 color prints valued at about $50,000 (=RM 125,000). According to German regulations a German version of an American movie produced in a foreign country is not allowed here. Therefore it shall be re-dubbed. The costs for dubbing exceed to about RM 40.000. This sum, however, can be deduced from gross revenues. The board will get an official confirmation in letter that neither there are objections against obtaining the film nor later against the exhibition. Seller's previous demand to buy additionally two Anny Ondra films[8] for Germany has been dropped.

Because this is an extraordinary color film the board approves the above mentioned conditions of sale.

While activities concerning the release of the movie in the German Reich were still being conducted, German Odeon music publishers during 1938 had already supplied all German record shops with the famous songs from *Snow White*. Electrola Music Publishers, too, produced for 1939 a *Snow White* potpourri played on two pianos by Peter Igelhoff and Fritz Schulz.[9]

The Walt Disney Company, of course, had high expectations for the European market. After releases in Britain, France, Belgium and the Netherlands, Germany was a key element in this marketing strategy. At least one American distributor, Paramount Pictures, even in 1940 was able to release four films to the German territory. Others, however, were less lucky. For there were anti–German films produced in Hollywood in the meantime, so called *Hetzfilme* (agitation and campaign pictures). Goebbels expected more information from Leni Riefenstahl, who in November 1938 visited Hollywood. She was granted a lukewarm reception there and soon realized that most studios ignored her. Only Walt Disney, still interested in releasing *Snow White* in Germany, invited her to his studio. (Although he politely declined having her Olympics films screened at the studio as his projectionists were members of the union and therefore refused to run them.) At the end of January 1939, Riefenstahl returned to Europe and was interviewed by a French reporter from *Paris-Midi*: "Three months in America, everywhere lustrous reception except Hollywood where she only was received by Walt Disney, but otherwise was boycotted at the instigation of the Anti Nazi League."[10]

On January 30, 1939, *Film-Kurier* reported about Hollywood's Anti-Nazi League under the headline "Filmhetze in Hollywood":

> An anti–Nazi League has established itself in Hollywood which was termed by Vittorio Mussolini [Benito's son] returning home from his research trip a "center of political agitation against the Fascist Idea."
>
> According to recent reports, for the time being they want to support needy émigrés before launching an all-out attack, increasing the film agitation against Germany.
>
> After all they have worked on a film in which Charlie Chaplin caricatures the Führer and hence wanted to ridicule him.[11]

On February 5, 1939, Joseph Goebbels noted in his diary: "Question if one should remove the American films. I am not quite sure about this matter.... This evening Leni Riefenstahl told me her exhaustive impression which is not pleasant. We have no chance over there. The Jews rule with terror and boycott. But how long?"

> Filmamerika 1938
>
> The anti–National Socialist and anti-fascist angle of the mainly Jewish [*verjudete*] American film industry emerged from several agitation and campaign films [*Hetzfilme*] which we have pointed out repeatedly in FK [*Film-Kurier*].
>
> The Jewish Anti Nazi League in Hollywood has a pressure upon all who have a different opinion [*Andersgesinnte*] so that, for instance, nobody else except Walt Disney recently dared to receive Leni Riefenstahl publicly in the American film town.[12]

The minister reacted with a ban of most American films (although behind closed doors he screened and adored them for himself, including *Gone With the Wind* and *Mrs. Miniver*, which he considered high propaganda), but he still would have permitted *Snow White*. American producers themselves, however, refused to cooperate any longer.

Indeed, there was a German-language dubbed version of *Snow White* already prepared which was released to German-speaking territory after World War II. It starred Paula Wessely as Snow White, Otto Wallburg (who was murdered in 1944 in Auschwitz) as chief dwarf, and Aribert Wäscher, as the Magic Mirror. Technically, the dubbing quality was poor by today's standards but the actors were of higher caliber than in any of the later German dubbings. Sadly, Disney made the film unavailable, although it is still available in private archives as a collector's item. In 1939 this version ended under Deposit No. 3828 in Berlin's Reichsfilm Archives.

With negotiations at an end, the official party language started to diminish Disney and his work for being too American for German taste. German fairy tales, official reviewers said, are strictly "German matter" (*Film-Kurier*, June 1938). However, behind the curtains there was some speculation about Disney's family background and even an attempt to "Germanize" him: Was he American or European? On inquiry by Dr. Günther Schwarz, Reichsfilmkammer, in a letter dated May 5, 1941, documentary filmmaker Dr. Hans Cürlis falsely assured that he had heard Walt Disney was born in Germany, baptized "Walter Distler," and had worked for some years in Germany. Others located the place of Disney's birth in Spain. And was not Disney himself a crypto anti–Semite? Didn't he once call one of Hollywood's movie moguls, apparently Louis B. Mayer of MGM, "a fat Jew," and didn't he please anti–Semites by including a gag in his most famous cartoon, *The Three Little Pigs* (1933), in which the Big Bad Wolf tried to outsmart the pigs by dressing up as the caricature of a Jewish peddler? That scene was later deleted from the original footage and substituted with one that seemed more politically correct — though the Wolf still had a Yiddish-sounding accent.

The failed Disney deal helped a small distributor, Willy Wohlrabe's Jugendfilm Verleih in Berlin, and Hubert Schonger's Naturfilm Company to issue their own low-budget live-action version of *Snow White* in 1939 starring a declared Nazi actress, Marianne Simson. She later shared some scenes with Hans Albers in a high-budget Agfacolor fantasy, *Munchausen*. That extravaganza was made on the occasion of the 25th anniversary of Ufa. The Nazis made it to rival Korda's *Thief of Bagdad* and the Disney epics that were secretly screened, analyzed and scrutinized by Dr. Goebbels and his cohorts.

When a Zurich cinema dared to screen Disney's *Fantasia* the Nazi reviewers fumed and criticized it as "a malapropism of sublime German cultural goods, of Bach, Beethoven, and Schubert, that in this grotesque form only is possible in the mental state of North-

America which is going to deliver Germany's greatest musicians to colored trickfilm drawings of the most stupid substance."[13]

Nevertheless, the Disney shorts acquired before *Snow White* remained in German cinemas until 1941. And after the war, of course, Germany became an important ally and source for Disney to launch films, comic books and merchandising through the Mickey Mouse Company headed by Horst Koblischek. In the 1960s, for a brief time, they had their own *Walt Disney Filmverleih* in Frankfurt am Main (with Hans Muth as head of distribution) to relaunch *Snow White* in German territories in a newly dubbed version which included Uschi Wolff and the singing talents of Susanne Tremper and René Kollo.

5
Global Power for German Trickfilm

Twelve months before the American premiere of Disney's *Snow White*, *Lichtbildbühne* had speculated under the headline "Deutscher Trickfilm weltmarktfähig" about why German trickfilm hadn't achieved worldwide recognition (*Weltgeltung*).

> Doesn't the German animator have imagination? Does he have only inadequate technical equipment? Don't exhibitors want to see his films or don't they want to pay for them? Or are there other invisible resp. unknown factors? How did it come that Mickey Mouse and Felix the Cat enjoyed us so much, that the Silly Symphonies amazed us, cinemas brought us whole series of Betty Boop, the spinach-eating sailor Pop [a.k.a. Popeye] or the little pigs and have booked them mainly for box-office? Was it only a single factor or was it a combined effect?
>
> Well, the German is known for his imagination, for his artistry. German animation stands only look differently outwards than the equipment in Hollywood and other movie capitals whereas the aerial-view camera operated by a single-frame motor including lighting of the glass by incandescent lamps, the film stock and the tracing paper including cells and ink is the same all over. But don't they watch in Paris, London and Rome Reiniger's silhouettes (for instance the marvellous Prince Achmed)...

[At this point the author reminds us of the many successfully animated commercials with animated objects and advertisements that moved frame-by-frame and sometimes created more excitement among the patrons than the feature film.]

> Do they think they don't have enough talent or don't they dare to "sacrifice" a few hundred feet of film and the fee for the trickfilm trainees? Animation stands are relatively inexpensive to buy or to produce in the facilities of a big production company. Also camera and lighting equipment one will get cheaply. So this cannot matter. Are the cinema owners the ones to put the blame on? Well, they wouldn't be smart if they would pay good money for stupid, boring trickfilms but — that is for sure — for good, attractive little supporting films they are gladly willing to pay. The motives are quite obvious! One has not only to rely to film the irrepressible Wilhelm Busch (although he has invented sheer film types) but our fairy tale characters are numerous; one also can choose animals, for instance a cute terrier, a duck, a parrot etc., give him an attractive name and throw him into all kinds of adventures. In the USA and England they have started with well-known comic strip characters as they still run them in the big magazines etc. in inexhaustible sequence. May it be a cart horse or ape, duck or pelican always it has to do with delightful sense of humour, skills and

inventive mind to bring the artificial character to life. Sure do we have enough of such men and women among our filmmakers. Let them work, all those who are obsessed by trickfilm. Then German animation in brief time will be weltmarktfähig [ready to enter the world market]. Then it will compete—supported by German color film techniques and German art of music—with Felix, Mickey Mouse and all the other film animals from USA, the "country of the already limited possibilities."

6

Puppet Films: Starevich, Mecki the Hedgehog, the Diehl Brothers and Jürgen Clausen, the German "Pal"

One way to bring Germany to power in animation was to use different animation techniques than Disney, for instance puppets and stop-motion. In this field Europe and, even Germany, had far more to offer than Hollywood.

The Color Puppet Trickfilm: What it is—what it could be—what it will cost?

During the war, under that headline, two writers, Herbert Pohris and Jürgen Clausen, provided a memorandum for Tobis Filmkunst in December 1941.[1]

Jürgen Clausen had approached Tobis on May 30, 1941, and offered to produce color puppet films as well as establish a color film studio. Clausen was an expert in both fields: As business and production manager of Gasparcolor Werbefilm G.m.b.H. and Gasparcolor Naturwahre Farbenfilm G.m.b.H. he knew about color film stock. And as he had been involved in processing stop-motion films (Clausen re-issued Fischinger's *Composition in Blue* in a special screening "Color Advertising Films" on October 30, 1938, in Hamburg's Waterloo Cinema) and particularly George Pal's Philips shorts as well as cooperating for some time with Alexandre Alexeieff and Ladislas Starevich, he seemed to be the right choice for Tobis heads Ewald von Demandowsky and Julius Fritzsche who offered him a one-year contract, beginning July 1, 1941, with a monthly payment of RM 2,500.

Herbert Pohris, co-author of the memo, was a Berlin painter and member of N.S.D.A.P. since 1931 (no. 724 929). For a monthly fee of temporarily RM 1,000 he was hired as consultant, writer-director and artist-designer. With their memo both men wanted to talk Tobis into setting up a puppet film studio like Pál had done in Eindhoven (if only to please the animated ambitions of the Minister of Enlightenment and Propaganda and his many children). In the end the plan, however, failed, but what was suggested is, beyond all propaganda, still food for thought.

> *One is allowed—yes, one should! The Color Puppet Film?*
>
> Is one allowed today, as German people not only fight for their economical and political existence but even more for the culture of the Occident, to bring up such question? Namely, as in this case, for the direct purpose of founding and systematically establishing a very

special and in Germany only little noticed let alone acknowledged production, the production of feature-length color puppet trickfilms?

Well — if you are allowed to do so or not, government is going to decide. And that here we got order to hoist the colours of the art even — and even the more — during the war is prerequisite of our planning and working.

Art is food — Joy is strength.

Art often is more important to war than army bread: every soldier who once he was out of the trenches will confirm this, got into a front theatre. In this regard every discussion is superfluous.

But only in this regard. This includes the right acknowledgment of the puppet trickfilm.

Who has seen a puppet trickfilm?

There are not many people in Germany who have seen a good puppet trickfilm. Among those who have not one will not find too many who possess enough imagination to acknowledge this special type of form and creation (by filmic means) as art, only if they regard it similarly high as a live action feature.

Prejudice renders blind!

How does it come that occasionally also film experts cannot link much with the puppet trickfilm? Could it be that they consider it an unreasonable amount of playing around? Such kind of misunderstanding would be possible. However, prejudice shouldn't be declared a dogma. — In spite of its relationship with other cinematic means of expression the puppet trickfilm is something truly special. And regarding the artistic rating: if ever a film could claim to be more than "light muse" — then it would be the color puppet trickfilm. — We shall try to prove this as much as possible in the limited space we have here.

[...]

A Difference — and a proposal

Here we want to insert the elemental differences between hand-drawn animation and puppet animation for the common distinguishing mark "two-dimensional" — "three-dimensional" is not sufficient; more likely the comparison Flächen-Trickfilm [flat trickfilm] and Raum-Trickfilm [spatial trickfilm or dimensional animation]. (We would also like to introduce this term to give the puppet animation the advantage by which it wouldn't be ridiculed — perhaps this only happens for the use of the term "puppets"or "dolls" — as a kind of "childish play").

What kind of man am I?

There are two ways to see pictures: the "flat" and the "spatial" kind. — Instead of "flat" in this case we might better term it: "plakatig" [poster-like], and instead of "spatial": "in depth" [tiefenmässig]. — As far as I enjoy plakatig, i.e., poster-like (hand drawn) trickfilm I am regarded more an intellectual-witty kind of man without the right sense of humour, also ober-flächig [superficial] (this is no rating). As far as I am going to enjoy puppet or spatial trickfilm I am a spiritually sensual man and have humour. Everybody who has the ability to watch himself will agree to this. — Hand-drawn animation addresses more the intellect. The ideas or improvisations (the American calls them "gags") have only little to do with humour but more with its brilliant superficiality, the *joke*. Hand drawn animation most often deals with malicious caricatures and likes to parody (the cheap kind to get a feeling of superiority). It is not childlike but more childish. For this reason, notabene, as long as hand-drawn animation will remain 'plakatig' or poster-like it will provide an awkward situation to retell German fairy tale content in this particular style (see Snow White by Disney!). It doesn't seem advisable at all to film fairy tales, legends and also novels in this way for each content is tied to a certain expression, on its form.–

Hand-drawn animation has more to do with distortion than with grotesque, it invites more to bemusement than guiding us to bonhomie which is reflected in the smile (actually about oneself, i.e., about the own "Menschlichkeiten"[humanness] which step out of the mirror of artwork).

Is this a condemnation of hand-drawn animation?—Yes and No! Yes,—regarding the style of previous animation films, and No—regarding the possibilities that lie dormant in this technique. Primarily the following: to give up the "moving poster" and create moving pictorial ornament (without deep illusionistic backgrounds!). As "moving poster" the hand-drawn animated film is an American matter, as moving pictorial ornament it can be as Germanic as, say, a Gothic church window,—and in spite of two-dimensionality so "profound" like this. This way, however, lies still ahead!–

Disney makes caricature posters

Americans have transferred the plakatig hand-drawn animation to its highest degree. This style comes from feuilletonistic comic drawings. The previous hand-drawn animation is—Disney.—Our own Fischer-Koesen, Kaskeline etc. by far don't reach the final perfection of poster style [plakatig] and the American humour—they are no Americans, that's it!

An information:

Now what is the puppet trickfilm?

Here the matter is totally different.—Like feature film, as "photographed theatre," has a tradition that dates back to age-old cultural spaces (tragedy, mystery or miracle play, cult dances and so on) the spatial trick is tied to everything that has to do with moving puppets. A cultural value so far which is as old as culture itself.—If we think of the wooden Egyptian crocodile with its movable mouth—from the second millennium -, or the Turkish and East-Asian shadow plays or the mechanical playworks of the 16th century (Peter Döpfer, Daniel Bertel for instance), the Kasperle hand puppets and marionettes (about these Kleist has made a final statement) and last but not least about the masks of South German Perchten Runs, yes—the nativity plays, gargoyles, chimes figures up to the truly world-dominating German toys—all this lives in us, excites us and binds us when we start to think about making color puppet trickfilms.

Only in Germany!

The puppet or spatial trick is located in European cultural space and no other country can be its more natural home than Germany. The German is deeply spatial-romantic, profoundly imaginative, he is dreamy and contemplative. None other succeeds that well in *humorous* grotesque (see Wilhelm Busch) so definitely that one can count it almost into classic art—classic in a sense of perfection of expression. All of this means a splendid, not to say decisive predestination for the spatial trickfilm and—an obligation. Space and depth oblige the German-Nordic identity. Therefore important results will be accomplished much faster with the German spatial trickfilm than hand-drawn animation which is burdened with Disney's virtuoso style.

Puppet trick artist?

First one has to name the Diehl Brothers in Munich. They come from the simplicity of rural wood cutting and have achieved in their kind perfection: the lovely carved childrens' puppet animation. A further development, even by use of color, one cannot expect here.

Furthermore: Starevich, the former taxidermist, whose Reineke Fuchs [Renard the Fox/The Tale of a Fox] a few years ago gained attention in Germany too. Starevich masters an animation film technique (mimic expression) which one has to call almost eerily-naturalist.—What one could accomplish if one could open this technical routine and will practice to an artistic form! For Starevich is a tinkering artist—no artist.—The experience and the animation talent of Starevich should be saved for Germany.–

An artist is Alexeieff, from nationality a Russian, regarding race a Nordic man. This is expressed mainly in his film *Eine Nacht auf dem kahlen Berge (A Night on Bald Mountain)* which makes use of a completely new trick mechanics invented by him. In its nature, particularly in this film, he is near to spatial trick. Alexeieff is a subtle man thinking in depth and space.

Then we know: Fischinger, Hangeler, Klemm, Thallmeyer and—Georg Pál.

We have to proceed from Pál technique!

Georg Pál is a Hungarian with a specific Balkan joy for the color and love for good-natured grotesque. He comes from hand-drawn animation, but has produced color dimensional trickfilms for many years. Almost exclusively commercials for Philips, Holland. Although he lost much of his original instinct—in the service of advertisement he has become a little bit Americanized—even his most abstract ideas reflect a little bit the child-like narrator. Therefore, too, his films are so sympathetic to us in spite of their American outfit.

What appeals most to us Germans is the special wood puppet style of Pál's films and the precision of his stop-frame technique. Behind the moving grotesque there is an, albeit originally more technical than artistic, seriousness and diligence. If one observes a Pál animator at the making of technical blueprints, one could think that it would be about the construction of valuable machines.

Color Dimensional Trickfilm will enlighten the whole process of filmmaking—especially color feature films

Pál's films today represent not only an outstanding achievement in the field of color dimensional trickfilm but—and this is essential—in this technique rest possibilities of expression resp. shaping of incredible simplicity and depth. The solution of these tasks will raise the puppet animation film finally into the ranks of artistic high-grade spatial trick creation, and so will demonstrate what essentially a Film-Spiel [Picture Play] is. ("*Film-Spiel*" should be written as motto above the whole process of filmmaking!)

If one reminds that not only an according score (in German tradition) will be added but also the color of these simple wooden forms (one should think only about Cézanne's space principle of painted space, of "cone, ball and cylinder") will achieve the most glorious, striking performance so that finally, what hasn't been tried before, one can go to a kind of synchronized element of color and its *dramatic* assessment—not only aesthetical—(which color film development needs so badly) ... if one considers all of this than one will understand why we should proceed from Pál's technique and should acknowledge it as a textbook example sine qua non by those offices responsible for German culture.

Who will win — has to dare!

We Germans have to make up a lot in the field of trickfilm: today and particularly after this war which burdens us a pleasant as well as heavy responsibility for all of Europe.— We have the power and the artistic impulse to create exemplary things: open the road — as generous as possible!— An operation like this should not be introduced with calculations of profitability: otherwise it will never make a profit.–

Planning in advance

Although one has to make estimates of cost and find out about all financial possibilities — it should be done due to the dimensions of such a project. In this regard we should learn from the American who is not glued on the maxim that time is money but modifies it occasionally:

A big business — much time, much money!

For sceptics, finally this suggestion: run Pál's films in a cinema ... when one realizes the excitement of the audience and the box-office receipts, each objection would vanish and would be replaced by insight and understanding:
Color dimensional trickfilm as feature-length film play
will have a bright future.

About style

Which people tied in tradition — contrary to people who are conscious and aware of tradition — might consider at first that the times of Baroque and Biedermeier are finally over. One should remember the way fashion has become in the past thirty years, architecture, machine building, yes — how could it be else — our style of living and, especially, the form of state: more and more our whole life tends to simplicity, the outspoken, the clear.

"Deutsch sein heisst klar sein," the Führer once said: "To be a German means to be clear."

Pál's technique proceeds from such clarity, onto purity of style — in its field of cinematic dream world.

A Postscript:

Puppet trickfilm and German toy industry.

In regard to American animation film, a unique insemination of the toy has occurred, which results for instance in the fact that after release of the Mickey Mouse or Pig films and later after Snow White and Pinocchio not only children's books were published in millions of copies based on the artwork and characters of the Disney production, but also toys, puppets and records invaded European countries (bijouterie: necklaces, buttons, stickers etc.). In Paris, for instance, many shop windows were decorated with characters of the Snow White picture. The same is true for the George Pál production in Holland. Here too the most prominent characters from various Pál films were absorbed by the toy industry and were exploited.

The German toy industry up until now was leading the whole world, especially the German children's puppet industry. We are absolutely sure that out of German puppet film production an equally extensive as well as necessary insemination of German toy industry will result, so that later an interaction will occur: puppet trickfilm will support toy industry and vice versa. Add to it that Pál's technique (use of simple work forms like cone, ball, cylinder etc.) is well suited for mass production. This is the technically best prerequisite for animated film featuring plastic color bodies and on the other hand simplifies the transfer into efficient production methods of the toy industry.

The toy industry will have to learn from color spatial trickfilm if it wants to play the role again, particularly as an export industry, in the wide world as it has done before.–

The paper states that while Pál himself already had moved to America two years previously [*Puppetoons* and *Madcap Models* series were Paramount releases] his collaborators, mainly from Holland, were still available. Some were working in the movies, others have returned to their original craftsman jobs. He wrote:

> Three leading artists of George Pál's have been hired by Tobis a few months ago and will form the nucleus of future production. I have let them work under the supervision of a German artist, Herbert Pohris, in the past months to secure German influence. Above that, I am in touch with former Holland co-workers of Pál's to hire them too. This group mainly consists of special effects craftsmen.

In a span of one and a half years Clausen estimated he would be able to work mainly with German artists who would have been trained sufficiently by the experts from the Netherlands. Puppet film production, he concluded, had a basic character that was mainly craftsman-like. He then suggested moving production to a town which had a background in toy manufacturing and came up with Sonneberg in Thuringia, provided the crews could find enough working and living space.

Clausen's clear objective was to create feature-length puppet films in color. A puppet feature wouldn't be more expensive than a regular feature, he concluded. Movies starring Emil Jannings would be more expensive. He estimated RM 1.5 and 1.7 million per puppet feature.

In October 1941 a former restaurant called Zur Linde in Berlin Gatow was inspected. Maybe Tobis could transform it into a stop-motion facility. On month later, on November 26, 1941, Studio Heuken, Berlin, Kurfürstendamm 180 was placed at Clausen's disposal. Karl Neumann (Deutsche Zeichenfilm G.m.b.H.) followed Hans Hinkel's suggestion and supported Clausen's plan to start production on a budget of RM 315,000 as Dr. Max Winkler let the Ministry of Enlightenment and Propaganda know. But in August 1942 Clausen's ambitious plans for puppet animation were vetoed by the Film Department of the Ministry of Enlightenment and Propaganda for reasons caused by the war. During his tenure at Tobis, and still owning his Gasparcolor facilities, Clausen had experimented with a project about a thin lion who devours the "treasures" of other countries, obviously meant to be the British lion. After ceasing puppet film production Tobis used the footage to assemble an anti–British short film, *John Bull in Nöten* (*John Bull in Distress*).

After putting a halt to all puppet film activities Clausen was asked to focus entirely on the production of color feature films. In his color film studio in Berlin Grunewald, Eichkampstrasse 152 he did extensive research for Tobis' first big color production, *Das Bad auf der Tenne* (1942–43), but he didn't get along with Tobis director Fritzsche with whom he was engaged in a personal feud.

Apparently a convinced National Socialist, Clausen tried to run Fritzsche down when Tobis lost Herbert Selpin, the defeatist *Titanic* director: While preparing his film of the ship's disaster, Selpin, drinking heavily, had blamed Germany's "fucking soldiers and fucking army in front of a fucking lieutenant," screenwriter Walter Zerlett-Olfenius. The upset writer had nothing better to do than to run to his friend SS Obergruppenführer Hans Hinkel and denounce Selpin. Selpin was immediately ordered to Goebbels' offices. The minister tried to give the *Titanic* director a chance to avoid a charge of treason but Selpin refused to take the bait and ended being strangled to death on July 31, 1942.

True to party principles, on September 6, 1942, he wrote to Reichsfilmintendant and complained "that Herr Fritzsche had described this case as a symptom of beginning GPU conditions in Germany. I told him that I immediately would bring charges in each similar case that I would hear of which would have nothing to do with denunciation." He called Fritzsche "a man of the old school who had difficulties to get accustomed to National Socialist conditions."

In a letter dated September 11, 1942, addressed to the Propaganda Ministry, Fritzsche proceeded to attack and characterized Clausen as "handsome negotiator who appears confident. I consider him a man who easily can sell goods as a travelling salesman. He isn't provided, however, with any organizational skills, at least not for assignments in the film industry, in which sums of RM 1 mill. or more are absorbed in production in a few months and pass the hands of the responsible production manager. He describes himself as extremely sensitive, particularly against reproaches. At every convenient time he threatens with complaints at high and highest authorities. He urges the people he is closest to, to write letters and telling how competent he is and how wonderful it is to work with him.

"Clausen today is still sole owner of Epoche Gaspar Color, an advertising company. In the middle of the previous year he apparently feared to get drafted and negotiated a passage in his contract to declare him *u.k.* [indispensable] as we are a state-controlled company. This is exactly what happened."

A few days later, on September 14, Clausen was fired. On September 17 he received a restraining order which prohibited him from entering Tobis' house.

On March 14, 1944, Film-Kurier reported Clausen's death in combat, as a newsreel cameraman.

The only ones who remained a household name in the small world of German puppet films, and thus ended up as sort of puppet monopolists, were the Diehl brothers. This author remembers vividly a screening of the Diehls' feature-length *Sieben Raben* (*Seven Ravens*) at the Berlin Film Festival in February 1985 to which he invited visual effects star (and stop-motion fan) Dennis Muren of Industrial Light and Magic fame. Muren was quite astonished by the heavy naturalism the feature employed, although he disliked Diehl's slow style. Diehl himself, when Rolf Giesen asked him, chalked this up to his own circumspect nature.

Under the headline "*The Diehl Brothers' idiosyncratic creation of art: Film Studio for ... Puppets—A well-organized fairy-tale world little known to the audience*," a trade film magazine in 1941 reported about Diehl's production:

> br. Munich, 17 January. Our fourth visit with Munich filmmakers this time takes us outside of the city gates, to Gräfelfing. There everybody knows the house and the small studio of the Diehls, the birth place of many fairy-tale puppet films which thanks to their superior artistic quality stay in the leads. Alas, with the exception of the fairy-tale picture

The 7 Ravens almost none of their work has reached the general audience as these Munich filmmakers for years work exclusively for Reichsanstalt für Film und Bild in Unterricht und Wissenschaft.[2] [...]

Maybe it is no coincidence that, particularly, Munich artists are leading in puppet films if one considers that Munich can look back onto many decades of traditional work in the field of puppet theatre. In Munich Count Pocci and Father Schmid worked as promoters and revivers of the puppet play.[3] The Diehls have adopted this art form and have translated it into the cinema. Today, the residency of the Diehls from top to bottom is filled with workshops of all kind. Also an appropriate studio, with several adjoining rooms, has been equipped. Only the congenial joint venture of all family members, however, made the creations of the Diehls possible who complement each other in a unique way.

The Diehls originate from an old family of violin-makers. So they unite artistic and mechanic, workmanlike skills in perfect form. The first to find the way to the movies was Ferdinand Diehl, today the reliable director of his puppets. At former Emelka, he began as scenic painter to end soon after in the animation department. He called in his younger brother Hermann, the creator of the magnificent puppet heads who at that time was art and painting student of Prof. [Angelo] Jank in Munich. After the collapse of the old Emelka the two decided to go independent. An older brother, grammar school professor Dr. Paul Diehl, joined them as poet and a first film was developed in 1928/29, the silhouette picture Caliph Stork (4). After this artistic success and financial failure they had the idea of puppet films. They created the nice supplement films of the Wupp series which focused on a little whizz-kid. Six pictures for the old Bavaria followed according to scores after Pfenninger's (5) sound system of "Tönende Handschrift" [Sound Handwriting], then five different short films and the feature The 7 Ravens. In 1936 they started work on films for education. These were: *Von einem der auszog das Gruseln zu lernen*, *Tischlein deck dich*, *Sterntaler*, *Handwerkerlied*, *Wettlauf zwischen Hase und Igel*, *Stadtmaus und Landmaus*, *Der Wolf und die sieben Geisslein* and, at the present time in work, *Der gestiefelte Kater*.

Behind these outside stages of development and build-up there is an enormous sum of painstaking and intense work. The basic conditions to produce a puppet film had to be provided and one will notice on a tour through the workshops of the Diehls at every turn all possible inventions in the field of mechanics.

Dr. Paul Diehl was our obliging guide. Himself a teacher he knows of course about the likes of children and has proved himself a formidable screenwriter. He is an exception among all film writers because for the peculiarity of the puppet film his screenplays are filmed word for word, syllable for syllable without the slightest change. The puppet film necessitates the production of the soundtrack first for the mouth movements of the puppets have to be adapted exactly to the previously recorded dialogue. According to the soundtrack the so-called exposure sheet [technisches Manuskript] is developed, an ingenious record of each frame of puppet mouth movement. But let's return to our tour. Actually nothing is missing what we have in a "large" movie studio! For instance, the birthplace of the actors. Here we enter the realm of Hermann Diehl. More than 1,000 puppets rest in shelfs. Under the artist's hands of sculptor Hermann Diehl always new puppet heads are developed. In another room the bodies are prepared; brass ball-and-socket armatures guarantee unlimited movement. After a puppet actor has been finished he is transferred to the skilled hands of the Diehls' mother. The old lady wraps the armature in soft cotton until the projected corpus has been ready which then is being enclothed. What the skilfull lady accomplishes in this regard would fill a book itself. For Puss in Boots we saw Rokoko ladies and cavaliers in clothes so perfect and stylished as in the best of historic prestige pictures. Three female

> assistants work temporarily in dressmaking. In the upper rooms there are more workshops. Here the sets are developed; there they glue, paint, solder, saw, gild, gold-plate and nail everywhere. Here we find true master pieces of painstaking architectonic work. We saw parts of a throne room with real parquet floor; on the abundantly with ornamentation decorated walls miniature paintings. Tables, chairs and other furniture of a bewitching reality. Actually the Diehls are proud to achieve such utter realism in a miniature world. Their team consists of special workers who are fully prepared for their tasks, each a master in his department. 10 to 15 persons are permanently employed in the facilities, and a fourth brother, the painter Robert Diehl from Trier, has joined recently. The house includes a projection, trick and editing room and one has to say that nothing is missing what one will find in real film facilities.
>
> Across the residential building with the various workshops is the studio. Here, too, everything is like in "real movies." Considerable lighting equipment, torn down and built up sets, various backgrounds and a cyclorama. The studio is very spacious including a lighting bridge and all kind of tools needed in movies. Right now the outer front of a castle entrance is being made. Unnoticed in a corner of the studio a magnificent golden king's coach is displayed drawn by two marvellous white horses; a masterpiece of applied arts. The prop shop, a goldmine of painstaking artistry, is filled under the roof with sets and props of all kind. More adjoining rooms include the actual joinery and a darkroom laboratory to develop the film strips. This is necessary as a trickfilm consists of too many sources of error which have to be checked immediately. One should imagine what it means to re-adjust 30 to 50 puppets frame by frame! Of course, all cameras have special stop-frame motors, which were invented by the Diehls too.[6]

The puppets of the Diehls usually were about 43 cm (16.9 in), about one-quarter life size. The mice of *Die Stadtmaus und die Feldmaus* (1939), however, were only 14 cm (5.5 in) each. Facial expression and mouth movements were made possible by exchangeable puppet mouth parts. On June 12, 1935, Ferdinand Diehl applied for a patent "*Puppe mit lösbaren auswechselbaren Teilen zur Herstellung von Filmen nach dem Einbildaufnahmeverfahren*" (Puppet with soluble, exchangeable parts for film production in stop-frame process, patent no. 404937, Reichspatentamt Berlin).

In the case of *Erstürmung einer mittelalterlichen Stadt um das Jahr 1350*, the stop-frame reconstruction of a medieval town under siege, which was begun in 1942 and finished in 1944 (interrupted by air raids, shortage of coal and other material, and affected by call-up orders for almost all male employees), Ferdinand Diehl used up to 60 puppets. By 1940 the company had 18 employees. The Diehls' main collaborators were cameramen Hans Asen (until 1935), Hans Schmid and Alfons Lusteck and composer Hilmar Georgi (until 1937) and Ernst Brandner (starting in 1948).

A stop-motion hedgehog seems to have been responsible for Ferdinand Diehl not being drafted in World War II. When a draft arrived the Führer was informed that this was the man who did Germany's most outstanding puppet films. Hitler himself then decided that Herr Diehl was *unabkömmlich* [indispensable] and should continue in his puppet work. At least this is what Diehl's daughter Monika Gruss in 1985 told Giesen.

The hedgehog and his perennial antagonist, the hare, from Diehl's short film *Wettlauf zwischen Hase und Igel*, which was produced two years after the Berlin Olympics in 1938, were released to German schools and fronts in 1,600 prints by Reichsanstalt in late 1939.

Then unnamed, after the war the hedgehog himself became known as *Mecki* in TV papers (drawn by Hans Held for "Hör Zu!" which resulted in a dispute over license fees), postcards (photographed by Ferdinand Diehl's son Toni), 8 mm films and as doll manufactured by Steiff. Congratulatory letters from soldiers who had seen Diehl's films in cinemas at the front were published by *Film und Bild*, the magazine published by RWU:

> In our front cinema which regularly screens cine-films from your *Kreisbildstelle* [local film rental] at first we have seen two films from the German fairy tale world: *Tischlein deck dich* and *Stadtmaus und Feldmaus*. At the beginning my comrades smiled a little. But then there was evidence that the fairy-tale pictures had to offer a lot more for the soldier. Not only was it an hour of entertainment, forgetting all sorrows and trouble of our battle. Many thought deeper. Since the days of our childhood for the first time something plastically rose before our very eyes. We recalled the long forgotten days of our childhood and youth. Our comrades who are family fathers thought about the content of the pictures and at the same time were reminded of their wives and children at home. Because of that the fairy-tale films moved anybody notwithstanding the deeper meaning behind the plot. We said to ourselves that these too are cultural treasures of our people which we must preserve for a future generation by defending our native country, even by risking our life. War last not least is fought not only for material but for cultural goods. And therefore these films have conveyed to the soldiers the meaning of their present life task and have awakened their enthusiasm[7]

A pupil in eighth grade who saw the Diehls' puppet version of *Tischlein deck dich* wrote a school essay[8]:

> Yesterday to much laughter of the undergraduate class we saw the picture *Tischlein deck dich* [Table-Be-Set]. For us grown-ups the fairy-tale, however, provided more than entertainment and joy. For in every fairy-tale there is a deeper meaning. Today we discussed with our teacher the deeper meaning of this fairy-tale.
>
> Two tailor's sons acquired, according to the fairy-tale, by hard work prosperity and wealth, one in the form of a "Tischlein deck dich" [Table-Be-Set], the other in the form of an "Eselein streck dich" [Gold-Donkey]. Happily they returned home. But the evil and envious landlord robbed them of prosperity and wealth. Luck seemed to have deserted them.
>
> The third brother, however, put an abrupt end to the fraud of the host through the "Knüppel aus dem Sack" [Cudgel-out-of-the-sack]. This demonstrates that for the maintenance and security of prosperity and wealth a strong Wehrmacht [military] is necessary, just a Cudgel-out-of-the-sack. It alone is able to regain for the others the lost treasures.
>
> The three sons of the tailor come, according to the fairy-tale, from Dingsda [Dingbat]. Dingsda, however, is somewhere in Germany, it can be anywhere. So the three brothers represent our whole German nation which has to master life as the three apprentices do. The little goblin, however, who lives in fairy tale land and gives the brothers work and pay, represents the luck that everybody needs. For a time it seemed as if luck had abandoned the good three brothers; but then it returns to them forever.
>
> The treacherous host, however, who hoped to get rich by employing swindle and meanness, faced the fate of punishment. He resembles the eternal Jew who wants to profit from the work of the diligent and capable without moving a single finger. He is a Schmarotzer

> [parasite] who only wants to suck the others and exploit them. In spite of his smartness he can't escape punishment; for there is the Cudgel-out-of-the-sack.
>
> So at the end of our review we have come to the conclusion:
>
> 1. By work people German people acquire prosperity and wealth.
> 2. The evil Jew wants to rob the German people of prosperity and wealth.
> 3. German people, however, secures its prosperity and wealth by a strong army.
> 4. Only a hard-working nation is lucky in the long run.
>
> So this fairy-tale strengthens and invigorates us in our unruly believe in the Endsieg [final victory] of Germany in this war. Its "Cudgel-out-of-the-sack" drums heavily on the back of our enemies until all who have called upon the cudgel will buckle like the malicious host did.

A constant nemesis to the Diehls, however, was the powerful shadow of stop-motion pioneer Ladislas Starevich. They accused him of spoiling the market for puppet films, which is not true. In fact, they envied him for he got a German distributor (Ufa) for a seven-year-old movie, *Le Roman de Renard*, while they were left empty-handed after the failure of their *Seven Ravens*, which played only matinees, if it played at all. They were dependent on a loan (RM 14,000.-) by Aktiengesellschaft für Film-Fabrikation (Afifa) in Berlin until they found world distribution by Tobis-Cinema in January 1938 and finally were able to secure the services of a German distributor, Jugendfilm-Verleih G.m.b.H., in September 1938.

While the Diehls remained stiff, Starevich was lively, although in a rather meticulous way. One could call him the entomologist among the animators, or the alchemist of ephemeral stop-motion. Not only was he a naturalist like the Diehls were, though perhaps in a naive sense, he was also a true, incorruptible artist whose protagonists primarily were animated insects and animals. But few know that for some time he worked in Nazi Germany and was married to a German woman. Five years after completion of his *Reineke Fuchs*, Starevich still needed dubbing and a musical score, and Ufa was willing to pay for it (RM 39,300.-). At the end of September 1936, Ufa board member Meydam visited Starevich in Paris. Starevich had some hope that Ufa would hire him to do more films and suggested a puppet film about dogs, but Ufa declined politely. They were only interested in releasing *Reineke-Renard* as a feature or alternatively cut into three short films.

In April 1937 *Film-Kurier* reported on "Starevich in Berlin":

> We appreciate that Ufa now intends to hire one of the most renowned spearhead of novel film thoughts and to support his work.
>
> We think of Ladislas Starevich, who currently is in Berlin, to finish his last feature film, Reineke the Fox, in creative collaboration with general music director [conductor] Dr. Julius Kopsch, who composed the score. (Parts of this film, although silent and with work still in progress, were successfully screened by Dr. Allendy in the Paris "Sorbonne"). In the meantime Dr. Kopsch has finished the score....
>
> Ufa will release the picture in the new season — and we have to admit that the approach to hire and support an artist who for 25 years works cinematically and whose name is known for a long time to all serious film aficionados deserves special appreciation.
>
> Starevich who had lived in Russia where he had studied natural history (he is National Pole and has married a German wife) entered the movies for scientific reasons. He wanted to photograph a fight of beetles but as these beetles fought only at night he had to reconstruct all events. In painstaking work he filmed frame by frame — and became enthralled

in the whole technique. Soon after he made a similar picture, *La cigale et la fourmis* (Die Grille und die Ameise/The Grasshopper and the Ant)—in remembrance of Lafontaine's fable—and then began a career in feature films.

He filmed plays by Pushkin, Gogol—starring Tourjansky (as actor), with Mosjoukine, Gaidaroff and Michael Chekov. One day he was visited by Olga Tschechowa and reminded her of her talent.

Russian revolution dispersed Starevich. Over Crimea, Constantinople, and Italy he came to Paris where he started in 1920 (making a virtue out of his lack of language) to produce "marionette films." These founded his fame, and from this basis he grew in creative work. [...]

Starevich stressed on the occasion of his visit that he has won high confidence in the reliability of German film work and the cooperation with German forces. The chance to work here would come close to his inclination. The modest, great artist said it quietly and softly and while doing so opens his heart. We feel truth and shake hands,—wishing that his work with us will continue and, as we knowingly expect, will be fruitful for our German efforts in the art of film[9]

On May 5, 1937, *Film-Kurier* reported about Starevich in the Lessing Academy:

That a "surreal picture" can be highly successful too, one will witness this autumn at the premiere of the great Starevich work, Reineke Fuchs. We have seen the whole movie in these days, right after its finishing—it is a grand work of about 2,000 metres and if I say directly after naming its length that there is no hint of any "lengths" then much is said. [...]

For two years, Starevich, the creator, has worked on it, has created all animal characters by himself, moved them frame by frame, occasionally, in mass scenes, we see up to hundred animal characters who simultaneously are moved.

The previously silent opus has been arranged in cooperation with Ladislas Starevich by general music director Dr. Julius Kopsch. He has tightened up and concentrated where Starevich might have become too epic and for our impression made it more effective. Dr. Kopsch also did the excellent score which avoids cheap illustration but interprets the work emotionally and dramatically and, integrating itself to the whole, re-structures its line reasonably and artistically expressively.

Leo Peukert speaks clearly and passionately introduces the events of the picture, the charming verses by Wilhelm Krug about the adventures of Reineke, the cunning fox.

Some small clips from the movie, well selected, were screened yesterday at the "Film Seminary" of "Lessing-Hochschule" as well as another, smaller film by Starevich, *Fetiche se marie* (Püppchen heiratet/Little Doll Marries) which gained equally abundant and frenetic applause. Dr. Kopsch who in the past time, by close cooperation with Starevich, got to know the modest, quiet, great artist and his thoughts interpreted them for Starevich himself was not to be moved to say something. So only by the words of Dr. Kopsch we learned a little about the good cooperation—and, as for the rest, the screened clips of a "surreal film" (so the topic of the evening) gave a perfect and complete image of the high quality, the importance and the artistic peculiarity of Starevich.[10]

A year later, in September 1938, Frank Maraun visited Starevich in Paris:

Starevich is known to everybody in Germany who is interested in good films for his Reineke the Fox. In the silent film era, over ten years ago, one could see here his short film, The Grasshopper and the Ant, an image of life of the world of grasses and flowers that mesmerized by its tender characters and their movements, so delightful in its luminosity and uniqueness of its imaginative world. It was poetry in images and in art and imagery ranks equal to that of Lafontaine's words. Reineke the Fox, too, might claim for itself to be equal to the poetry of Goethe on the level of cinematic. Starevich has created a true piece of art that in its poetic content and in the characteristics of the different animal figures proves congenial to the intent and expressiveness of the poet to complete the profound portray of human and all-too-human in the mask of the animal outfit and animal face in splendid simpleness and exceptional clearness of images. It is the ardent simplicity and the dreamy-bright clearity of fairy-tale.

Starevich, today a man aged over fifty, but with eyes that reflect the belief in miracles of a child while he speaks about his plans — Starevich is a true fairy-tale-teller. Originally he started completely different. In his Polish home[11] he was natural scientist. By that he entered the movies: He wanted to film the fight of stag beetles. After he succeeded in doing so (1910) he couldn't get the movies out of his mind anymore. He became a director of live-action films. [...] After his flight from the Bolshevist revolution which led him over Crimea, Constantinopol and Italy to Paris he returned to the film with no humans. He was forced to do so because he didn't speak French. His daughter who speaks fluent German as well as Polish and French is indispensable to him as interpreter today, particularly if he talks to a visitor about his films and wants to express more difficult thoughts meticulously. He lives in a small cottage in a Paris suburb. There he lives withdrawn like a hermit, in a cocoon of his imaginary world, entirely occupied with his pictures. For two years he has worked there in a studio that is no larger than a living room on Reineke the Fox. The animal sculptures his hands have formed, cloth and rags and a 15-ampere lamp were the only tools besides the camera.

Starevich belongs to those few artists who use the film like a painter uses brushes and colors, alone and without assistants, an uncompromitting mediator of his imagination. Here not literature is being filmed but moving images are recreated from scratch. [...]

A film creator like Starevich can afford what no man of the industry can afford: He can wait for inspiration. He can play with his figures and thoughts. Although completely playful on the other hand he builds up his films strictly logical. He is natural scientist but one who observes nature with the eyes of a poet and with the perception of the fairy-tale: at the same time real and symbolic, concrete and transcendental. The development of a film happens with him as kind of a process of crystallization. He makes an observation while he goes for a walk or observes a community of insects which hits him, infiltrates his mind and moves his imagination. This observation or the thoughts deduced from it he will enrich by new ideas. [...]

He is the actor of all his characters. If he is in the right mood he carefreely can start and freely follow his imagination: the elastic,malleable material that provides the "sculptures animees" as he likes to call them allows any nuance of mimic and gesture. It allows him to remain in the mood and to immediately realize each idea. Until he came up with this method Starevich needed ten years. He first employed it in Reineke Fuchs which he therefore considers as kind of journeyman's work, as a highlight and starting point towards unlimited possibilities of expression. His previous method to use exchangeable masks for various, already abundantly graded basic forms of mime had something static and mechanical in their line up of finished expressions. [...]

To answer the question for a concrete example for his way to conceive a film Starevich mentions his newest fairy-tale *Abenteuer zweier deutschen Jungen* [Adventures of two German Boys] in which for the first time he is going to use color (and in the future he will continue to work exclusively in color). But why German boys? This question is on the tip of the tongue for a Pole who works in Paris. Starevich explains that the German boys possess a better feeling for the nature than any other boys in the world for in no other country there are so many natural science books in the vitrines of the bookstores as in Germany. [...]

Two little boys, one from the countryside, the other from the city, each with his dog, meet and walk alongside — Max, the farmer's boy, searching for physical work, Fritz from the city more sportly and well equipped with intelligence, both of them supplementing each other. So they come to a sleepy miller whose possession is in a lamentable state: mill and house are ruins, garden and acre uncultivated, overgrown by weed and looted by vermins [schädliches Viehzeug]. The miller has two little daughters, Minna and Gretchen, whom he promises both boys as wives provided they will do the work he will apply to them. Max and Fritz are eagerly involved with thirst for action. They have to battle the weed and parasites. The littlest plant, the most minor corn has to be protected and defended from a whole army of parasites. The ferocity of the various enemies is equally strong as is their number and their destructive activity. But the vigilance and the active courage of the boys who ally with the useful animals and insects overcome the enemies and put them to flight. Mill and rooming house, too, are restored. Finally after all strain comes the harvest of fruits, the joy. Order and fertility rule again in the realm of the miller. Max marries Minna, Fritz marries Gretchen, and many little Max and Fritz and little Minna and Gretchen will populate the freshly cultivated acres.—

Of these enchanting effects of images one can assume what Starevich says: that he can make entirely visual pictures. Occasionally he makes them — advertising films to make some money. But this is not his ideal "because there is no heart in it." He wants to touch emotionally — children and adults alike -, to make them sad or happy. Although he esteems Disney in his kind and doesn't minimalize him he dislikes hand-drawn films. They are not to his taste. Drawings in a film, he says, will remain caricatures: with all amusing characteristics, however caricatures. They are not living entities who touch the soul. The flatness doesn't allow expression of soul. The drawing cannot have a soul, for it you need a body. The body alone is bearer of the soul, it necessitates three dimensions. In a hand-drawn animated film a man's head can be ripped off and moved back again, and the audience will laugh. To living sculptures you cannot do that: "Od sent de la peine," one will feel pain. Contrary to Disney the animals are no little machines but living entities, almost human.

Who has seen Reineke Fuchs and who knows Disney will find this differentiation very affecting. Starevich's film, compared to Walt Disney's animal grotesqueness, has the advantage of an unlikely higher level of liveliness and naturalism. In his finer, tender, saturated tone of fairy-tale, he is nearer to our feeling. Against the saucy, clean step of civilisation of the American, the Pole represents convincingly the old Europe with its culture grown in emotion and so rich in tradition. About Disney one can laugh and marvel but Starevich one has to love.[12]

7

An Animation Pioneer with a Non-Aryan Background: Wolfgang Kaskeline

UFA Feuilleton #8, February 25, 1931:

"Each cinemagoer will know the name of Wolfgang Kaskeline because he is credited with most of UFA's advertising films. If it appears on screen one will know that now one of those amusing commercials will unreel in which objectivity and humour, farce and fantasy will mix, in which colour, form and sound, scene and schematic illustration softly and evoke a general impression which will leave, apart from the propaganda effect, a pleasant artistic delight for each receptive eye." Then Kaskeline is quoted himself: "I cannot freely and unconditionally express an artistic idea. The basic idea is always connected with the propaganda object. This is a specific thing, and believe me — for a true painter this reference to a subject, this responsibility to the real — is a delight. I'm not permitted to interpret something into an object which is doesn't tell me, otherwise it will become crooked and forced — not real. [...]

"As a painter — and only as a painter — [...] I am an enthusiastic Don Juan. That is, I love *each* object. Only the one who loves to explore the final secrets and only if I have put my ear and my eyes to these last secrets I can reproduce the importance of an advertised object in a way that it will have an impact on the spectator: novel, thrilling, convincing.

The wish to possess it must be awakened in him for this is the essential thing in all advertising.

And now to the technique of the art of advertising films — no, I better shouldn't begin. It is like a country's government — the better, the less one has to talk about.

I have approximately 20 employees. They are who transform my sketches and preproduction art technically with remarkable diligence and — this is the key to the art of animation — accuracy.

Since I have been the first who has created a color sound image I constantly endeavour to vary the use of sound in all of my advertising films. The Expressionist, allegorical film requires different sound, different score than the grotesque cartoon where all objects will become living beings and all living beings will become creatures of magic and jugglers."

Cartoonist Gerhard Fieber, who for some time worked with Kaskeline, remembers one particular incident: "Kaskeline made a completely new type of film, he played with colors. Then people from Muratti came, a very dignified lady with her staff, and asked to see the film. So we screened the film for them. Then she said, 'May we see the film again?' Then she said, 'Can I stay with my family alone?' We had to leave, Kaskeline and myself, and when we returned she said that she will not accept the film, that she didn't like it. One of the directors said, 'Madam, may we put forward a proposal? We will show the film tonight at Ufa-Palast am Zoo, then you will see yourself how the audience will respond to this novel idea in color.' She couldn't deny that of course. We arranged to meet that night, 8:00 P.M., at Ufa-Palast am Zoo. The film received tremendous applause. Why? We had sent all who were available for 5 Mark to the cinema to applaud and act as claquers."[1] The applause, however, at least according to Fieber, turned out to be real and spontaneous.

But then, when Kaskeline had reached the peak, problems arose. On November 1, 1933, the National Socialists revised the Reichskulturkammer (Reich Culture Chamber) Law. According to section 4 all artists and technicians involved in the making of animated films were requested to register their company with Reichsfilmkammer. Their employees had to apply for membership in the section Reichsfachschaft Film (Reich Film Department). Wolfgang Kaskeline did so on January 25, 1934.[2]

On December 19, 1934, the Kontingentstelle (contingent office) of *Reichsfachschaft Film* reported:

> Re: Wolfgang Kaskeline, Aryan origin
>
> After consulting the Reich Ministry of Interior, Amt für Rasseforschung [Bureau for Racial Investigation], I advise you in the matter of Kaskeline that the Amt für Rasseforschung has sent a questionnaire to Herr Kaskeline on November 22, 1934. This wasn't returned until today (four weeks).
>
> On November 1, 1934, the Contingent Office wrote to Kaskeline:
>
> Regarding your letter dated October 30, 1934, I regret to tell you that a further prolongation is out of question as you had had enough time since fall of the previous year to provide the necessary documents.
>
> May I indicate that further petitions of Ufa no sooner can be submitted to Reich Ministry of Enlightenment and Propaganda until certificate of your Aryan parentage has been received completely.
>
> On November 6, 1934, Kaskeline submitted a petition to the Amt für Rasseforschung re: settlement resp. sourcing of the missing documents. Concerning the failure to fulfil obligations and the fact that the questionnaire of the Racial Bureau was not returned by Herr Kaskeline one might recognize at least a protraction.

In fact, Kaskeline had problems producing such documents to prove a so-called Aryan background.

On September 17, 1935, the UFA Board of Directors discussed this issue: "Mr. Grieving announces that Reichsfilmkammer has prohibited animator Kaskeline from continuing work as non–Aryan. The Board assents to pay his fee until end of this month. Also Kaskeline should receive an interest-free loan up to RM 5,000 on October 1, 1935. The loan is not repayable provided that Kaskeline succeeds in obtaining the renewed accreditation in the next one and a half years. In case of renewed accreditation the employee's contract with Ufa which now has to be terminated will become valid again. The loan will be immediately payable if Kaskeline would accept trick assignments from third parties. Mr. Grieving is authorized to terminate Kaskeline's employment relationship on that basis."

On September 23, 1935, Reichsfachschaft Film reported to the president of Reichsfilmkammer and denounced Wolfgang Kaskeline:

> Subsequent to our letter of December 19 we have to tell you that it was determined post hoc that Wolfgang Kaskeline (advertising film cartoonist and director) is non — Aryan.
>
> In the marriage certificate his father is registered as Jew.
>
> Kaskeline has suppressed this fact in his application to Reichsfachschaft Film on January 25, 1934, and indicated parentage as: German Protestant.
>
> We request herewith the expulsion of said person from Reichsfilmkammer resp. Reichsfachschaft Film.

On October 1, 1935, Reichsfilmkammer wrote to Wolfgang Kaskeline and asked him for his comment within three days. Nevertheless, the manager of Reichskulturkammer, Hans Hinkel, allowed to employ Kaskeline "*bis auf weiteres*" (for the time being) until the fundamental question how to deal in the cases of so-called Halb- & Vierteljuden (Half- and Quarter-Jews) has been resolved.

On October 26, 1937, Mr. Grieving reported to the UFA board of directors that Kaskeline had to be dismissed summarily as there was evidence that he had accepted an assignment from third parties:

> With letter from December 11, 1937, Reichsfilmkammer asked a number of persons to testify in the expulsion proceedings against Wolfgang Kaskeline, Berlin-Tempelhof, Manfred von Richthofen Str. 34 on Friday, December 17, 1937, 11:00 A.M.: Ufa animators Kurt Blank, Hermann Groth, Bernhard Huth, Georg Leutke, Alfons Ley, Egon von Tresckow, advertising artist Curt Schumann, Mr. Staab (Tobis Filmkunst), Dr. Kraemer (IMAGOTON Film G.m.b.H.).

With a letter dated December 24, 1937, Reichsfilmkammer informed its president:

> Re: Wolfgang Kaskeline (non–Aryan)
>
> By decree from September 25, 1935, it was decided that there are no objections against further employment of war invalid Wolfgang Kaskeline for the time being.
>
> On October 25, 1937, Universum–Film AG. (Ufa) has filed an application for expulsion of Kaskeline.
>
> The main complaints that Mr. Kaskeline, contrary to his contract with Ufa, has recommended an animator known to him, Miss Jacobi, for the production of animated titles for the Tobis movie Die Fledermaus to Imagoton-Film G.m.b.H. resp. Tobis and that he himself during his office hours has produced part of the preproduction in his Ufa studio resp. has them produced by subordinated animators and photographers. Furthermore, Ufa complains about the improper demeanour, personal and business, of Mr. Kaskeline.
>
> The principal result is documented in a file memo from 20th of this month (p. 91). From that it is certain that Kaskeline is to be blamed for breach of contract and betrayal of confidence as far as Ufa is concerned and that his personal and business manners are not always regarded as impeccable.

The writer, however, concludes that expulsion proceedings are out of the question and instead recommends revoking of the special permit. A special permission like that in the case of Kaskeline, however, is regarded a benefit which doesn't necessitate the same strict requirements. Although he agrees that Kaskeline's behavior is to be regarded as blameworthy, it doesn't exceed the liberties that prominent artists sometimes presume in business matters: "There is, however, another issue to be considered," the writer pointed out. "I don't know if there are similar cases in point at Reichskulturkammer: According to our investigations there is no doubt that Kaskeline has an affair with Jacobi. This is not liable to prosecution according to the *Rassenschutzgesetzgebung* [Law for the Protection of the Race]. However, both would need to contract a marriage according to § 3 of the First Regulation on Implementation of the Law for Protection of German Blood and German Honor from November 14, 1935, and therefore would require the permission of the Deputy of the Führer and the Reich Minister of the Interior. As is known from previous administrative practice this permission which is necessary for contracting the marriage was always denied."

On February 26, 1938, Reichsfilmkammer wrote Kaskeline that although he was guilty of breach of faith concerning Universum-Film A.G., the president of Reichskulturkammer had decided to let the matter rest with a one-time but final admonishment.

Nevertheless, Ufa terminated the contract. Kaskeline had to apply for work elsewhere and found a niche with Epoche Gasparcolor-Film A.G.

One year later, on March 4, 1939, the special permission from September 25, 1935, was cancelled: "You have lost the right to become active in each field that belongs to the domain of Reichskulturkammer. The decision is final as it is based on a decree of Herr Reich Minister for Enlightenment and Propaganda. I ask immediately to abandon your commitment with company Epoche Gasparcolor-Film A.G. and report after having done so."

But this time Epoche Gasparcolor intervened on Kaskeline's behalf. On March 14, 1939, Reichsfilmkammer reported to the ministry that the company would be damaged if Mr. Kaskeline would be forced to resign immediately: "I endorse the petition that the advertising film assignments will be finished by Mr. Kaskeline and he is allowed an adequate deadline.

Concerning the represented issue that Kaskeline is of Jewish birth I ask for decision if an expert report from *Reichsstelle für Sippenforschung* [Reich Office for Hereditary Research] has to be obtained and if Mr. Kaskeline, until advance of such report of *Reichsstelle*, should be given a working permit."

On March 22, 1939, Reichkulturkammer informed Epoche Gasparcolor-Film A.G. that the removal of the special permission cannot be revoked: "Regarding the deadline I am prepared to accommodate you."

Epoche Gasparcolor-Film applied for a deadline of nine months, but a prolongation of only five months, until September 30, 1939, was granted. Simultaneously they tried to file for hereditary and racial investigation at Reichsstelle für Sippenforschung.

On June 5, 1939, Reichsfilmkammer forwarded a petition to *Reichsstelle für Sippenforschung* (Berlin NW 7, Schiffbauerdamm 26):

> Re: Proof of descent of trick film artist Wolfgang Kaskeline, born September 23, 1892 in Frankfurt am Main, residing in Berlin-Tempfelhof, Manfred-von-Richthofenstrasse 182.
>
> I herewith submit the attached documents:
>
> 1. Petition of Epoche Gasparcolor-Film Aktiengesellschaft, Berlin W 9, Schellingstr. 7, dated May 6, 1939, for a hereditary and racial investigation of above mentioned person,
> 2. Affidavit by Mrs. Katharina Kaskeline dated March 9, 1939 (mother of testee)
> 3. Affidavit by Mrs. Katharina Kaskeline dated March 27, 1939 (mother of testee)
> 4. Affidavit by Bruno von Alt-Stutterheim, Lieutenant of the Reserve ret., dated March 27, 1939 (brother-in-law of testee), residing in Berlin-Tempelhof, Thuyring 68,

5. Affidavit by Mrs. Olga von Alt-Stutterheim dated March 27, 1939 (sister of testee), née Kaskeline, born on December 14, 1890 in Frankfurt am Main,
6. Copy of petition which is addressed to Herr Reich Minister for Enlightenment and Propaganda by Mrs. Katharina Kaskeline dated March 9, 1939 (mother of testee),
7. Copy of letter by Epoche Gasparcolor-Film Aktiengesellschaft dated March 10, 1939 addressed to Herr President of Reichsfilmkammer, Berlin W 35, Bendlerstr. 35,
8. Copy of letter of Epoche Gasparcolor-Film Aktiengesellschaft dated April 22, 1939 to Kanzlei des Führers/Chancellery of the Führer, c/o Mr. von Hegemann (the family name is wrongly recorded; the correct name is: von Hegener), Berlin W 8, Reichskanzlei/Reich Chancellery,
9. Questionnaire by Reichsstelle für Sippenforschung (with paternal grandfather and 3 certified photos of testee),
10. Questionnaire of Reichsstelle für Sippenforschung with legal paternal grandfather,
11. Passport photo of father,
12. Passport photo of mother,
13. 2 passport photos of brother Raimund Kaskeline, engineer, born Frankfurt am Main on March 14, 1888, residing in Rome,
14. Passport photo of maternal grandmother,
15. Passport photo of daughter Sigrid Kaskeline, born on December 3, 1918 in Berlin,
16. 2 passport photos of son Horst Kaskeline, born on December 11, 1919 in Berlin,
17. 2 passport photos of son Heinz Kaskeline, born on January 24, 1926 in Berlin,
18. Passport photo of paternal grandmother,
19. 2 passport photos of maternal grandfather,
20. 2 passport photos of maternal grandmother,
21. Folder containing
    a) 51 documents
    b) 2 document copies,
    c) 1 certified copy.

All above mentioned passport photos are not required to be certified by police.

The animation artist Wolfgang Kaskeline made false statements to our office re: his pedigree paper in 1934/35 and tried to conceal the Jewish descent of his father. On November 5, 1934, Universum-Film-Aktiengesellschaft forwarded, inter alia, the copy of a petition by Herr Kaskeline addressed to Reich Minister of Interior, Amt für Rasseforschung [Bureau for Racial Research]. [...]

Wolfgang Kaskeline — Berlin S 19, 11/6/34
Universum-Film — Krausenstr. 38/39
Aktiengesellschaft
To Reich Minstry of Interior,
Bureau for Racial Research, Berlin.

The undersigned asks for recognition of his Aryan descent according to §2 decree for the screening of foreign films dated June 27, 34, next-to-last passage, because he, as he explains below in more detail, is not able to submit documents about the actual Aryan descent of his father and grandfather who both came from Finland.

I was born as German citizen on September 23, 92 in Frankfurt a.M. and baptized Protestant as son of merchant Viktor Samuel Kaskeline and his wife Katharina née Scherf. My father, who already as a young man had immigrated from Finland and was German citizen, died in 1931 in South Italy. My mother lives in Berlin. I have forwarded the hitherto missing documents concerning the parents of my mother to the contingency office for information.

In spite of all my great efforts I myself, my brother who lives in Rome, and my brother-in-law Bruno von Alt-Stutterheim were not successful in collecting any document concerning the birth of my father and grandfather Kaskeline and about the marriage of my parents in Genoa. The Kaskeline family origins, as the name says, from Finland and, as is known to my family, generations ago immigrated from Toscana. Any two generations in Finland were glass painters and glass burners and due to their profession had travelled frequently around the world.

Because of the political change of system in Finland research regarding the Russian time is extremely difficult, especially as my father, who died in a foreign country didn't leave any documents because he wasn't interested very much in family history. Certain, however, is only that there is no evidence of Jewish blood in our family. I leave this issue to an expert assessment. My only brother who entered the war as volunteer, became a pilot and left as lieutenant, lives in Rome for 8 years. I myself entered Elizabeth Guard Grenadier Regiment on August 1, 14 as war volunteer, came to Jnft. Regt. 203, 11. Kpg. and was severely wounded on October 26, 14 in the battle of Dixmuiden. I was made private and received the E.K 2.[3] After a two-year stay in military hospital I was released as 70% war invalid because of my wound (stiffening of the knee joint, shortenage of the right leg, Peronnaeus paralyzation and Fascialis paralyzation) and received a pension from relief ogranization.

The past 7 years I worked for Universum-Film Aktiengesellschaft as an artist and now have to attest my Aryan background according to the mentioned contingency decree. Therefore I ask politely to certify that I am of Aryan descent.

I am married to Minna Kaskeline née Berg since 1917. She comes from Buchwald i. Riesengebirge [Giant Mountain range in Silesia] and is of pure Aryan descent.

Mit deutschem Gruss
signed, Wolfgang Kaskeline.

Regarding the origin of his father the testee explains that he is not able to prove and submit records of the actual Aryan descent of his father and grandfather who both come from Finland. His father (Viktor Samuel Kaskeline) who already as a young man immigrated from Finland and was German citizen died in 1931 in South Italy. In spite of greatest efforts, the testee writes, he, his brother, who lives in Rome, and his brother-in-law, Bruno von Alt-Stutterheim, were not successful in collecting birth certificates of his father and grandfather Kaskeline and the marriage certificate of his parents from Genoa. The Kaskeline family origins, as the name says, from Finland and shall have immigrated, according to a tradition only known to the family, generations ago from Toscana. Any two generations were glass painters in Finland and glass burners and have travelled due to their profession all over the world. "Certain, however, is only that there is no evidence of Jewish blood in our family. I leave this issue to an expert assessment." "Therefore I ask politely to certify that I am of Aryan descent."

These statements of the testee are lies. The same false statements were also made concerning the pedigree paper of Reichsfilmkammer. The father Viktor Emanuel Kaskeline comes not from Finland; he was actually born on December 28, 1858 in Teplitz/Bohemia as son of the Jewish couple Ludwig Kaskeline and Linna Schlesinger. The marriage of the testee's parents was not contracted in Genoa but on March 30, 1887 in Frankfurt am Main (according to marriage certificate No. 336 of the register office in Frankfurt am Main, disctrict I, issued on August 3, 1935). This certificate was located by Abstammungsnachweis (proof of descent) of Reichsfilmkammer without any problems and with it the statements of the testee disproved. The mother of the testee, Mrs. Katharina Kaskeline née Scherf, who lives in Berlin, could have told her son and son-in-law if asked about day and location of their marriage.

The request of Wolfgang Kaskeline (dated November 6, 1934) addressed to the Office for Race Research, to confirm that he is of Aryan descent, is, considering the (false) statements, a manifestation of greatest audacity.

Also the affidavis by the testee's mother, the brother-in-law, Bruno von Alt-Stutterheim, and his sister, Olga von Alt-Stutterheim née Kaskeline, deserve greatest doubt and mistrust. In his affidavit the brother-in-law, Bruno von Alt-Stutterheim, states: "It is known to me for some time that my father-in-law Viktor Kaskeline, who passed away in 1931, actually is the son of a Teplitz castle owner who was in close contact with his mother (Linna Kaskeline née Schlesinger). This fact was told to me occasionally by my father, forester Wilhelm von Alt-Stutterheim, who was a friend of my father-in-law."

From the letter of Wolfgang Kaskeline dated November 6, 1934, results conclusively that his brother-in-law, Bruno von Alt-Stutterheim, tried to get a pedigree paper for his wife. His father, Wilhelm von Alt-Stutterheim, has died on November 28, 1922 in Rengersdorf district Sagan according to telephone information by Mrs. Olga von Alt-Stutterheim. The testee's father and father-in-law of Mr. Bruno von Alt-Stutterheim, Viktor Kaskeline, died on April 5, 1930 in Riva/Lake Garda. The knowledge of Mr. Bruno von Alt-Stutterheim concerning the misstep of Linna Kaskeline née Schlesinger must stem from the time before the case of death of his father (November 28, 1922). He could have used this knowledge in 1933 or 1934 and not yet on March 27, 1939.

The statements of Wolfgang Kaskeline in the letter from November 6, 1934, are contrary to the statements of Mr. Bruno von Alt-Stutterheim from March 27, 1939. Also the affidavit by the mother, Mrs. Katharina Kaskeline née Scherf, is no proof; on March 27, 1939, she explained: "It was not known to me that my son could be regarded as non–Aryan. I didn't know about such a possibility." This statement seems to be unreliabale. At the marriage contracted on March 30, 1887, in Frankfurt am Main her husband, the merchant Viktor Kaskeline, was of Israelite religion. Mrs. Katharina Kaskeline knew already in the years 1933/34 that her sonwould have to keep a record concerning his descency. She must have used her affidavit issued on March 9, 1939, back then. This she had omitted.

Deutsche Zeichenfilm G.m.b.H. (DZF): An unfinished *Walzermärchen* (1944) by Wolfgang Kaskeline.

The pictures submitted by the testee (passport photos) are insufficient. Mrs. Katharina Kaskeline explains under oath: "My husband had no similarity with his siblings who had the Jewish father as documented; he was blond and had glaucous eyes." Mrs. Katharina Kaskeline must have known the brothers of her husband resp. possess photos of her husband's brothers. There were no photos of her husband's brothers attached, however, which could serve to substantiate her statements.

According to his marriage certificate the testee is "art teacher and artist" and since 1927 active in the film industry as animation artist. Therefore he has respective knowledge of camera and photography. It is our guess that the testee may have photograped his family (wife and children) and his parents repeatedly. Instead of attaching photos of his father from recent times, however, the testee submits only a passport photo of his father that was made approximately 1887.

Above we have determined that the attached affidavits in important issues cannot be regarded as well-founded.

You will have to check the petition and decide if regarding the poor and doubtful material the application for hereditary and race file of Wolfgang Kaskeline can be approved. We have refrained from asking the testee to submit more means of evidence as requested.

Heil Hitler!
REICHSFILMKAMMER
Pedigree Paper
signed by proxy, Dr. Jacob.

By special permission of Reich Minister for Enlightenment and Propaganda dated July 25, 1939, at any time revocable, Wolfgang Kaskeline was allowed to continue in his profession, until conclusion of the current investigation of his descent by Reich Office for Hereditary Research.

On February 1, 1940, Reichsfilmkammer reported to Fachschaft Film:

Re: Wolfgang Kaskeline

The Reich Ministry for Enlightenment and Propaganda announces by decree from January 27, 1940, as follows:

"After receiving now pedigree paper from *Reichsstelle für Sippenforschung* which has arranged for a hereditary and race investigation at the *Poliklinik für Erb- und Rassenpflege* [Polyclinic for Hereditament and Race Cultivation], Berlin-Charlottenburg, in the case of Wolfgang Kaskeline the above mentioned is *Vierteljude* ["One-Quarter Jew"].

Thus there are no objections against his registration as fully-valid member of your Chamber."

Nevertheless, Kaskeline's career in the Third Reich had virtually come to an end. On February 1944 he was recruited by Deutsche Zeichenfilm G.m.b.H. to work with 16 artists on an unfinished short *Musikfilm: Walzermärchen* [*Waltz Tale*] and very likely for military training films by Mars-Film G.m.b.H., then restarted business in Berlin as independent producer of advertising films and commercials right after the war. Years after the war Kaskeline still tried to get back his personal assets that were left in the bombed rooms of Deutsche Zeichenfilm G.m.b.H. and maybe were taken away by others but his efforts were to no avail.

8

The Phenomenology and Psychology of Cartoons

Analytical Investigations (Analysis) of the Phenomenological, Psychological and Artistic Structures of the Animation Group: This was the title of a thesis published by Reinhold Johann Holtz. Holtz was born on June 19, 1913, in Hamburg-Harburg. He was admitted to college in 1933. After a brief period at Freiwilliger Arbeitsdienst (voluntary fatigue duty) he was allowed to enroll at the Philosophical Faculty of Hansische University in the winter semester of 1934–35.

His thesis evolved in cinematographic colloquia and lectures held by Professor Anschütz and inspired by his color-sound-congresses. He attempts to explore the category "cartoon" within the context of its phenomenology, psychological and artistic significance. In the introduction, the author welcomes the upheaval of the collective mind and feeling through National Socialism and the state's recognition of valuable films. He turns eventually to the topic of trickfilm. He names the most popular cartoons from America, Disney's Mickey Mouse and Silly Symphony series as well as his imitators, Curt [sic! Max] Fleischer and his hero Popeye the Sailor, Paul Terry and his characters, Farmer Falfa al Falfa and Kiko the Kangaroo.

In Germany the author sees no overall trend to series, but unique efforts like those of the Fischinger brothers (especially Oskar) and their synesthetical abstract films, Lotte Reiniger's fairy tales in silhouette, Kurt Stordel's animated cartoons (especially fairy tales like *Purzel the Dwarf*), the Diehl brothers, *Das tapfere Schneiderlein* (*The Brave Little Tailor*) by Schwab and Gerhardt and so on. Regarding in abstract animation he points out Oskar Fischinger's *Composition in Blue*.

The category of cartoons should be subdivided into the following, he suggests:

- abstract film
- silhouette film
- *Sachtrickfilm* (animated objects)
- cartoon
- visionary film.

The visionary film is mainly represented by Alexander Alexeieff's classic short *La Nuit sur le Mont Chauve*. If the focus of the work is predominantly the creative process, that is, its impact on the audience, a number of conclusions and observations remain important to the cinematographer.

The editor's intention is the synesthesia composed of drawing, motion, sound and color that differs from any other cinematographic category concerning its perfection. There is a compilation of 31 newspapers, as well as magazine articles on the subject of cartoons and on 76 typical cartoons (unfortunately, there are no data concerning the year of publication), including 39 by Walt Disney.

9

Hans Held, Troublemaker

Hans Held was a well-known caricaturist and the one who did some of the best Mecki cartoons for *HoerZu* after World War II. Many Germans remember Mecki as the hedgehog puppet character brought to life by Ferdinand Diehl's stop-motion animation. Held was an accomplished animator himself, and was one of the few animators who was also an actor in pencil.

In 1940 Bavaria Filmkunst released an animated color short with certain propaganda value: *Der Störenfried* (*The Troublemaker*) by Hans Held. In the film, the forest animals unite against the red intruder who troubles the peaceful Teutonic environment: Hedgehogs wearing *Wehrmacht* helmets as well as wasps forming Stuka squadrons attack the fox, who turns out to be the foe.

Hans Held in 1933 (courtesy Erika Held).

Who is Hans Held and where does he come from?

He was born in Holzminden (May 25, 1914).

He went to school in Osnabrück and, in gymnasium, began to draw on blank film without knowing anything about the technique.

Early on he realized the importance of movement as means to express what he had in mind. To command movement was his main goal.[1]

He volunteered at the Municipal Town Theatre in Osnabrück: He did intensive research in scenic painting, costume design and theatrical sciences and was educated in scenic art by Friedrich Prätorius.

When hired as actor and scenic

artist by the Municipal Theatre Brandenburg for the first time he could make practical use of his newly won experiences. From there he tried to connect with trickfilm.

In his creative work he could make good use of his early activities as sportsman. During his school days he had already excelled in Youngster and Glider piloting (1930 glider license).

Flying is his main interest; the scenes involving birds and wasps in Einigkeit macht stark [retitled *Der Störenfried*] reveal the results.

He has made his license (1932) as motor glider and built aircraft himself not only for gliding but also motor gliding.

An active guy who sticks at nothing and wanted to become a parachutist, but didn't make it. Nevertheless he has jumped at least once, "in high spirits" as he recalls.

The technical aspects of his art had taught him about humans: their actual disposition has made him recognize nature. Rightfully he calls nature his great teacher.

Whenever possible he tramped in free nature: on bicycle and motorcycle, and to earn some money even tried car racing.[2]

When Hans Held learned that Ernst Röhm's (Sturmabteilung) organized a flying squad in Osnabrück he joined them in December 1931. He even felt qualified enough to command this squadron. In an interview in 1988,[3] he denied being politically minded at all. He was interested only in his flying career. This, he claims, was his only reason to join the SA and, a few months later, on November 20, 1932, the Nazi Party. But then someone else was chosen to head the Nazi squadron: a former pool attendant. For a moment, he recalled, he thought about quitting, but his passion for flying was too strong and eventually he became squad leader. (Finally, of course, he would make a career not in the Luftwaffe but in movies and animation.)

At the second Election Day in 1933 the National Socialists needed every vote. They organized an extensive service to escort registered party members to the polls. On Election Day Held's doorbell rang. The night before he had drunk a little bit, and he was escorted to the polling station. In his tale he still wore dressing gown and slippers. And voted "No." In his denazification form in 1945 he faithfully answered every question. Only: "Did you vote for N.S.D.A.P. in 1933?" he answered "Yes." Nobody, he thought, would have believed that a member of SA and Nazi Party would have possibly voted "No."

Hans Held: *Der Störenfried* (1940), pencil sketch (courtesy Erika Held).

As the theatrical stage in Osnabrück seemed too small for someone like him, he moved to Munich on July 9, 1934. He rented a small flat in Schwabing, an artisan's district, at Zieblandstrasse, 27. Besides studying with Professor Prätorius, he attended lectures in theatrical sciences with Professor Kurt Kutscher, and in the afternoon drew artist postcards for the Hanfstaengl Company. Much time was spent with his fellow student Liselotte Fürst-Ramdohr at Starnberger See. (Liselotte later became a supporter of White Rose, a students' resistance group.)

In October 1935 Hans Held entered the movies with a special permission issued by Reichsfachschaft Film (German Film Guild) County Office Bavaria, and played a Russian orderly in a Bavaria Film production, *Der andere Perbrandt* (*Henker, Frauen und Soldaten*). In Schwabing he met a bank clerk, Waltraude Quentin, and fell in love with her. Then he moved to Berlin. In Brandenburg he found an apartment with the Seiler family at Grosse Gartenstrasse. 5, and got a contract from Municipal Theatre Brandenburg as scenic artist with acting commitment. Eventually he rented an apartment in Berlin Spandau, Weinmeisterhorn 17. Waltraude followed from Munich, and they married. On January 10, 1936, he officially had joined Reichsfachschaft Film. The same year he was registered with Reichsfilmkammer, Fachschaft Film, for a welfare account and in December applied for a loan of RM 30,-: "For several days I have no means now — no parents to turn to. Because I will have some jobs with several companies over the next weeks I can repay the sum very soon (January 1, 1937)."

Result of judgment: Refused. Reason: Didn't make a contribution.

As a struggling actor in Nazi Germany Held racked up debts repeatedly.

On March 9, 1937, one Heinz Benda[4] protested at Reichsfilmkammer:

> Re: actor Hans Held
>
> Alas, I have to turn to you with a complain about actor Hans Held. Mr. H. in October of previous year has introduced himself as animation cameraman and given an address in Berlin Spandau. Located there, however, is only a small summerhouse currently not used by himself and his wife. For an important business trip to the Rhineland he has loaned from me RM 250. This money he needed urgently as some big order for him depended on this trip. Later I learned that these specifications were false. He had agreed to pay off on November 1 previous year but didn't observe.
>
> As he didn't get in touch with me the following weeks, neither in letter nor verbal, I tried to do some research on my own.
>
> He had stated that he had rented a large office in a house on Friedrichstrasse 8 from the landlord and that craftsmen already were at work. I learned, however, that although he apparently had rented this office since September he didn't pay any kind of rent. The craftsmen who had worked there still try to get their money. Only one of them, the bricklayer, has enforced the payment of his bill by threat of a warrant. In the meantime I have learned from another film company, Ultra-Film G.m.b.H., that he has made himself guilty for breach of contract and breach of trust in connection with wilful libel and therefore is to be persecuted.
>
> When I recently met him in Friedrichstrasse he gave me his new address but this statement was not true either.
>
> May I ask you to pursue this matter and take legal proceedings against Held.
>
> I have to add that then as security he left a not very valuable animation film camera.
>
> Mit deutschem Gruss!
>
> Signed

In a letter dated March 12, 1937, Reichsfilmkammer answered creditor Benda:

> We herewith confirm the receipt of your letter from 9th of this month but have to tell you that we ourselves have no option to proceed in your matter because it is an entirely private loan.
> Heil Hitler!
> Signed on behalf

The animation camera mentioned in the letter was a proof that Held already had moved towards animation. In 1935 Kurt Maetzig had opened a small studio in Berlin making credits and advertising. There Held, who had become sort of a pupil, learned the basics of animation, editing, sound and camera technique. In 1937, however, Maetzig was forced to close his studio, for his wife was Jewish. Hans Held lost a lucrative job. In 1937 Paramount Film A.G. Germany confirmed "that Mister Hans Held was active for us as actor in two pictures, *Farm am Mississippi* and *Assistenzarzt Dr. Kilder.*" Hans Held's acting career ended in mid–1938 with a bit part in *Wenn in Werder blühen die Bäume* for which he received a fee of RM 50,-.

In this time his problems with creditors increased. He was always on the run. Looking for money he met a Berlin animator, Max Wuestemann. Together they founded an animation studio at Friedrichstrasse. 19. They intended to do an animation short after a poem that Friedrich Schiller had written in 1797, *Der Handschuh* (*The Glove*).

Hans Held: *Der Handschuh* (1938–39).

In its December 25, 1938, issue *Der Stern* reported:

> Der Handschuh
> Not by Schiller
> A new color cartoon is being made
> Forthcoming a new German color cartoon will see the light of the screen. A team of artists under the supervision of artist Hans Held has created in long, meticulous work approximately twenty-thousand little images from which they are going to make a 500 mtr long animated color feature. The artistic preproduction has lasted almost a year for every tiny movement necessitated a new frame. The film which had cost this enormous sum of artistic effort will enroll in fifteen minutes. A German subject is the premise, the ballad of the "Glove." A "Prelude in the Sky" introduces the Old German world of knights, kings and beautiful noblewomen. The play is a mix of seriousness and serenity. There the honourable squire strides out in shining armor, with sword and panache, into the lion cage, there jump spotted leopards, there creep snarling tiger cats, there flaunt and throne majestic lions. On high balcony the court resides. Colorful and funny a forgotten time is being revived. And besides coarse humour German poetry will enlighten this picture.

After months of intensive work to no avail, Hans Held and Max Wüstemann suspended their project as "sort of finished" and offered another short, *Caliph Stork.*[5] However, the mountain of debts increased and they parted in a bitter quarrel. Hans Held kept the film, including all rights.

In the meantime, Waltraude Held had mobilized their Munich relatives. Her husband needed a full-time job very soon. One uncle with some influence had good contacts to Bavaria Filmkunst. Bavaria at that time was commissioned by the Film Department of the Ministry of Enlightenment and Propaganda to provide their own short films. Hans Held approached them with the idea of producing cartoons.

On August 2, 1939, Held signed the contract for *Einigkeit macht stark* (*Unity makes strong*). They planned to finish the 250–450 meters color cartoon until March 31, 1940. According to his contract, Held would receive RM 35.000 after finishing his work. For a few months Held could now work freely on the fourth floor on Friedrichstrasse, where Bavaria had its Berlin offices. There he was joined by nine other animators and colorists. During a meeting in the Ministry of Propaganda, Reichsfilmintendant Fritz Hippler asked about Held's experiences in the cartoon business. Four days later Bavaria answered by shipping a demo reel of Held's *Glove.*

Held's creditors, however, now approached Bavaria Filmkunst. Above that, the production costs for Held's new short already mounted to more than RM 70.000. At the end of March 1940 there was no hope that the production would wrap soon. Hans Held was *K. v.* (*Kriegsverwendungsfähig,* which meant that he could be drafted any time) and, like many other members of the German film industry, didn't receive UK status (*unabkömmlich,* indispensable). So besides his duties on finishing the cartoon, he had to serve in the German Luftwaffe [air force].

Production manager Ernst Mosich, at Bavaria's Berlin offices since 1939 (in 1943 he would move to Munich, but still remained in charge of animation production in Berlin), had his lawyers work out a plan to redeem Held's debts by granting him a credit of RM 15.000. A condition was a long-term contract with Bavaria, including an agreement that Held would pay off RM 800–1,000 of his monthly fee to his creditors. Above

Hans Held: *Der Störenfried* (1940).

that, all his rights on *Glove* should go over to Bavaria. Thanks to this support, Held was able to pay off all his debts by the end of September 1940, and focus thereafter on finishing his cartoon. On November 4, 1940, *Der Störenfried*, as *Einigkeit macht stark* now was called, passed the Board of Censors (No. 59626) and received the rating *volksbildend* (people educative). It was first screened as a German entry at the Biennale in Venice in 1941. As Geyer Laboratories in Berlin were not able to deliver prints on Agfacolor film stock, in September 1941 prints in the Gasparcolor process were shipped to Venice. Prints were also given to the army's transportable cinema wagons for troop entertainment. While finishing *The Troublemaker* Held was already preparing the next short, *Die Abenteuer des Freiherrn von Münchhausen* (*The Adventures of Baron Munchausen*), and planned to put finishing touches on *The Glove* too. *Film-Kurier*[6] announced two more shorts: *Winter Olympics* and *Puppet Fairy*. Held's staff then consisted of Freiherr Bernhard von Friesen, Anneliese Boas, Erika Clausen, Olga Grzimek, Beate Koch, Freiherr Kurt von Lamezan, and Elisabeth Lehne.

Eventually, however, competition arose named Deutsche Zeichenfilm G.m.b.H., and made working conditions difficult.

10

Kurt Stordel and Purzel: A Self-Proclaimed German Walt Disney and His Dwarf

When J.P. Storm visited *Ullstein Bilderdienst* in Berlin to do some research on Walt Disney and Germany between 1927 and 1945, he unearthed the name of Kurt Stordel. When he asked for Stordel's file he only found a small black-and-white pass photo. After some more research he found out that Stordel was still alive and well and living in Hamburg. He visited him at the end of 1985 and was astonished that Stordel lived in a small flat that also served as his studio. He was still active, and even dreamed of new projects in animation. However, talking to the 80-year-old proved that Stordel's memory more than occasionally failed. Also he seemed to feel uncomfortable when questioned about his activities at Ufa in the 1930s and 1940s. Eventually he produced a folder of press clippings.

Stordel, a book illustrator and graphic artist, became interested in animation in 1926 after witnessing the audience response to a Felix the Cat cartoon. Although he had no experience in animation, he was commissioned by a Hamburg-based advertising company operated by the Flach Brothers to draw a trickfilm. They were looking for an artist who could animate a dog cartoon published in a Danish newspaper. With an old camera turned into a stop-frame device Stordel began his first experiments.

The idea to found his own animation company came to Stordel after attending the screening of an early Mickey Mouse cartoon in a Hamburg cinema. Because of the economic crisis he failed to make any profit. The year 1932 was not a prosperous one, neither for society nor an animation studio. Stordel mainly did advertising to survive, but refused to do pornographic cartoons which then were sold in South America. His objective was the animated fairy tale.

In 1933 he got some assignments from Ufa-Werbefilm, but his business connections in Switzerland were cut by export limitations dictated by the Ministry of Enlightenment and Propaganda. On September 8, 1934, Stordel applied for membership in Fachschaft Film as Trickfilmzeichner [animator]. In mid–1935, supported by an associate of Hansa-Film, he opened a studio for documentary, advertising and animation films in the Klockmann Building in Hamburg. Together with his wife he developed the idea of a German fairy tale cycle (Deutscher Märchenkranz) and announced as first entry *Graf Habenichts*, an adaptation of Puss in Boots: "Referring to the grotesque style of Walt Disney was consciously avoided. Stordel's films shall be funny, romantic, folksy. The background of the individual sequences is rendered in grey water colors to evoke soft color tones."[1]

Kurt Stordel: *Purzel der Zwerg* (1938).

Besides his work on advertising films he turned out more entries in the German fairy tale cycle and produced a number of black-and-white animation films, among them *Sleeping Beauty, The Bremen Town Musicians,* and *Hansel and Gretel.* By that time he had moved his company, which was strictly a family business and included his wife Elli and son Peter, from Hamburg to Berlin Charlottenburg, Bismarckstrasse. 82/83. He also intended to do *Brave Little Tailor* and film works inspired by fantasist E. T. A. Hoffmann.

A journalist of a trade paper visited Stordel and his wife in their apartment in Berlin. He wrote:

> In the big city of Berlin, in Moabit, the young artist Kurt Stordel lives with his wife in a middle-class 4 room flat. The young couple, however, doesn't belong to those quiet people for whom the Sunday chicken in the pot means the fulfilment of all earthly wishes. They are imaginative people who on top of it are in league with film.
>
> In a room there are long tables which are covered with drawings. On the walls hang flashy watercolors and cardboard boxes are filled with all kinds of colorful characters which are carefully cut out. Kurt Stordel is a self-made man.
>
> Clearly contrary to foreign animators who mainly focus on gags and for whom the idea is essential, Stordel proceeds from content and from strong romanticism. This shows in his work. Instead of sharp outlines he prefers the watercolor, instead of hard color, stains and blots the more effective but more difficult nuances. The key frames he draws himself. His wife supports him in tracing them onto cels.
>
> His wife takes the cue of romanticism: "Yes, my husband is a romanticist.... He completely goes up in the work on his fairy tale world. While such a movie is developed there is nothing else for him.[2]

One of Stordel's creations was Purzel, a dwarf in Magicland. *Völkischer Beobachter* hailed *Purzel, Brumm und Quack*, announced to the public as *Ein Märchen* (*A Fairy Tale*), as a first-rate German cartoon: "Nobody should ask which fairy tale shall be filmed. There is no answer to this question. Nothing will be turned into a film what German people possess in treasures of fairy tales. Stordel borrowed his creatures from cartoonists, draughtsmen and painters and one should let them go as they were conceived by their creators. If we weren't able to newly invent nice and funny plots things would be looking bad for us. The trickfilm is an absolutely modern invention and so the contents which he deals with have to be new and topical."[3]

"One should be anxious to see if Stordel will succeed in breaking Walt Disney's present autocracy over the 'German fairy tale forest.' In fact, in the interest of German filmmaking it should be wished that this gap in the field of short films will be filled if one considers the many excellent attempts for instance in the advertising films.[4] In another interview Kurt Stordel stressed that, good heavens, he doesn't want to become a Walt Disney.[5]

The renowned trade magazine *Filmwelt* let Purzel introduce himself:

> I take off my pointed cap and make a low bow. I am allowed to introduce myself to the readers of *Filmwelt*: My name is Purzel the Dwarf and I am a film actor. Do not compare the size of my body impression to my abilities as an actor. What I am able to do and mean you will see yourself in the film theatre where my first picture will be premiered around Christmas. Without any doubt I am a talent for I have formed myself quietly. Nobody foresaw my coming. I appeared all of a sudden. All famous movie people are being interviewed now, but I myself as a creature of fable cannot communicate with humans. I must take the miracle of Christmas for help. My father lived for a long time in Hamburg, studied at the Academy in Berlin, read years ago a newspaper advertisement that they were looking for artists to make an advertising film, bought himself a camera, opened a studio in the kitchen of his home and thus entered animated films and finally got the idea to film me. At Ufa he trained himself in trickfilm technique, for Tobis he made a film *Der gestiefelte Kater* and now for Terra has drawn and painted the first color fairy tale featuring myself. As you all know I have predecessors. In America, besides the Mickey Mouse, many colorful characters have been brought to life on screen. I myself do not want to be confused or identified with them. It's very important to me to stress that I am German. My father in his pictures consciously strives for mood and not only mere grotesque. Contradictory to the Americans he prefers not the contour drawing but water colors. He designed me as well as my partners, Quack the Frog and Brumm the Fly, with whom I have in the pic-

Kurt Stordel: *Purzel der Zwerg* (1938).

Kurt Stordel: *Purzel der Zwerg* (1938) (courtesy Thomas Stordel).

ture "A fairy tale by Kurt Stordel" immense adventures with the deadly enemy spider and in a strange kingdom. I save my life and that of my comrades and provide the King with a beautiful wife.[6]

Soon after, Terra commissioned a second Purzel cartoon: *Purzel, der Zwerg, und der Riese vom Berg*. The sequence list, which gives away a rather peculiar way of storytelling, reads as follows:

Purzel the dwarf talks to a tree which he admires for its bigness

The tree lifts Purzel onto its branches — a raven flies by and lets him look through his glasses

Purzel sees a mountain and wants to stay on its peak

The tree and the raven laugh at Purzel

A gust of wind comes and carries Purzel to a vineyard where God Bacchus sings: *Klingklang, goldener Wein*

The vine goblins are dancing. Purzel is allowed to drink from God Bacchus' glass. He starts to dance. Purzel falls asleep. God Bacchus sings: *Es war einmal ein Wicht.* The vine goblins carry him out

Purzel wakes up and sees a giant from the mountains and beside him a snow man who places him onto a sledge to bring him to the Ice Princess

Purzel watches the dance of the ice elves and slips down

***Quick macht Hochzeit*: Abandoned Ufa project supervised by Kurt Stordel in 1940.**

Book illustration by Kurt Stordel (1944) (courtesy Thomas Stordel).

The snow man holds him up and places two skis under his feet so that he can whiz down the chasm of the mountain

Purzel gets stuck and sees the giant from the mountain; the sun melts an icicle off his nose

The icicle falls onto Purzel's skis. He is lifted upwards and ends on the head of the giant from the mountains

The giant from the mountains shakes. Purzel rolls down the mountain in an avalanche and lands on a field of snow

The foehn wind frees the field from snow

Purzel sees the fairy of spring approaching who produces the flowers by magic

Purzel is happy and wants to pick a gentian flower

The giant from the mountain shouts to Purzel that one should only look at this flower but mustn't pick it

Purzel watches the other flowers and disappears dancing and singing

On September 25, 1939, Stordel wrote State Secretary Hans Hinkel of the Reich Ministry of Enlightenment and Propaganda a meaningful letter:

> Dear Comrade Hinkel,
>
> As a young member of K.d.d.K.,[7] I have heard your remarkable roll call to the members of the comradeship.
>
> I am a professional illustrator and painter and as such have notably worked for the German film resp. animation film.

> I have particularly commissioned myself to replace the production of American Disney films by own German films. The beginning was successful after overcoming big obstacles the previous year. Commissioned by Terra Filmkunst I have already produced two color fairy tale pictures. The first, A Fairy Tale, got the ratings "künstlerisch wertvoll" and "volksbildend [educative]," the second, Purzel der Zwerg und der Riese vom Berg, was equally rated "Künstlerisch wertvoll." The pleasant launch of this new production which was greeted and cheered equally by all of the press has naturally in this time come to a standstill as there are more important tasks for pictures.
>
> Nevertheless, I want to offer my services and my manpower furthermore to propaganda in pictures. I have the plan to edit a kind of grotesque newsreel or two newsreels that means to illustrate political events which are suitable for grotesque recording and interpretation in a short, funny animation film.

Signing *Heil Hitler!*, Stordel asked for the support of the ministry. Hinkel referred him to Dr. Fritz Hippler, who by then already was preparing the infamous propaganda "documentary" *Der ewige Jude* which made use of some graphic animation by Svend Noldan. Although Hippler didn't agree with Stordel's project he referred him to Ufa. Ufa wanted to open a new animation studio and was looking for a unit. On January 3, 1940, production chief Ernst von Leichenstern announced this plan to the Ufa board of directors. General manager Ludwig Klitsch applauded the project.

In March 1940, after a non-public screening of Disney's *Snow White* in the cinema of the Propaganda Ministry in Jägerstrasse, Kurt Stordel received an offer from Ufa to join its newly founded trickfilm studio. A staff that had already worked on another Ufa trickfilm at Krausenstrasse in Berlin, titled *Pitsch-Patsch*, was to join the project soon. Although he wanted to stay independent, in July 1940 he signed a contract, primarily to avoid getting drafted. Stordel was selected to helm Ufa's prestige project under the supervision of Horst Kerutt who was hired as supervisor in March 1940: the animated *Pitsch macht Hochzeit* or *Quick macht Hochzeit* (*Quick Marries*). Their staff consisted of:

Gerhard Fieber	Artist	July	1940
Hildegard Greiser	Artist	July	1940
Elisabeth Gröhn	Artist	July	1940
Ursula Harms	Artist	July	1940
Erwin Kramp	Camera	July	1940
Anna-Luise Subatzus	Artist	July	1940
Annemarie Ullner	Artist	July	1940
Kurt Blümel	Artist	October	1940
Ellen Brade	Artist	October	1940
Sergei Sesin	Artist	October	1940

Stordel, an autodidact, was impressed with the new Ufa Animation Studio that was set up in Babelsberg near Ufa Movie Studios. But a year later, in July 1941, Horst Kerutt's production was cancelled. Ufa had decided to focus on a feature-length cartoon, not with Stordel but Fischerkoesen, who turned out a rising star.

After his failed Ufa venture, Stordel, who, being a heavy drinker, didn't seem to be very reliable, continued in book illustration and advertising films. To avoid getting drafted, on July 29, 1940, he joined N.S.K.K. (NS-Kraftfahrkorps). He was sent to the front as a private but returned for reasons of health to Berlin on July 1, 1943. He supplied animated short film footage for Schongerfilm, Jugendfilm-Verleih Berlin and Roland-Film. On January 22, 1945, he was still able to watch and study the *Snow White* and *Pinocchio* prints kept by Reichsfilm Archive. A month later Stordel and his family headed for Brandenburg. When the Soviets occupied the city and learned that Stordel made animation films, they commissioned him to design red banners for them. As a reward he received special ration of groceries.

On October 26, 1945, Stordel applied at Chamber of Culture Filmmakers. He wrote: "As painter and graphic artist I strive to support the German animation film born from German mentality and to create own artistic ideas cinematographically, free from previous tutelage and dictation in this field of creative art and free from copying superior American animation films."

Rübezahl project, 1940.

Top and bottom: *Armer Hansi*, 1943.

Münchhausen, 1942 (courtesy Erika Held).

Verwitterte Melodie, 1943 (courtesy Dr. Hans Fischerkoesen).

Verwitterte Melodie, 1943 (courtesy Dr. Hans Fischerkoesen).

Verwitterte Melodie, 1943 (courtesy Dr. Hans Fischerkoesen).

Der Schneemann, 1943 (courtesy Dr. Hans Fischerkoesen).

Das dumme Gänslein, 1943 (courtesy Dr. Hans Fischerkoesen).

Top and bottom: ***Das dumme Gänslein***, 1943 (courtesy Dr. Hans Fischerkoesen).

Das musikalische Auto, 1943 (NIAf collection).

Original artwork for advertisement films produced by *UFA Werbefilm* (early 1940s).

Top and bottom: **Original artwork for advertisement films produced by *UFA Werbefilm* (early 1940s).**

11
Towards a German Disney Empire

The narrative domain to which the color cartoon feels attached, and so enables it to fulfil itself its promise in the most beautiful way, is the fairy tale. In Germany, however, one couldn't imagine until recently the production of independent fairy tales in cartoon style for reasons of insufficient economical profitability. In particular, this is because the talents growing in this field were required to limit their working ability by advertising films, and were well stocked with assignments months in advance. The production of commercials in the past decade has increased six-fold. Even war hasn't impaired or reduced production and artistic completion of color cartoons. For in commercials, color has clearly succeeded already, not only considering the growing number of films made in color but also in the powerful impact they leave on the audience....

In the past months in Berlin, an operation was founded which gathers the most skilled artist power, and has started with them a large-scale production of color cartoons. According to the guidelines, the first work of this production will be the awakening of Rübezahl, the folkloristic ghost from Riesengebirge [the Giant Mountain Range of Silesia], into cinematic life. The preproduction is already finished. The designs are now ready to enter production. But before the finished films are submitted, we can proudly look onto the simple fact that this operation was started in the middle of the war. It proves anew to the world that the German film, in the decisive battle of existence for the nation not only undiminshedly maintains the standard of production during peace, but above that is going to break new ground and make it fertile out of European tradition and spiritual outlook for Europe.[1]

In 1940 Tobis Filmkunst had set up a small animation film studio in Berlin Dahlem, Unter den Eichen, for this task. Supported by Deutsche Kulturfilm Zentrale, *Rübezahl* was going to be their first entry. In cooperation with Bernhard Klein, who was assigned as set designer, painter and animator, a rough draft of 76 pages was developed which detailed 217 shots.

Introduction Screenplay *Rübezahl* [Old Nip, Watcher of the Woods, his original name means: *Turnip Counter*] according to production papers left by Tobis Filmkunst in 1940[2]:

Since 1662 a mountain ghost, Rübezahl, has found his way out of the secret mutterings of spinning rooms and long winter nights into printed literature — to which he was introduced by Johannes Praetorius under the Latin title "Daemonologia Ruebenzalii Silesii" both, solemnly as well as awkwardly — he lives his double existence in the mind of our people:

To big and small children he is known as well as to those who did not get tired of doing research about his nature and his origin. The cornerstone to this work was laid in 1782 by a former Pagenhof master and later professor at Weimar gymnasium, Karl August Musaeus.

The manifold literature about Rübezahl published up to present day was studied to find a legitimate reason to transfer Rübezahl as a mountain ghost back to life in our days.

In the present version he is interpreted as mountain ghost of all German mountains. All treasures which rest in these, he protects for the benefit of mankind. Coal and ore, healing waters and herbs are subordinated to him as well as the fertile ground and farmland and the forest. He is the underground "Reichsstatthalter [Reich governor]" and "trustee." Executors of his will are the dwarves who are subordinated to him. He is the father and friend of the well-behaved and hard-working, to the lazy and "antisocial" however, he is a really threatening "mountain ghost."

Character Design for Rübezahl film.

The mountain ghosts, who are Rübezahl's subordinates, are called in collective term dwarves. Regarding their special duties in the empire of the mountain ghost Rübezahl, they are distinguished in

1. Gnomes
2. Goblins
3. Little Earth Men
4. Little Fire Men

They are graduated in the same order as their height. The tallest are the

Gnomes:

(I) Metallic workers and miners. The miners are distinguished in mineworkers and pit foremen. The oldest of them are Rübezahl's adjutants. They are put in charge by Rübezahl as reliable persons above goblins, little earth men and little fire men. The oldest adjutant is Rübezahl's deputy.

The gnomes get totally absorbed by their difficult work. Sincere slim guys with deeply furrowed faces which reflect a tranquil quietness. They are reliable and faithful.

The color of their skin is brownish-green like weathered rock. The hair shines silver-grey covering their foreheads and billows backwards onto the coat. Others have a fringe of hair.

While fulfilling their duties, the mineworkers wear a short dark green jacket with leather straps and equally colored short pants. Around their shoulder they wear a

Illustration from *Rübezahl* script drawn by Bernhard Klein in 1940.

Model sheet from Tobis project, *Rübezahl* (1940).

rope to which a climbing iron is attached and in the right hand a pickaxe which they also use as stick. Their feet are stuck firmly in hobnailed boots. On their forehead they have a sparkling stone or diamond fastened with a leather strap which serves as light while they work.

The pit foremen, too, wear a short sturdy jacket with leather straps, on the head is a round black cap with a black tassel which, on the front as a trademark, shows two little crossed hammers made of silver. On the side a heel hangs (like a sabre). On the breast they have an inflammable lamp with changing focus to light bigger distances. Furthermore, they have a second lamp in the hand with an incandescent bulb which from the outside is armed with iron rings which in case of diredamps will flash with violet colors.

Goblins:

(II) Their assembly is by far biggest number of employees. They have no special task assigned to them but will be assigned according to requirement to all kind of work.

They are vivid and always prepared for jokes, however, not ill-willed. They tease each other while working. Amongst them, however, there are also ill-willed, mean, crafty, work-shy elements who try to keep the others away from their work by any means. For that, they represent almost any version of human features. Their type is therefore less self-contained than that of the gnomes.

The color of their skin and faces is fresh, they have red jaws. Over the forehead swell brown curls. On the head they wear pointed caps sparkling in all colors which are pulled backwards. Their physique is slim, roundish or long and slim; others are small and stocky.

Their clothing is colorful (sparkling colors). They wear short waist-like tapered vests or smocks in all colors with broad leather belts and silver clasps. Their shorts extend to the thighs and are almost fully covered by the smocks. They wear no stockings but kind of curled up socks and tall large wooden slippers.

Little Earth Men:

(III) Strong guys, tough but friendly, hulky, not averse to crude jokes (occasionally), diligent.

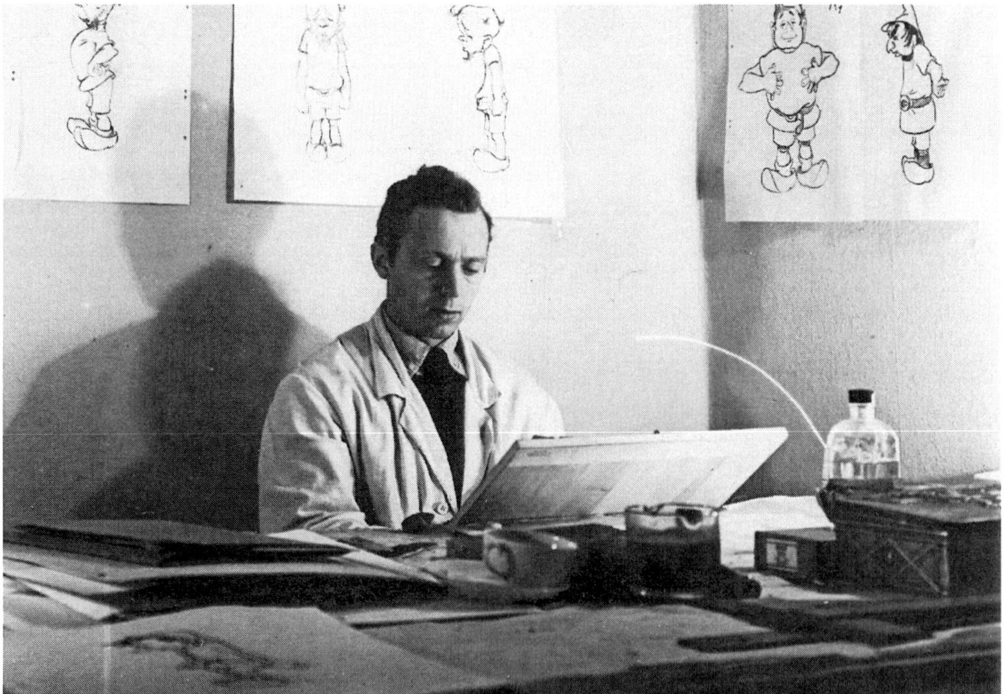

Rübezahl **animator Klaus Markus.**

Rübezahl **animator Karl Sonntag.**

They are gnarled, wiry guys. They have an unshaven stubbly chin and straggly tufts of hair which cover the temples. Some wear shaggy tufts of beards which stick out of their chins. On nose, ear and jaw they have fat warts covered with hair. The eyes gleam in a water blue teary liquid. The hands are clumsy and fissured and the fingers end in strong curved nails.

They wear a rough, greasy, green-yellow linen shirt with rolled up sleeves, long drill pants which stick in high boots. The pants are held by a leather strap. They have a mighty leather apron which is held round the neck with a simple noose.

Little Fire Men:

(IV)They are the smallest among Rübezahl's entourage, quick, cleverly swirling and twirling creatures who poke their nose into everything and know about everything.

The color of their skin is scarlet and shines like phosphorus light in darkness. The head is round about bald and on the skull there are flaming tufts of red hair which come to a head like pyramids upwards. The color of the eyes is piercing-saft green and therefore overshine the surrounding skin partien (the colors must fight each other).

The upper part of their bodies is naked. Around the hips they wear a ragged, frayed loincloth which hangs on one side deeper than on the other. They have little wooden blocks for shoes which are fastened with leather straps on the feet. Under the heel there is a large spring which enables them to jump into the height. In their hands they have big bellows.

The *Rübezahl* staff consisted of:

Friedrich Brunner	Animator	July	1940
Stephanie Steuer	Animator	July	1940
Bernhard Klein	Animator	October	1940
Klaus Markus	Animator	October	1940
Karl Sonntag	Animator	October	1940
Heinz Tischmeyer	Animator	October	1940
Hildegard Sascha Czekanyki	Animator	November	1940
Ane Melita Meinhardt	Animator	November	1940
Herta Schiller	Animator	November	1940
Ursula Schönherr	Animator	November	1940
Ursula Steneberg (Harms)	Animator	February	1941
Hildegard Greiser	Animator	April	1941

To head the operation, a true film pioneer with a fascinating background in national and foreign animation had been selected. At the end of August 1939, Louis [Ludwig] Seel was summoned back to the German capital from Rio, Brazil. With a special permission to join Reichsfilmkammer, Seel at the end of September 1939 had already produced a short animated film for Döring-Film-Werke, *Union-Melodie*, and in March 1940 a Gasparcolor short, *Tobis Karikatur I*, an anti-British propaganda satire which derided and mocked an already groggy British lion.

Rübezahl **animator Heinz Tischmeyer.**

On October 1, 1940, *Film-Kurier* reported on the early period of animation and published his recollections:

> As one of the pioneers of animated trickfilms, I take the liberty of adding some remarks primarily about the origins of American animation films which I have experienced first-hand from my own praxis.
>
> In 1911 in New York, the first attempts were taken. At that time I was political cartoonist of *Brooklyn Daily Eagle*, the biggest afternoon paper of New York. At the same time as my colleague Windsor McKay [*sic*: Winsor McCay] from *New York World* and several other cartoonists like Mac Cauly

Louis Seel, the artistic supervisor of Tobis Animation Studio.

and F. M. Follett we focused our attention on the work Analysis of Motion by [Eadweard James] Muybridge.

With the help of a specially constructed photographic (not kinematographic) device Muybridge succeeded in recording the movements of humans and animals which unreeled in the course of a second in 16 frames onto a photographic plate. Muybridge published these analyzed movements in a great volume which became important to sculptors, draughtsmen, painters and so on. As a film strip also records a movement of a second in 16 frames and the same process applies to a projection machine, 16 frames per second, the thought seemed very likely to photograph drawings or caricatures on a film strip, that means to draw an event which unreels in a minute in 60 by 16 drawings.

Thus originates the first American animation film of 150 mtr. length which consisted of 2,500 individual drawings. It was a simple "story." One saw the head of a sleeping man and a mosquito pecked him in the nose.[3] The movie was screened as biggest attraction in vaudeville theatres while Windsor McKay spoke some introduction in front of the screen.

And this film was it for a long time. A few years later when the cinema industry had made considerable progress, when the building of many cinemas coincided with the foundation of distribution organizations, when the first American film epics (*The Battle Cry of Peace* and so on) were produced and when the screening of programs necessitated the short film, the industrial manufacture of animated pictures started in 1915.

For some years the *New York Herald* published the Mutt and Jeff cartoons of the genius cartoonist Bud Fisher.

Nothing was more obvious than to film this series. Weekly a Mutt and Jeff film of 150 mtr. length was turned out. The luminous advertisement of the Broadway cinemas for Mutt and Jeff towered above the advertisements of the feature film.

Only after 350 films Mutt and Jeff died of old age. In the meantime Bray Studios produced *Colonel Heezar Liar*, the Hearst Trust made *Bringing Up Father*, there were my own Screen Novelties and on and on.

As early as 1915 I became collaborator of Bud Fisher on Mutt and Jeff. In 1918 I supervised my own production and introduced title cards for distribution, in animated form, with tinted backgrounds.

In 1920 I introduced the animated cartoon in Germany. In association with Emelka in Munich the production of Münchner Filmbilderbogen [Munich Pictorial Broadsheet] was started.

Under my own company label, Seel-Thomas Film G.m.b.H., I continued the production. Every second week a film of 150 m was released. The yearly production of 26 Münchner Filmbilderbogen was released by Ufa and shipped per contract to 26 foreign countries, including America.

Between 1921 and 1924 my Münchner Filmbilderbogen not only had caught on in Germany but rivaled films produced in New York such as Felix the Cat by Pat Sullivan who before Disney was highly successful. With Pat Sullivan, alas, died Felix the Cat.

In 1925 I introduced production of animated cartoons in England and in 1927 in Rio de Janeiro from where I submitted trickfilms to South and North America. With my return to Germany, shortly before outbreak of the war, I was highly surprised that in Germany animated cartoon existed only as advertising films.

Since sound and color as new elements add an extraordinary appeal to trickfilms I didn't understand why animated cartoons in Germany weren't acknowledged as supplement features and immediately turned my attention to assure its importance in Germany and its value in export business.

Currently I head a company which pursues the objective to create our own European cartoon style which differs from the American in mental depth and inner imagination.[4]

Seel and his unit worked for almost a year but suddenly a rival turned up, the idea of forming a Geman animation film company controlled by the Ministry of Enlightenment and Propaganda itself. Ufa quickly closed down its *Quick* enterprise in Babelsberg and joined the new company. The ministry decided that Tobis should do likewise. The heads of Tobis Filmkunst, Julius Fritzsche and production chief Ewald von Demandowsky, were upset about the liquidation of their animation plant.

What, under Seel's supervision, was turned out in preproduction, Stephanie Steuer described as a "dark, eerie story" compared to Disney's *Snow White* (which was quoted occasionally). And more important, the relationship between Seel and Goebbels' loyal assistant Karl Neumann, who was in charge of Deutsche Kulturfilm Zentrale and was going to head Deutsche Zeichenfilm G.m.b.H., was stressed. When the *Rübezahl* project folded, Seel on July 28, 1941, applied for registration as independent producer of color fairy tales. A copy of his application went to Deutsche Kulturfilm Zentrale. Neumann feared competition and tried to prevent it.

On July 9, 1941, Ludwig Seel received an answer from Reichsfilmkammer, Section Cultural and Advertising Films, signed by Dr. Müller-Goerne: "Your application, dated 28th of this month for registration as independent producer of short and advertising films is herewith denied, due to decree of protection of economical film production issued on August 6, 1937, as the economical requirement for the enlisting of new film production enterprises (according to § 2 of this decree) does not exist." Seel was forbidden to continue work under the label Studio Seel and not allowed to sign any employees. He was allowed to work only as an employee himself.

As he didn't want to remain destitute or surrender to Neumann, on February 24, 1941, Seel signed with Epoche-Color-Film A.G. on a year's contract and produced some footage. Then, dissatisfied with the situation, in October 1941 he joined Josef Pfister who worked for AFIT (Prague Studio for Film Tricks). AFIT produced a cartoon set in the world of opera, *Orpheus in der Unterwelt*, then adapted *Der Zauberlehrling*, clearly inspired by Disney's *Fantasia*. In 1943 AFIT became part of Prague Film.

There were some activities to exclude him from Reichsfilmkammer, after his assumed flight to Prague as Epoche litigated for breach of contract. There was another contract dispute with Prague Film.

Seel's post-war activities remain in the dark. Seel died in 1958 in Wiesbaden.

12

The Futile Dream of a German Cartoon Factory: Rise and Fall of Deutsche Zeichenfilm G.m.b.H.

As Nazi Germany was not able to raise the money to buy and release Disney's *Snow White and the Seven Dwarfs* and Stordel, Held and others were not up to the task of truly becoming a German version of Disney, Goebbels during World War II decided to enter the ring himself and establish his own cartoon factory. As with the press and film in general, the minister again relied on the services of former mayor Max Winkler of Cautio Treuhand to prepare the deal. Money would be no problem.

While Mars Film G.m.b.H. focused on training films for Deutsche Wehrmacht, Goebbels felt that something was needed for general exhibition to rival American animation. On August 7, 1941, Deutsche Zeichenfilm G.m.b.H. (DZF), the German Animation Film Company, was founded in Berlin (authorized capital: RM 50,000.-). It offered in-house animation training for young artists. Although in May 1944 there were 94 employees and 151 trainees with eight teachers on the payroll, only one short, *Armer Hansi* (*Poor Hansi*), had been completed. This concerned the misadventures of a canary lost in freedom, which was a satire in itself if one considers that all of Nazi Germany was sort of a prison. Work was started on another feature starring some puppies, *Schnuff, der Nieser* (*Schnuff the Sneezer*). This became *Purzelbaum ins Leben* (*Forward Roll into Life*), and was redone and finished after the war.

Head of animation was Gerhard Fieber, born in 1916. Fieber was a soft-spoken, polite man who claimed to have had nothing to do with politics (but appearances are often deceptive as we shall see): "Never met Goebbels. Politics were handled by the production department, by Herr Oberregierungsrat Neumann." In fact, ORR Karl Neumann, a councillor, was a long-time trusted official of Goebbels' and a party member, who had nothing to do with art or animation. In fact, as usual with Nazi parvenus he was a complete layman. Neumann's career was based on accounting, meat and sausages. In Goebbels' eyes, however, this seemed to qualify him perfectly for his task as supervisor of German animation.

Neumann's biography[1]:

Bank accountant, Deutsche Überseeische Bank, Berlin
Clerk in a meat factory in Cologne

Floor manager, Rügenwalder Wurst-und Fleischwarenfabrik/Ostsee (Baltic Sea), another meat factory
Member of NSDAP since 1931
Member of SA, later SS
Full-time head of propaganda NSDAP Gau [County] Pommerania
Personal assistant, Reich Ministry of Enlightenment and Propaganda
In Charge of enforcement, Memorial Day 1935
Chairman *Reichsarbeitsgemeinschaft* [Working Pool] Safety Measures
etc.

Coming to the attention of Reich Minister Goebbels, he was assigned the task of reorganizing Cultural Films[2]:

> It has been necessary to organize German cultural filmmaking more strictly in political, ideological and organizational understanding and to relate the production planning for all producers of cultural films to our present time.
>
> For this purpose I have decreed the establishment of a department "Kulturfilmdramaturgie" [Cultural Film Dramaturgy] within the film department of my ministry as well as the "Deutsche Kulturfilmzentrale" [German Cultural Film Center] as subordinate office. As head of the department and of "Deutsche Kulturfilmzentrale" I have appointed Oberregierungsrat Neumann.

On August 6, 1940, Goebbels wrote in his diary: "Then a few cultural films. Very good. Neumann has whipped this into shape. I conferred a long time with him. This field we have to activate even stronger. There is a lot to do after the war."

Karl Neumann, head of Deutsche Zeichenfilm G.m.b.H. (DZF), in 1940.

Goebbels called Neumann's attention to another problem area: German cartoons. On October 10, 1940, Neumann submitted a memo for "Citation of Young Talent for Cultural Animation Film Production." Dr. Goebbels was pleased and agreed. Especially for this field, a referent from *Reichsfilmprüfstelle (*the board of film censors), Curt Reinhard Dietz, was assigned as official in charge. Right away they became involved with Paul Lehmann and Tobis and their troubled production of *Rübezahl.*

After a while Dr. Goebbels and his staff began to pay attention to rumors that Disney's studios in Burbank were on the verge of bankruptcy after a 1940 European export deficit of $1,259,798. Goebbels was willing to redeem in favor of German cartoons and Neumann reinforced him. On May 15, 1941, Goebbels noted in his diary that he had examined Neumann's memo about German cartoon film production: "I will support this because it is a good and useful matter." A day later he was prepared to give Neumann free rein in building a production company on a larger scale.

On June 25, 1941, Dr. Max Winkler wrote to the head of Ufa, Ludwig Klitzsch:

> The Minister of Enlightenment and Propaganda has decreed, as I have already announced, the etablishment of a German cartoon film production according to the suggestion of ORR Neumann.
>
> It shall be enforced within the framework of a special company, Deutsche Zeichenfilm G.m.b.H.
>
> It is necessary to found this company. Cautio Treuhand G.m.b.H. will acquire shares for RM 26,000 and Ufa shares for RM 24,000.
>
> First managing director of this company will be ORR Neumann. A board ad interim will not be appointed.

On August 7, 1941, the entry *Deutsche Zeichenfilm Gesellschaft mit beschränkter Haftung* is published in the Commercial Register of District Court Berlin-Charlottenburg, Abt. B No. 62 HRB 85 Nz.

As Neumann and his right-hand man, scenarist Frank Leberecht, who was a journalist and had been involved in cultural films, were novices to trickfilm making, both sought the advice of a specialist whom they found in Dr. Werner Kruse. In 1934 Kruse had established an animation company in Berlin. Kruse successfully studied Disney's early "rubber hose and circle" formula style as practiced in the basic creation of the Mickey Mouse cartoons to build cartoon characters. Kruse once was arrested by mistake because it had been reported that at night strange light signals were to be seen in his animation chamber. Eventually he convinced the police that this was due to the rostrum camera equipment he needed in photographing the animated artwork and he was released.

Karl Neumann in 1942.

On September 1, 1937, Ufa began to commission Kruse Film to do cartoons for them. With the outbreak of war, Kruse feared getting drafted, and applied for a job with Deutsche Zeichenfilm G.m.b.H. (DZF). To become part of DZF was highly attractive. Many commercial artists applied as it became known that DZF members were *UK-gestellt* ("indispensable, reserved occupation") and wouldn't get drafted for the time being. Even fashion designers coming from Berlin fashion schools tried their luck. The wages were state-controlled but, contrary to German industry there were special bonuses and raises that made work at DZF highly profitable, especially for the selected group of artists.

Dr. Werner Kruse, technical manager, DZF in 1942.

Dr. Kruse was hired as technical head, however to his dismay not *uk, unabkömmlich.*

On the lot of a Berlin company, Eier-Born, Rosenthaler Strasse 11–12, backyard, 3rd floor, Tobis-Filmkunst maintained some studio space. In August 1941 this was rented by Ufa and assigned to Zeichenfilm G.m.b.H. The choice didn't prove adequate as nearby egg dealers left an unpleasant smell outside. Searching for something more suitable, Neumann found larger premises on Kaiserstrasse 29/30 near Alexanderplatz, where a Jewish school had been located. Ufa rented the building and DZF moved into on November 1, 1942.

Here former Ufa and Tobis personnel was assembled. In the beginning there were 5 chief animators, 6 female animators, 1 head of color department, 12 colorists and 14 female tracers.

First the company finished a black-and-white commercial for a washing powder called Hexona that was a left-over from Kruse's studio.

Neumann's original idea was to concentrate all German animation activities under one roof, under his personal control, so to speak, but not all gentlemen of the ministry agreed. Neumann at first had to prove that he would be able to accomplish something. A few weeks after the foundation of DZF, on December 18, 1941, Neumann addressed a letter to State Secretary Gutterer (forwarded by Ministerialrat [Undersecretary] Dr. Hippler):

> Dear Mr. Gutterer!
>
> Thanks to your visit of Deutsche Zeichenfilm G.m.b.H. I am induced to submit what kept me very busy in the past time considering the establishment of Deutsche Zeichenfilm production.
>
> In the comments attached which, alas, are a little bit too voluminous, together with my collaborators Leberecht and Dr. Kruse I have touched upon those issues which need a plain decision by the Minister as soon as possible.
>
> Together with my collaborator Leberecht, after finishing the draft of the exposé dated May 12, I have thought over for weeks if we might be able to solve such a difficult task as the establishment of an animation film production in Germany would be in the light of

the regrettable failure of the film industry in this field. Only then we have dared and decided to submit the exposé because we could complete each other in a fortunate way and with Dr. Kruse we have won an expert in the matter of animation who for his long-time praxis and studies of music has the necessary prerequisites for his special task.

In taking this decision we had in our mind that nobody else would be willing to begin what had to be begun if Germany shouldn't remain behind in this important field of film.

Moreover essential for our decision was that we would find the most generous support. The patrons, however, had to be aware right from the beginning that the establishment of such an operation, with skilled workers lacking in number and quality as well as facilities, technical equipment etc., would necessitate considerable means and long patience before revenues would flow from the release of the finished films.

Thanks to your recommendation the processing of the voluntarily accepted task was assigned to me.

I know that for the Minister it is a matter of course to assign to Deutsche Zeichenfilm G.m.b.H. and myself within the framework of the re-organisation of the film industry that position that is necessary to solve such a task and master upcoming difficulties. You will understand my express request when you will have read attached éxpose. [...]

Exposé

About the current situation of German animation film production

Invalidation of unfounded attacks

Necessary decision re: the future route.

I.

From various comments I have learnt that objections were raised against the procedure of the establishment of a German animation film production which have to be once andforever invalidated; for recognition would let the recently started work get stuck in its early origins.

The kind of objections suggests that they completely go back to one source, most apparently a group of producers of animated advertising films who regard for the future an impair of their revenues if expertly trained skilled workers are being recruited and trainees gifted at drawing will be assigned by Deutsche Zeichenfilm G.m.b.H.

In detail these objections have following content:

(1) They claimed that the wages paid to the artists are way too high (on the other hand see Attachment 1: List of actually paid fees).

DZF drawing: studio neighbor Eier-Born (1941).

DZF: Letters to Santa Claus (1941).

(2) Following the methods of English propaganda they invent incredibly short dates of delivery and then sarcastically ask when the first feature-length cartoon will be finished.

(3) They spread the slogan that because everything that was tried in Germany in this field failed the new task would be condemned to fail as well according to natural law.

(4) The distribution head of a big state company explained that one could not reach what Disney had achieved as he is a unique genius. When Disney would die it would be over with animated films. Regarding the German plans the same film mogul remarked that nobody has asked him.

(5) In defeatist manner mouth-to-mouth propaganda has been employed that it (namely the establishment of an animation film production with the goal of producing feature-

Drawings from the files of DZF (1942).

length films) never would come true. The working methods would be too expensive and schedule for much too long preproduction. The whole issue was begun with too much grandeur.

In fact, all attempts of German film industry to create the German animation film were started with so inadequate means and such a capitalist focus that they necessarily had to fail. If the recently started work will succeed all those people who were not able to create the German animation film and considered him dead would be made absolute fools.

Their opposition has therefore personal motifs.

In the exposé dated May 12, 1941, which contains the proposal for the establishment of a German animation film production with the objective to produce feature-length cartoons, it is stressed that in the company a special working atmosphere should prevail, that special social measures would have to be taken and so on.

Since work started I have applied accordingly. This apparently has widely spread and has increased the above mentioned anti-propaganda.

So, for instance, Deutsche Zeichenfilm G.m.b.H. under the supervision of teachers of the capital's master schools classes has introduced evening classes for further training of the animation personnel.

The trainees receive furthermore during the whole working time an exclusive school education and are employed only internal as far as the objective of the training makes this necessary. Contrary to this — with few exceptions — the trainees of advertising film manufacturers are only trained for the earliest chance of exploitation. That Deutsche Zeichenfilm

G.m.b.H. to the annoyance of masters, derelict of duty, consequently has a big quota of trainees and other employees is obvious. Changes of trainees out of legitimate reasons have already happened.

Considering the self-proclaimed objective for which later a bigger and efficient crew is necessary one has to try to get out of a now still small core a much more qualified talent pool for executive positions. That these career chances have an attractive effect right now is the guilt of those who didn't offer equal chances.

Part of the animators' education towards professional ethics is that the trainees must not, as it still is the case, attend the technical college for dressmakers (!). From this the trainees of Deutsche Zeichenfilm G.m.b.H. will be excused soon due to meetings with the Municipal Main school office.

In this connection, a profession of animators should be created and this should not be integrated in the expert group advertising films (as is the case now) but in a newly to be founded expert group "animation" of the Reichsfilmkammer.

Instead of a trickfilm proletariat of technical supporting forces that without any passion and stoledly draws its lines, a special professional type of responsible and creative artist craftsmen of German animation must develop.

II.

If one considers that Disney has worked on the movie Snow White for two years with 500 men after training and expanding his employees over 15 years in the production of short films so one easily will understand that until the start of production of feature-length cartoons in Germany there is still a long way to go. It will be even longer if one one approaches the clearly manageable solution of the assignment less determined and less goal-directed.

Of course Deutsche Zeichenfilm G.m.b.H. can skip many of Walt Disney's years of apprenticeship provided one will not force upon it a narrow-minded, in too short deadlines limited, purely capitalist amortization.

In this sense I have understood the Minister's remark in the personal meeting on July 18, 1941, in which you took part and in which he said that in Germany it doesn't need to last so long as in Walt Disney's case.

In the current stage there are the following two possibilities how to proceed:

The performance of the company which at the moment consists of 50 animators is gradually improved and raised without facility and personnel expansion onto the out-put possible within this frame. It will get the chance to produce three films at a length of each 200—250 meters. (At least three films are necessary because a single subject doesn't contain all artistic and technical possibilities to prove the efficiency. Add to this that the quality can increase only according to the development of the working methods from film to film.)

The current company would need for the production of the mentioned three films a span of three years which will necessitate for the first film a longer production period than for the second and third one.

Until finishing the first three films facilities, technical and staff development for continuing on larger basis would cease.

One could therefore only in the fourth year (1945) proceed to create the conditions for the production of feature-length cartoons, i. e. to raise and train the necessary 500 animators gradually, to develop the working methods for them and to create the technical facilities.

This alone would last further 4½ to 5 years, approximately until 1950.

Drawings from the files of DZF (1942).

One already begins, during the production of the first short film, to expand the company in an organic way and slowly build facilities, technical and personnel until it has reached in 4–5 years the level of 500 animators (for comparison: Disney needed 15 years to reach this number of employees).

This would to 1) have the advantage that according to a rough estimate, three films would likely be finished in two years.

If, however, the gradually raised animation staff has been trained and integrated into the company it would have at least tripled at the end of the second year so that in a total span of three years six films in the above mentioned length could be produced.

Resume:

According to process	1) 3 films would be produced in three years
" " "	2) 6 films would be produced in three years.

One has to have in mind that one cannot for instance rent and equip rooms for, say, 100 artists, then for 300, then for 400 and finally for 500 artists. To save in the long run, one has to try under all circumstances to find as soon as possible the facilities for 500 and equip them to the current needs so that the company will slowly grow into these rooms.

It makes sense that method 2) would need considerably more input than 1). It will reach, however, the proclaimed objective much earlier. By exploitation in the evening program [of the cinemas] the invested sums would be recouped earlier. A budget only could be given after decision of the single steps and after solution of the question of facilities.

That such extension of staff could be started even during the war the daily increasing number of applications by draftsmen and female artists prove which includes a great number of invalids of this war. The question of facilities would to be solved by means of the proposed Jewish real estate and property where probably painter's and joiner's workshop would be provided. [...]

The past week we negotiated with the famed Norwegian commercial artist Damsleth who could make exact specifications about the state of Disney production at the beginning of the war. Disney worked then in his old facilities with 1,500 men. Included in this number are 300 men who exclusively work for non-film exploitation of his characters in picture books, for promotional campaigns and so on.

By that time his new studio was built which is laid out for 4,000 employees. One has to have in mind that Disney too without any doubt would need for the expansion up to 4,000 men several years if he will not do damage to the quality of his work. Disney himself confirmed this in earlier statements about his trainee school. Already in 1937 he annually trained 200 graphically skilled young people for his demands and integrated them due to their skills into his practical production.

Regarding Disney's large-scale planning there is evidence that he intends to release in the future several animated feature films per year.

If German Reich will approach the establishment of its animation film production with less initiative than private entrepreneur Disney we will fall behind even more than we already are.

This fact would be less than supportive for the reputation of German film especially in

Drawings from the files of DZF (1942).

> Europe which shows a big demand for American cartoons. For the German cultural propaganda it would be essential if we succeed to fill the existent gap in the foreseeable future and provide German cartoons to the open market.
>
> The chance that this objective will be reached in not too long time only exists if option 2) will be taken.

A postscript to the letter spoke of five- and nine-year plans for the large-scale establishment of Deutsche Zeichenfilm G.m.b.H.

Attachments compared monthly fees of animators being paid at Deutsche Zeichenfilm G.m.b.H. and Ufa-Werbefilm:

	Zeichenfilm G.m.b.H.	Ufa-Werbefilm
Colorists	RM 200 / 250	RM 120 / 200
Tracers	RM 250 / 285	RM 150 / 200
Animators	RM 250 / 285	RM 170 / 250
Inbetweeners	RM 325 / 350	RM 210 / 300
Chief animators	RM 325 / 350	RM 250 / 300
Background artists	RM 390 and above	RM 375
Supervising animators	RM 600 and above	—

Currently, the attachment concluded, there is no animator's tariff or pay scale. For the fees of DZF the fees of the former Tobis Animation Film Production served as guideline.

Attached was an "Approximate estimate of costs for the production of a feature-length cartoon":

Drawings from the files of DZF (1942).

Staff of 60 supervising employees (according to credits Snow White, Pinocchio):	
10 for RM 2,500 monthly	RM 25,000
20 for RM 1,500 monthly	RM 30,000
30 for RM 600 monthly	RM 18,000
140 additional employees for appr. per person	RM 121,000
	RM 194,000
Totalling per year	RM 2,328,000
*Live-Action shooting** (actors, cameraman, electricians, studio facilities and so on)	
*Rotoscoping process[3]	RM 100,000
Sound Recording and Musical Score: Orchestra, Choirs, studio etc. for 10 days	RM 100,000
Negatives and prints:	
Photographing pencil drawings (black-and-white) for checking animation etc.:	
10,000 m for RM 1 each	RM 10,000
Color negative film stock including processing:	
5,000 m for RM 2 30 each	RM 11,500
60 color prints (2,500 m) for RM 3,750 each	RM 225,000
	RM 2,774,500
20% general overheads (taxes, social insurances, real estate, heating, lighting, office, business trips and other fees)	RM 554,900
	RM 3,329,400
	===============

This estimate can also be seen as approximate calculation on the basis of previous experiences.

Less risk than in the case of, say, Ohm Krüger[4] because unlimited export will be possible.

According to a message by Vice President Melzer the animated feature film Snow White has recouped between Dollar 1.5 and 2.5 million in Europe alone excluding Germany.

Release period longer than 10 years possible, for children unlimited.

Released not only in Europe but also in Africa, Asia and South America.

Non-filmic exploitation [merchandising]: picture books, toys, post cards, Kasperle theatre [hand puppets, Punch and Judy show], advertising etc. (For Disney in this field of exploitation alone 300 men have worked at the time of exhibition: even handkerchiefs, children's clothing a la Mickey Mouse, ash trays etc.)

Not far away from the original location in Rosenthaler Strasse, in Jaegerstrasse, the Ministry of Enlightenment and Propaganda had its own cinema. Once a week members of DZF were asked to get together and study Walt Disney films, especially techniques like rotoscoping, in order to copy them in their own work.

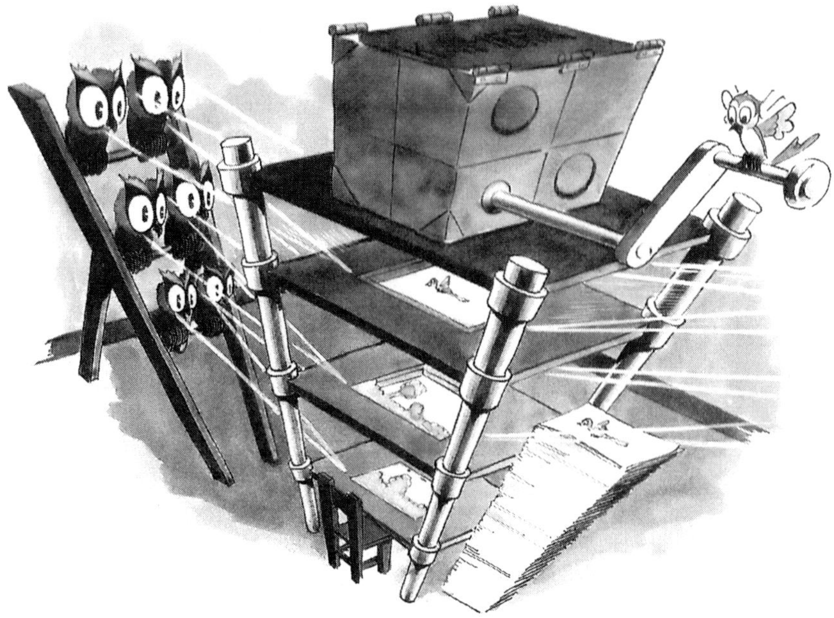

Drawing from the files of DZF (1942).

Searching for cartoon plots, Leberecht came up with Waldemar Bonsels' book *Die Biene Maya* (Maya the Bee) that had been a best-seller during World War I. Leberecht, joined by Kruse and Fieber, visited Bonsels at his home at Lake Starnberg, near Munich. Bonsels was skeptical about the prospect of his book being transformed into a cartoon and asked for time to consider. Neumann suggested hiring screenwriter Thea von Harbou, who had written a number of German film classics such as *Die Nibelungen, Metropolis,* and *M* for her former husband, director Fritz Lang. Harbou also was close to National Socialist ideology. Eventually Bonsels sent a contract stating he would be willing to sell the film rights for RM 15,000. ORR Neumann, however, did not agree to that sum and left with an option for RM 5,000.

Looking for alternatives to *Maya the Bee*, Frank Leberecht immediately summoned a circle of newspaper cartoonists. This *Künstlerischer Arbeitskreis* (working group) included:

Hugo Huber
Ernst Keienburg
Charlotte Kleinert
Hans Kossatz
Hermann Krause
Dr. Kurt Kusenberg
Leo von Malachowski
Hans Meyer-Dietrich
E. O. Plauen
Heinz Rommelt
Manfred Schmidt
Erich Will-Halle
Artur Zell

Conceptual drawing from the files of DZF (1941): ***Armer Hansi***

It also included Friedrich Luft, an aspiring film and theater critic whose voice would come to prominence after the war in Berlin radio (RIAS). This selected artists' group met in a restaurant and, over beer and wine, the renowned caricaturists discussed possible gags for future movies.

Hans Kossatz would continue to draw cartoons for Berlin papers after the war. Manfred Schmidt, after the war became famous for his Nick Knatterton cartoons in magazines and on television. Another artist, E. O. Plauen (*nom de plume* of Erich Ohser), who drew the famous strips of Father and Son, was sentenced to death for spreading defeatist jokes.

One of the most creative and inventive members of the group was Horst von Möllendorff, a popular Berlin cartoonist.

Usually six members of this working group would meet every second week on Wednesday at 6:00 P.M. in a Berlin wine tavern called Krüger, Jägerstrasse 19. Möllendorff said: "The meetings always were very funny. We sat for a long time drinking red wine, concocting the funniest gags for the respective film ideas. For each gag that was accepted we were paid RM 20 and RM 50."[5]

In October 1941, Möllendorff submitted his first complete cartoon film script to Deutsche Zeichenfilm G.m.b.H. It was titled *Luftikus im siebten Himmel (Luftikus on Cloud Nine)*. A *Luftikus* is a happy-go-lucky sort of fellow, a homage to Heinz Rühmann's popular 1941 feature comedy character *Quax, der Bruchpilot (Quax, the Crash Pilot)*: "*Quax, der Bruchpilot* is a war film. The plot follows the standard formula of dozens of war films, German or American: a misfit becomes a hero when he learns to overcome his individuality for the sake of a greater whole. Although the film takes place in 1928 with no overt references to war, a military atmosphere pervades the flight academy where the majority of the scenes takes place. The instructor declares that pilots form a 'stormy front' that 'fights for the idea.' They fly, he promises, not into the sky but into 'world history.'"[6]

In Möllendorff's project idea Luftikus, a pilot, not only would fly through the sky, he also would fly through the world of imagination: On a large airfield a little funny man is waiting in pilot dress. This is Luftikus. The engineer approaches and announces that the plane is ready to start. This is a funny little plane. When Luftikus boards with a big noise the propeller, motor and the pilot seat on which Luftikus sits fly out of the plane. When Luftikus looks back he sees the empty chassis. "Where is the control stick?" he shouts angrily, then grabs the control stick and strikes the unlucky engineer. The engineer, however, informs Luftikus that he has boarded the wrong plane. Finally Luftikus boards the right plane and is ready for take-off.

Through many cloud layers he comes to a signboard: Cloud Nine. Riding a white Pegasus there is a poet who passionately invents love rhymes. Luftikus invites the poet into his plane while the winged horse is leashed to the tailpiece of the plane where the animal faces some problems. Luftikus is so touched by the love poem that he forgets about the control stick. The plane nose-dives but gets stuck on Pegasus' neck. The poet falls out of the plane. Luftikus lands on the next cloud and releases the winged horse which immediately saves the poet while Luftikus takes a stroll on Cloud Nine. There is a bank and sitting on it Luftikus spots the girl whose praises the poet sang in his poem. He falls head over heels in love with her. He wants to present his heart and finally finds it in the back of his pants. She accepts and presses it to her heart. Apparently the girl is in love too but when he kisses her she fades away. Luftikus is amazed. He looks for her but cannot find her.

Still searching he comes to a wine tavern. A violinist plays. When Luftikus falls asleep the musician wakes him up rudely. As he wakes up Luftikus sees the girl again but when they hug and kiss she disappears a second time.

He empties several glasses of wine and with each glass a gray character rises from his body. "Who are you?" Luftikus asks the ghostly females. "We are your sorrows. The alcohol has driven us out!" He says, "Why are you sitting in so gloomy and melancholic mood?" Luftikus is getting merry again. "I want to see you dance." He takes the violin and plays to see the sorrows perform a dance.

Horst von Möllendorff in 1942.

Singing, he leaves the tavern, the characters in tow. On a rainbow bridge he meets the beloved again. She asks him, "Are these your girlfriends?" Angrily he throws one gray character after the other off the bridge. The girl wants to hug him for his brave deed but he urges her to be careful: Otherwise she might fade away again.

Then he puts the girl in a sack. He stows the sack in his plane and returns to Earth. But while he does so and starts to kiss the sack, it empties. Disappointed, he throws it out of the plane. But when he begins to land he sees the girl waiting on the airfield. He jumps out of the plane and hugs the girl. When he kisses her he won-

Armer Hansi **(1942): Ultraphan cel.**

ders why this time she doesn't vanish. Disbelieving he asks her, "Are you really here?" She confirms this: "I am here and I will stay with you for the rest of your life!"

Möllendorff had already suggested sequels with the same character: *Luftikus in Schlaraffenland, Luftikus und Adebar, Luftikus in der Walpurgisnacht.* Leberecht paid him RM 300 for the film rights.

On October 25, 1941, he wrote to Möllendorff: "Re: submission 'Luftikus on Cloud Nine': The idea of using the seven sorrows will possibly make a whole film without even using the character of Luftikus. This will be the story of a worrier who tries to get rid of his sorrows which have become personified. He succeeds in doing so with the exception of his best-looking sorrow: the jealousy."

On November 12, 1941, Möllendorff submitted another idea called *Frosch-Sinfonie* (*Frog Symphony*). The musical leitmotif is played by a saxophone with a number of saxophones substituting for the croaking chorus of frogs. A frog jumps upon the leaf of a white water lily. He wears swimming trunks and holds a sheet of music. In big pose he begins to sing. There is another frog under the water lily who sees that on the sheet there is only one single sound noted. Wearily he pulls away the leaf and the singer falls into the water.

On a nearby meadow a third frog in bathing trunks (they all wear them) picks flowers. He jumps onto a leaf and while he sings throws flowers onto the water lily. Again the frog in the water reacts irritably and pulls the water lily away.

Then a third frog turns up who is a master singer and even gets the applause of the resentful frog. A frog lady appears and holds out her hand to the brave singer. He takes it and kisses it galantly. Among the reeds a stork appears. All frogs flee. Only the singer continues as he doesn't realize what's going on and gets snapped by the stork.

***Armer Hansi*: Ultraphan cel (1942).**

Still in the stork's beak, the frog continues to sing. The other frogs, particularly the frog lady, start to wail, whimper and cry while the young storks in the nest are eager to devour the welcome prey. But when they hear the frog's saxophone solo they listen enthusiastically. All of a sudden the frog jumps into the rainwater gutter and escapes successfully, back to the lake.

The moon rises while he still sings. An owl shouts, "Quiet!" All the other birds, however, enjoy the music. Even the cow from the nearby meadow comes to the lake, as do ducks, geese, chicken, sheep and pigs. The guard dog even drags his doghouse. A nightingale joins in the concert.

Two gold fish drag the sea lily on which the lady frog sits to the festival. A fanfare sounds. The lover answers with a saxophone solo. She leaves her leaf and hugs him. Waves form that depict a heart.

On March 6, 1942, Frank Leberecht wrote Möllendorff that the sketch lacked a story, but he considered the basic idea charming, that a singing frog mesmerizes the storks and thus escapes being eaten. For this single idea he was prepared to pay RM 50. Möllendorff took the money and submitted a third story, *Klimbimbo*, for which he was paid RM 1470.

Other ideas were turned in as well. In *Waldemar* Dr. Ernst Keienburg told the story of a dog who would have liked to be a seal. Hugo Huber watched the chicken fashion house "Kiki" sell alien feathers in *Mit fremden Federn*.

In *Aufbruch zur Fahrt ins Blaue* Charlotte Kleinert told about farm animals who enjoyed an outing.

Then, in October 1941, Hermann Krause submitted an idea that seemed perfect: *Die Geschichte vom kleinen Kanarienhahn, der in die Freiheit flog*. In his cage Hansi, a canary, listens to the voices of freedom, love and adventure. Hansi hears the song of a chickadee

DZF Hansine for *Armer Hansi* (1942): Ultraphan cel

and carelessly leaves his prison birdcage. However, Hansi's wings grow weak too early. The tender wooing is rejected. Hunger, thirst, rain and finally a cat drive Hansi back to the safety of prison. In the end it all turns out to be a dream.

Having read the basic idea, Möllendorff suggested changes:

> Suggestions for the cartoon film Kanarienhahn
>
> I want to comment on two important issues:
>
> The canary who only dreams about the flight into freedom leaves an unsatisfied desire.
>
> The ending leaves an unfree feeling, the cage becomes a prison as the canary returns because he is unable to live in freedom.
>
> Therefore I suggest:
>
> Leave the desire for freedom as core of the plot but give the whole another basic idea as follows:
>
> **The wish to swap with the life of another**
>
> 1. This would give a different meaning to beginning as well as the ending.
>
> 2. The canary wants to swap his life with a sparrow, and this not in dream but in real life.
>
> After they have lived the life of the other they are happy to become their old selfs and change again.
>
> My thought is: He doesn't swap at the end freedom for prisonship as in the original story but he exchanges the other life for his own.

Möllendorff's idea was not that new: We find it in the story of Doctor Faust, who trades his soul, or Robert Louis Stevenson's *The Bottle Imp.*

The heads of DZF didn't agree completely but they changed dream for reality and at the end allowed Hansi, who returned to his cage, a Hansine as consolation.

Anyway, National Socialists didn't seem to understand the freedom aspect. The revised story, on the contrary, appealed to the National Socialist way of thinking: A canary escapes into freedom, gets sick of freedom and returns into his cage where he is safe.

Until November 9, *Künstlerischer Arbeitskreis* [working group] had to fill some holes and inconsistencies in the story. On December 1, 1941, a 20-page first draft was ready that contained 94 scenes. It was now tentatively titled *Hansi, Abenteuer eines Kanarienhahns (Hansi, Adventures of a Canary)* and eventually would become *Armer Hansi (Poor Hansi).* Hermann Krause, Manfred Schmidt and Libertas Schulze-Boysen were the ones who were chosen to finish it. With the sequence list completed, the characters had to be redesigned. Möllendorff agreed to do some designs for *Hansi, der Kanarienhahn*. "These designs," he wrote, "will have to depict the main character in 7 different situations." He promised to submit the finished drawings sized 21 × 28 by January 5, 1942, and asked for a single payment of RM 400. If required, he also offered another 12 drawings within three weeks for RM 1200. Deutsche Zeichenfilm G.m.b.H. took only the seven originals, and on April 20, 1942, paid the asking price of RM 400.

Möllendorff said, "For myself it was important to explain to the artists that not the punch line was most important but the evolution of the story. Wilhelm Busch stories consist of punch lines and therefore are not well suited for cartoon films. Therefore I always thought of original ideas."

On May 13, 1942, Leberecht asked Möllendorff to sign a new contract: "The previous experience necessitates renewing cooperation with the members of Künstlerischer Arbeitskreis. We strive for either full time or free cooperation from case to case. Therefore we terminate our contract for renewal till June 30, 1942."

By then Möllendorff was drawing a monthly fee of RM 300 from DZF, but he decided against renewal and left DZF. Others left too. Möllendorff would later sign with DZF's competition.

In autumn 1942, the heads of DZF were told that one of their writers was a member of the resistance group Rote Kapelle (Red Chapel). Frau Libertas Schulz-Boysen had worked in Neumann's office, then got in touch with Frank Leberecht. She was born on November 20, 1913, as third child of art professor Otto Haas-Heye and his wife Viktoria, née Countess zu Eulenburg, in Paris. From 1933 to 1935 she was employed in the Press and Propaganda Department of the Berlin branch of Metro-Goldwyn-Mayer Film A.G. In July 1936 she married an employee of Reichsluftfahrtministerium, Harro Schulze-Boysen. On January 12, 1937, she left NSDAP. Between July 1940 and November 1941 Frau Schulze-Boysen wrote film reviews. Then she returned to Kulturfilmzentrale as scenario editor.

On August 31, 1942, her husband was arrested. Libertas was at this time in Bremen and was arrested in the train on her return on September 8, 1941. Both had been founding members of Red Chapel. Both were sentenced to death on December 19, 1942, and executed three days later.

***Armer Hansi* (1942): Ultraphan cel.**

There were high aspirations,

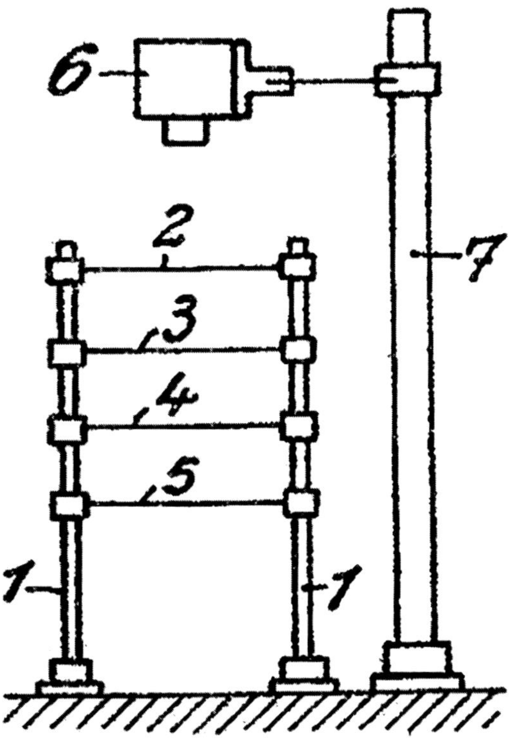

Erwin Kramp: camera patent (1942).

if not content-wise, at least technically: Like Fischerkoesen the company was going for Fleischer's technique of mixing cel animation with three-dimensional (miniature) background as well as a German version of Disney's Multiplane process.

On December 4, 1937, *Film-Kurier* had reported that the original Disney Multiplane Camera, which at its time represented the ultimate in rostrum camera technology, had cost $ 70,000.

The Ministry of Enlightenment and Propaganda ordered several research groups to collect information about Walt Disney and his working methods. One of these groups found out that Disney's Multiplane Camera hadn't been patented for German territory. So Franz Hendrix (DZF) and other technicians were assigned to copy and rebuild it for DZF. Before they did so DZF had to check, however, with the registered design of another German cinematographer, Erwin Kramp, who had registered a similar device (D.R.G.M. No. 1520 819, 57a, June 3, 1942). DZF interviewed some of their employees who had been involved in some stages of Kramp's development while working at Ufa. Kramp was associated with Kurt Stordel for a while, and he worked for Ufa's Kerutt trickfilm unit from March 1, 1940, until the end of September 1941, as independent cameraman. Chief technician Dr. Richard Schmidt (Tobis Tonbild-Syndikat A.G.) recommended simply ignoring Kramp's claim as Disney's superior technology was widely published. Tobis then took Hendrix's version under its wing and allowed the Dutch cameraman a bonus of RM 100. In 1944 the Hendrix Multiplane version was sold under German patent to various European studios.

Artists were always welcome at DZF if they could draw Disney characters. One of those was Gerhard Fieber. Like Kramp, Fieber, as we have seen, had worked with Kurt Stordel on the ill-fated *Quick macht Hochzeit*, then went to DZF and, although still a "youngster," carved out a career. They all served Nazi animation for mainly one reason: good salary. Fieber received a monthly paycheck that totalled RM 1,500. Neumann made RM 3,000. Fieber, who had a good working relationship with Neumann, was selected to design the Hansi models. As Disney's artists did with *Bambi*, Fieber partly relied on live animals, two canaries named Kasimir and Nepumuk. However, during production Fieber's designs turned out to be rather difficult for a number of artists, so Fieber had to do corrections for several weeks.

Armer Hansi was considered a sample film. For the period 1943–44, two short films were planned, for 1944–45 three, 1945–46 six, and 1946–47 eight. Until June 30, 1942, DZF got monthly subsidies from Cautio Treuhand, then was funded by Ufa-Film G.m.b.H. out of the funding program for cultural films granted by the Reich Ministry for Enlightenment and Propaganda.

From memory Gerhard Fieber later compiled a document describing the structure and set-up of DZF but sometimes his memory failed:

Supervisor/General Manager:	Karl Neumann, Councillor Berlin
Scenario Supervisor:	Frank Leberecht, Berlin
Personnel Officer:	Fritz Böhme, Berlin
Technical Consultant:	Werner Kruse (1 year), Berlin
Supervisor Unit I:	Gerhard Fieber, supervising animator
Supervisor Unit II:	Kurt Blümel, color supervisor

Members of the creative unit (ideas and character design) were writers Frank Leberecht, Friedrich Luft, Hermann Krause, cartoonists Gerhard Fieber, Horst von Möllendorff, Dr. Kusenberg, H. Malakowski [*sic*], Manfred Schmidt, the painters and graphic artists Kurt Blümel, Bernhard Klein and composer/musical supervisor Friedrich Schröder.

The production set-up consisted of six animation studios:

studio 1: Fieber	studio 2: Tolle	studio 3: Tischmeyer
studio 4: Sesin	studio 5: Coolen	studio 6: Savaniac [*sic*]

Studios 4, 5 and 6 consisted of foreigners from Russia, Holland and France.

One was equipped with the most recent animation equipment and animation stands and was supervised by Jan [Franz] Hendrix and his wife, both Dutch. Each studio had about 10 animators: one animation director, one supervising animator and 8 in-betweeners. All studios were assigned to the head of unit 1, Gerhard Fieber (animation director) regarding design, animation and consistency of characters in acting, facial expression and movement.

Fritz Böhme, DZF proxy, in 1942.

To deal with thousands of pencil drawings from six different studios they had one Ultraphan Tracing Dpt. Here the pencil drawings were traced, then inked in black or color outline onto transparent cels. After inking cels were transferred to the

Left to right: Animators Sergei Sesin, Stephanie Steuer, unknown illustrator and Gerhard Fieber in 1942.

Painting Department. Here the cels, according to color model sheets, were painted on their reverse sides. All in all, there were about 60 animators, about 30 cel artists (tracing artists) and 30 painters.

Meanwhile, in Kurt Blümel's background art department, the color backgrounds were designed and finished on the basis of layouts. This studio had four highly skilled background artists.

According to the exposure sheets of the respective studios, the finished cels and background art were composited on Hendrix's special animation stands frame by frame using Disney peg bars and photographed with dynamic action (mostly single-frame).

The animators were able to continuously check their work. Before clean-up a rough pencil test of each sequence was photographed on black-and-white film stock. Timing, facial expression and character design were checked, approved or corrected by the supervisor of unit 1, Gerhard Fieber, in cooperation with scenario head Frank Leberecht.

Two shorts were produced, *Armer Hansi* and *Purzelbaum ins Leben*, each 450 meters in length, running 18 minutes. Each meter had 52 frames × 450 = 23,400 frames.

With usually three characters on screen this meant about 70,200 frames. Excluding stills, cycles and the like, this meant 60,000 frames to draw, to trace onto Ultraphan cels, 60,000 cels to paint, and 60,000 frames to photograph.

The score for both films was composed by Friedrich Schröder of Berlin, well known for his songs and operettas. Members of orchestra and sound effects team were O. Sala, Willi Stech, Willy Mattes.

Deutsche Zeichenfilm established its own art school (training workshop) for aspiring talent. This was assigned to supervising scenario head F. Leberecht and, in terms of art, the supervisors of unit 1, G. Fieber, and unit 2, K. Blümel. Each class had about 20 students:

Group I:	Painting	Supervisor: Prof. Sommer
Group II:	Drawing	Supervisor: Prof. Cernak
Group III:	Background Art	Supervisor: Prof. Schön

From this training workshop the most talented students were selected for the six studios. The cooperation worked beautifully. Very good talent was trained and specialized.

In late 1943, commercial pioneer Wolfgang Kaskeline joined the set-up and tried to do a short on his own, but the project was canceled.

Not all press cartoonists, however, had the talent for animation. In the beginning it was rather difficult, and some were drafted during the course of the war.[7]

Due to war and an increasing state of *Luftterror* (air terror, meaning Allied air raids against the Reich and especially the German capital), DZF was forced to hire foreign talent to guarantee their *kriegswichtige* (strategic) production. Animators and artists from France and Holland volunteered and offered their services. Of course, before being hired they were checked for their Aryan background. As special bonus a return trip [*Heimaturlaub*] was offered, which a few used for courier services on behalf of various underground organizations.

In the beginning Dr. Werner Kruse acted as mastermind and talent scout. In summer 1942 he went to Paris to secure animation equipment and Disney material. After the German Reichswehr had occupied France in 1940, the Gestapo, coincidentally, took its Paris headquarters in the very building that housed the French branch offices of Disney. The German occupants, of course, showed high interest in continuing ties with Disney. After doing some business at 104 Champs-Elysées, the French office of German Filmtechnische Zentralstelle (Central Office for Film Technique) which collected the requisitioned film material (here Dr. Kruse bought drawing paper, cels, paints and cameras), Kruse immediately visited French Disney representative Wally Feignoux, who literally shared his offices with the Gestapo at 52 Champs-Elysées. Since 1936 Feignoux had represented Disney's

Art instructor Professor Sommer DZF in 1944.

interests in releasing RKO films to continental Europe. Feignoux seemed to be open to Kruse's requests. He even recommended an artist who was about to be conscripted for *Arbeitsdienst* (fatigue duty) and serve as graphic artist for Siemens in Berlin. His name was Robert Salvagnac. According to Feignoux, Disney had been prepared to hire Salvagnac a few months ago and bring him over to America. Dr. Kruse was able to get Salvagnac off the list and have him and his wife signed by DZF. Neumann welcomed him with open arms. On May 15, 1942, his boss, Dr. Goebbels, had noted in his diary: "Exceptionally gifted talent in French film must be hired by us as soon as possible." Salvagnac's influence on *Hansi* was nevertheless minimal.

Although the Disney studio contributed to the American propaganda and war effort with cartoons like *Der Fuehrer's Face* and *Education for Death,* one of the best anti-fascist films of its time, and the feature-length, partly animated *Victory Through Air Power*, Feignoux remained on post.[8] Some of the Disney films, however, were dispatched to DFZ in Berlin for further research and translation.[9]

Many Dutch citizens, some of them with Pál background, volunteered for DZF:

Johannes Antonio (Jan) Coolen was hired as animator on May 1, 1942.

Geradius Fransiscus Antonius (Franz) Hendrix as cinematographer on May 1, 1942. He was the one to design a Multiplane device.

Hendrik S. van Manen as cinematographer on May 1, 1942.

Jacobus (Jan) Schadee, who was a teacher, as apprentice animator on June 1, 1942.

Joanna-Maria Hendrix as assistant cinematographer on January 15, 1943.

As of September 30, 1943, Salvagnac earned RM 800, Schadee RM 600, van Manen RM 1370, and Coolen and Hendrix each RM 1,400.

The budget of DZF was RM 50,000 in the first year, and it doubled each following year. In 1942 the company had 72 employees, a year later already 263. All in all there were 119 trainees.

From memory Fieber listed the company's leading employees as follows. The left column lists position in the company; the right, each person's professional background.

General Manager	Karl Neumann	Oberregierungsrat	
Deputy	Frank Leberecht	Scenario Supervisor	
Chief Accountant	F. Böhme	Finance Accountant	
Technical Consultant	Dr. Werner Kruse	Advertising Film Producer	
Head of Department I Painting — Graphic and Background Art	Gerhard Fieber	Press/Film Cartoonist	
Chief Animators	Gustav Tolle	Animator	
	Heinz Tischmeyer	"	
	Luis Seel	"	(U.S.–German)
	Jan Coolen	"	(Holland)
	H. Schadee	"	(Holland)
	Sergei Sesin	"	(Russia)
	F. Fannier	"	(France)
	C. Salvaniac	"	(France)
	J. Mongazon	"	(France)

Effects Technician	van Mahnen [*sic*]	Technician	(Holland)
Camera	Jan [*sic*] Hendrix	Camera	(Holland)
	Mrs. Hendrix (assistant)	Camera	(Holland)
Background Artists	H. Olberts	Fine Arts Painter	
	Bernhard Klein	Fine Arts Painter	
Chief Animator (employed 1943–44)	Wolfgang Kaskeline	Advertising Film Producer	
Head Animation School I	Prof. Cernak	Art Professor	
Head Animation School II	Prof. Schön	Art Professor	
Head Animation School III	Prof. Sommer	Art Professor	
Composers	Friedrich Schröder	Schlager/operetta	
	Willi [Willy] Mattes	Schlager composer	
Writers	Friedrich Luft	Critic, film writer	
	Hermann Krause	Writer (*Armer Hansi*)	
	Dr. Cusenberg [*sic*]	Writer	
Freelance designer	Manfred Schmitt [Schmidt]	Press Cartoonist	
	H. von Möllendorff	Press Cartoonist	
Studio Dachau			
Official Supervisor	H. Wöhrle	Oberamtsmann (senior civil servant), Munich	

In the beginning Dr. Kruse acted as mentor of eight apprentices who were the first to enter the newly founded Lehrwerkstatt (training workshop) of the company. A Professor Sommer was selected as teacher. He was a former member of Moscow Art Academy, who focused on water colors and not animation. With his students he made field trips to Berlin's greenest areas and asked them to capture nature with their brushes.

When the company moved from Rosenthaler Strasse to Kaiserstrasse the number of apprentices increased to 30, then to 60. A good number of trainees had already become involved with finishing *Hansi*. Finally a new training ground was found on the second floor of Kaufhaus Horn, a department store located at Alexanderplatz 2. Three classes (A, B, C) were arranged. Starting on April 1, 1943, they were led by teachers Heinrich Zernack (who supervised nude drawing and used models from the ranks of forced laborers and war invalids), Max Lingner, Max Kaus, Wilhelm Hübner-Lauenburg, Egon Stolterfoht and others.

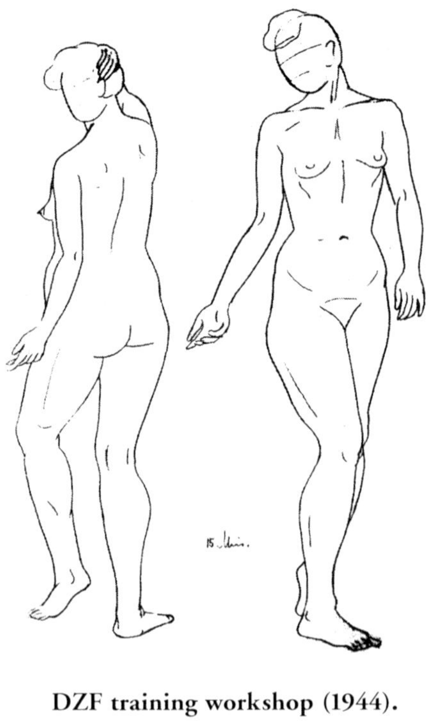

DZF training workshop (1944).

When a visitor from Propaganda Ministry saw one of the sacred Führer portraits among nude models, Professor Rudolf Schön was called in and asked to remove it immediately.

On November 1, 1943, Deutsche Zeichenfilm G.m.b.H. published a fact sheet about choice of employment:

> Boys and girls who demonstrate their drawing skill will be accepted once a year for a three-year training period. Ten teachers instruct in object and figure drawing (including nude study and anatomy), perspective, culture and style research, animation and stop-frame technique, rhythmic education, aural training and handicrafts. Objective is the development of sight and motion, to master a character and the laws of movement as well as free design within the context of the language of animation.

By that time, Kruse, the "Aryan" who was married to a Jewish wife, was no longer a staff member of DZF. On August 27, 1942, Reichsfilmkammer reported to *Fachschaft Film*:

> Re: my inquiry at Gau Staff Council of NSDAP, Gauleitung Berlin, I today receive the following note:
>
> "Volksgenosse Kruse is a member of both, NSV and Reichsfilmkammer. For the efforts of NSDAP he shows no interest, however participates in social activities of party and state. His wife is first grade Jewish half-breed. There is no guarantee for his political reliability on my part."

On November 13, *Fachschaft Film* phoned Neumann. Neumann already had talked to Kruse. Both agreed to terminate their contract. Kruse, however, was allowed to continue at Ufa. There he was assigned to a project called *Brot für Europa* (*Bread for Europe*). All involved were married to Jews and agreed that this project should not be finished before the end of the war. Thus Kruse was able to save his wife from arrest and deportation.

DZF trainee Sigrid Koop in 1943.

Gerhard Fieber recalls that in 1942 they started to search for new topics and characters and as a potential animation project even unearthed *Rübezahl* (Old Nip, not to be confused with the project originated by Tobis in 1940–41): "However, our cartoonists were not able to get something to please the ProMi [Ministry of Enlightenment and Propaganda]. For them it didn't look very Aryan, not enough blond hair. So *Rübezahl* was cancelled."

The ministry clearly considered DZF a war-important facility.

Contrary to Ufa, Tobis or Bavaria, no DZF member was able to quit. By signing a contract everybody had to sign a service obligation. If somebody wanted to change employers he or she would have to present a special certificate. Several artists tried to change, of course.

ORR Neumann in spring 1943 was released from his duties as civil servant at his own request, but he continued in his position and played the big boss. "If this isn't going to work as I want, I am always able to send you for service in the armament industry," was a typical threat. He also devoted himself to female artists, who made 70 percent of the employees. If women bucked the system he had them denounced, such as tracing artist Ingeburg Ammon in a letter to the personnel officer at Reichsfilm Intendant dated January 27, 1943[10]:

> The above-mentioned declared in summer her desire to leave our studio. A job had been offered to her for the same fee at an institution of higher education in Tegel as art teacher. She would have to work there, however, for only four hours a day. Her request to quit her job was not approved. It rather was arranged with Herr [Horst] von Hartlieb — legal department of Universum-Film A.G. — to induce a service obligation if Miss Ammon should insist to leave. Deutsche Zeichenfilm G.m.b.H. relies on the few skilled employees who are available and who have been trained gradually in-house. It would turn out to be a catastrophe if indispensable workforces would be lost.
>
> Subsequent to denial of her request, Miss Ammon repeatedly made derogatory statements

Stephanie Steuer and Gerhard Fieber at Deutsche Zeichenfilm G.m.b.H. (DZF) (courtesy Stephanie Steuer).

Moosschwaige Dachau, 1944.

about work and company. She didn't recoil to repeat these statements in the Duerer House where she had been employed previously. As a result, the managing director has talked to her in confidence about three months before Christmas and seriously cautioned her. She was told that she would disrupt the labor peace and that the path she would tread would not lead her into freedom but possibly into a concentration camp.

Shortly before Christmas the brother of Ms. Ammon was killed at the front. Ms. Ammon was in hysterics while in the room of the managing director and demanded vacation because she couldn't leave her mother alone. After some consultation, this vacation was granted to her. On this occasion, too, she said that she couldn't fulfil her tasks and that we should let her go.

On Monday, 18th of this month, after both English air raids in Berlin, in the cel department they talked about the air raids and the resulting damages. During this talk Ms. Ammon was reported to have said: "Why is this Saftladen [dump] not hit by a bomb so that I will be free again." This statement has been testified by the department head, Brigitte Quass, Berlin-Kaulsdorf, Hoenowerstr. 63, sitting next to her. All other staff members who with the exception of Ms. Ingeborg Wichert are befriended with Ammon according to Ms. Quass, claim that they haven't heard this statement. The members of the department have testified as follows.

Gisela Hütten, Berlin-Schlachtensee,

who comes from Bochum has called the attacks on Berlin ridiculous. Otherwise she cannot remind anything.

Anneliese Herdt, Berlin-Schlachtensee,

can recall that there was some talk about damages in Zaehringer Strasse. Miss Herdt admits the often-repeated statement made by Ms. Ammon that she had something else in mind.

Ingeborg Wichert, Berlin-Weissensee,

claims that she hasn't heard that statement, however she gives her credit for doing so. Ammon fumed at the company because she didn't get a release. Miss Wichert has heard from Miss Meinhardt that Miss Amon wanted to leave under all circumstances.

Melita Meinhardt, Berlin NW 87,

was told by Miss Ammon often that she wanted to leave at all events although, according to Miss Meinhardt, she has tried the wrong way.

Christa Kuntzen, Berlin-Wilmersdorf,

who is Ammon's closest friend, claims that she hasn't heard the statement. If she [Ms. Ammon] has made it it would have been childishness according to Miss Kuntzen. Miss Ammon might have lost her temper because of her brother's death.

Miss Quass hat testified that in December the whole department and particularly Miss Ammon have asked her to degrade the efforts of Ammon in the face of the managing director so that she would get a release. This was rejected, of course, by Miss Quass.

After all these statements and for the resulting continuous disturbance of labor peace Miss Ammon is no longer sustainable in the studios of Deutsche Zeichenfilm G.m.b.H. If she would get a simple release then she would have achieved her goal. We therefore ask to induce her immediate transfer as tracer to an electric company. It would be appropriate if she wouldn't be transferred to Borsig where presumably her father is working as graduate engineer.—As told in our last phone conversation, it has been abstained from demanding more serious steps because Ms. Ammon has obviously suffered a lot caused by her brother's death four weeks ago.

This company has not induced any steps against Ms. Ammon. She only has been suspended and has house ban.

In November 1943 the building that housed DZF was hit by bombs. During an air raid on November 22, the training and apprenticeship workshop, located in Berlin C 2, Alexanderplatz 2, was bombed and completely burned. In November 1943 the Ministry decided to split the whole company into five independent animation units located in Berlin, Vienna and Dachau near Munich.

Some of the leading employees changed quarters. In Berlin remained Sergei Sesin in his studio with 17 other employees to work on *Das Feuermännchen*,

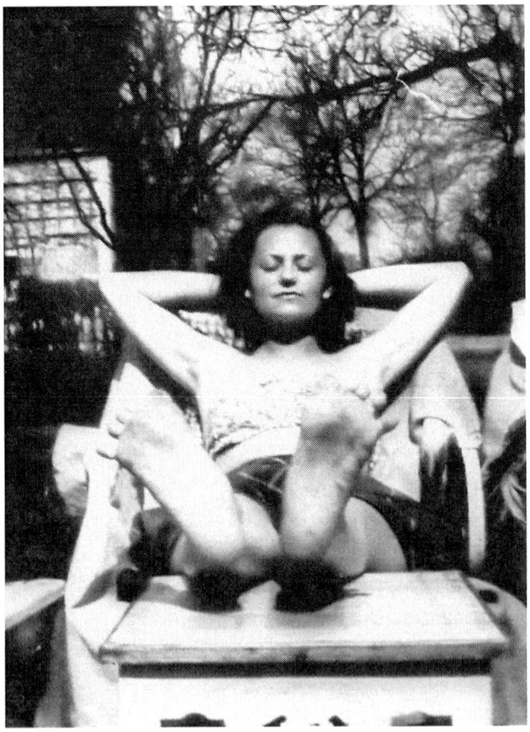

Break at Mooschwaige Dachau, 1944.

a dance humoresque starring a fire manikin and a water drop, which remained unfinished, like most of DZF's product. In the main building there were also 12 tracers, among them six war invalids and one Dutchman.

Fieber said: "Due to bombing and other problems in Berlin, production was outsourced to Dachau in 1944. Work continued at 'Moosschwaige.' Assisted by 20 artists from Berlin, I finished the second short for Deutsche Zeichenfilm, titled *Purzelbaum ins Leben*, in Agfacolor. Running time: about 15 minutes."

Mooschwaige Dachau: Studies (1944).

In early 1945 the complete cels, negatives, equipment and so on were shipped back to the headquarters of Deutsche Zeichenfilm in Berlin, where they suffered war-induced fire damage.

"During my activities in the DZF Dachau studios in 1943–44," continued Fieber, "I met the famous cartoonist Olaf Gulbransson at Tegernsee where the Norwegian artist and his student Franziska Bielek lived and worked. For myself this was quite an event since both were famous for their work for the magazine *Simplicissimus*.

"As directing animator I got the impression that all male artists during the war were happy and relieved not being drafted, including myself.

"The foreign colleagues, as far as I know, had been *dienstverpflichtet* [they were under service obligation]: Frenchmen, Dutchmen, Hungarians, Belarusians (exiled Russians). Our cooperation in Berlin, Vienna and Dachau worked out admirably. I have the highest praise for these very skilled professionals of the trade. As humans they were impeccable. For instance I was very impressed by Jan Coolen from Holland, a great character animator. Following my designs Salvaniac [*sic*] from France drew wonderful sequences for *Armer Hansi*. Frenchmen Frannier and Mongazon were brilliant animators and a great asset in character and dynamic animation. The exiled Russian Sergei Sesin was highly intelligent, spoke fluent German and supervised the chief animators of his unit superbly. His female in-betweeners were enthusiastic.

"The special camera department I left confidently in the hands of Jan [*sic*] Hendrix, the top technician from Holland, and his talented wife. He came with Mahnen [*sic*] and Schadée from the Philips Holland commercial agency. Artist Luis Seel (U.S.–German film pioneer), Horst von Möllendorff as scriptwriter and cartoonist, Dr. Werner Kruse (technical supervisor) as well as Manfred Schmidt left earlier for various reasons—(differences, conflicts amongst writers, drafted etc.). The leading German cartoonists, press artists or commercial filmmakers Kaskeline (since 1944), Tischmeyer, Tolle, Blümel, Klein, Olbert and Fieber finished both short film projects assisted by German animators, the foreign unit and teachers of the school."

After Dr. Kruse had left, Frank Leberecht took his job and supervised the artwork for *Armer Hansi*. The minister immediately realized the weak points when saw the finished result.

The second project, *Schnuff, der Nieser* originally was going to be a feature film and had 500 artists recruited for it. That was too much to ask for at the end of the war. To assist in the completion of just a short version, even the rival Fischerkoesen studio was called in. At the same time, scripts for other projects were developed: *Frische Fische, Vertauschter Schatten, Gerücht,* and *Innerer Schweinehund.*

Schnuff had similar structure to *Hansi*. Fieber replaced the canary with a puppy, Nies, that sneezes and is catapulted out of the warm house into the rain. Another dog, family *Purzel,* tries to get the puppy back to safety and has all kind of adventures including an encounter with a dog catcher. One of the puppies, a yawner, infects the dog catcher with its tiredness.

Mooschwaige was a recovery home for Munich artists supervised by caring householder. Tischmeyer and 10 other artists who had been at *Moosschwaige* earlier left after Fieber's arrival to Vienna to begin a short film called *Frühlingslied* (*Spring Song*) that dealt with a joint venture by animals to get rid of winter and welcome spring. Some weeks later, Fieber was joined by Jan Coolen, who brought with him nine DZF staff members (most Dutch, with one French background artist) to start preproduction on another short about the adventures of a little bear.

Schnuff der Nieser **(1943).**

Dachau, was the new home of German animation, but from the other side of the street there came an offensive smell like the smell of old meat. They noticed barbed wire fence and livestock wagons drawn by men. A female French artist got to know more when she got in touch with some SS men who let her see what was going on inside the refinement.

Schnuff, der Nieser **(1944): Model sheet by Gerhard Fieber.**

When she returned, none of her colleagues wanted to believe what she had to report. Actually, the protected area was a concentration camp.

At that time DZF separated from Frank Leberecht. On May 8, 1944, Karl Neumann wrote Dr. Max Winkler:

> As I indicated in our last personal meeting, difficulties have arisen between the Minister and Herr Leberecht. Although after our talk and submission of documents he has acknowledged altogether the previous achievements and called our first film a good start, the Minister

asked for a change in the artistic line of our work and close cooperation with Herr Roellenbleg [Deutsche Wochenschau]. Alas, Herr Leberecht tried to defy this for reasons I do not understand. He will be dismissed from his post very soon.

DZF then tried to seek the cooperation of other scenario specialists and hire Ernst Holub, who for several years (since 1939) had worked for Wien Film as dramaturge, but that company's production chief, the versatile Dr. Karl Hartl, intervened and protested successfully. Holub was needed for feature film production.

The new production manager for the DZF studios in Berlin, Dachau and Vienna, Dr. Friedrich Bernhard Nier, was hired for a monthly fee of RM 1,500,- on May 19, 1944. Now Neumann himself came under fire. From the minutes of a management meeting, Ufa-Film G.m.b.H.:

Mayor Dr. Winkler puts his veto on contemporary state of affairs. Herr Neumann is unable to lead creatively and inspire people. Relying on diligence, hard work and theory won't accomplish much in the long run. After all, Zeichenfilm currently costs mill. 2–3 annually; as long as a spiritual leader is missing a target rate of return is not to be expected.

Behind the curtain, rivals in Roellenbleg and Möllendorff were pulling the strings. Möllendorff would have liked to become the key principal writer, but in spite of his successes this was not going to happen.

In a letter dated July 13, 1944, addressed to Mayor Dr. Winkler, Roellenbleg, who then was head of Sonderreferat Kulturfilm (Special Department of Cultural Film), estimated the total for Deutsche Zeichenfilm G.m.b.H. at RM 4,200,000.

Included in this sum are the following line items:

Studios, refurbishments etc.		RM 325,000
Equipment..................................		RM 200,000
Training workshop................................		RM 500,000
Drawing material..........................		RM 75,000
Current account......................................		RM 400,000
	total	RM 1,500,000
Actual production costs during the 3½-year work span of Deutsche Zeichenfilm G.m.b.H. from beginning 1941 until today.................................		RM 2,700,000
	total	RM 4,200,000

Regarding that only one single short has been produced, this sum is at a first glance way too high. To reduce the costs for future films of Deutsche Zeichenfilm G.m.b.H. to a level we are used in our other studios, it seems to be necessary to apply some drastic organizational measures.

The training workshop has devoured — according to above breakdown — previous costs of almost [*sic*] half a million. It has, however, nothing to do with actual production. Therefore it would leave a wrong image if these costs would be added to actual production costs. [...]

For this reason, I would recommend to continue the training workshop in the future as an independent enterprise with its own budget besides a German animation studio.

As far as I can oversee, the conditions at Deutsche Zeichenfilm G.m.b.H., the high production costs and the low output of film production in many cases might have had to do with wrong disposition which resulted in twice and triple assignment of manuscripts, musical scores and animation drawings.

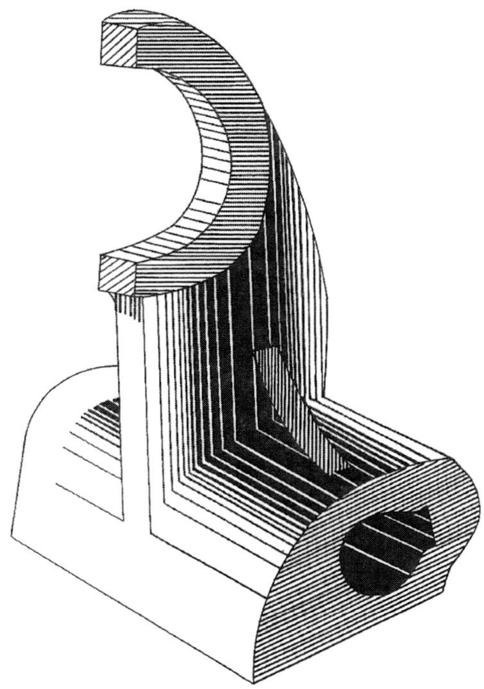

Drafting: Instruction at DZF.

"Here some gentlemen without initiative have to be replaced," Roellenbleg added for consideration. Roellenbleg said that Neumann had proven himself adequate in matters of sheer organization, in the establishment of a production machine, and in the establishment of a training workshop:

> Otherwise, in the management of the company an active, artistically minded personality focused on animation production is missing. There is evidence that the single studio heads of Deutsche Zeichenfilm G.m.b.H. don't dispose of the necessary sovereign manner and mental powers to shape a topic independently. Concerning ideas, they are creative only to minimal extent. They are efficient in their profession, however in the majority no more than executing draughtsmen and heads of a production studio. The objective judgment of quality and artistic instinct on how to develop a topic is mostly lacking.

Roellenbleg clearly had ideas of his own that we will discuss later.

On July 25, 1944, Deutsche Zeichenfilm G.m.b.H. had 201 female and 96 male employees on the payroll. Due to total war, it became necessary to shut down animation studios and employ the artists in armament factories. On August 4, 1944, the Propaganda Ministry announced that the company would be closed for the war efforts: "To keep the precious manpower the company will continue in its own service rooms on behalf of Rhein-Metall-Borsig trust. The head of Deutsche Zeichenfilm G.m.b.H. is accountable that no animation work will continue on the side." Only Fieber was allowed to continue on *Schnuff der Nieser*. *Schnuff*, however, was not finished under the Nazis. It was transformed into a DEFA production after war and retitled *Purzelbaum ins Leben*.

In September 1944 Ufa stopped payments to Deutsche Zeichenfilm G.m.b.H. "as the company was shut down for matters of total war."

On November 17, 1944, the Court of Auditors of Deutsches Reich complained:

> The efforts of the company are in evident contrast with money spent. In a period lasting from August 7, 1941 until July 25, 1943, i.e. in roughly 2 years, the company has finished a single cartoon (length: 438 m).
>
> The means which were granted to the company out of Kulturfilm-Förderungsfonds until

May 31, 1943, amount to RM 2,046,166, out of which RM 332,888 were not used; until May 31, 1943, RM 1,713,278 were spent. These subsidies amounted until October 4, 1943 to RM 2,748,914. Regarding the exorbitant launching costs the question has to be brought up if the establishment of such a special company with highly paid managers and proxies was not precipitant.

Neumann was a realist when he said that the route towards feature-length cartoons from Germany would be a long one. The Americans were 20 years ahead. Neumann expected to give it a try in 1947. However, when it finally happened in postwar Germany, Neumann was no longer alive. He had been denounced, and on May 14, 1945, he was arrested in his apartment in Berlin-Tegel. He was brought to an internment camp in Weesow, near Werneuchen, where he was found hanged in a toilet a month later.

The remainings of DZF (valued at about RM 17,000) were confiscated in East Berlin by Soviet occupation forces and consigned to Zentralverwaltung für Volksbildung, Film-Aktiv.

In a letter dated August 3, 1946, one of the staff members of Deutsche Zeichenfilm, Bernhard Klein, who was married to a Jewish woman, complained bitterly about his experiences. Klein had a background in theater and painting (the paintings of his older brother, César, were classified as Entartete Kunst — Degenerate Art — and banned) but took an early interest in animated cartoons. He had decided to experiment with animation and produce his own cartoon.[11] In 1938 he came to the conclusion that it would be best for his wife and himself to emigrate. He finally saw a chance to do so in 1941. To raise some money he tried to sell his finished cartoon film and found himself trapped in the network of animation under the swastika:

> In the meantime, prompted by Disney's Snow White success story, German film industry had become wide-eyed. The Cultural Film Center arranged immediately that my film was accepted by Tobis and released successfully. Then, however, they launched their own production and followed my example, initially under the roof of Tobis, where still a certain artistic atmosphere dominated, later under the label "Deutsche Zeichenfilm G.mb.H." which was supervised by a scenario-wise completely obstinate chief dramaturge (Leberecht). At that place happened exactly what I always had feared. Advertising filmmakers and commercial artists were entrusted with the task which was tantamount to assigning poster artists to do a painting.
>
> Under these circumstances I wasn't interested anymore to try to prevent that the Zeichenfilm company would have to make experiences the hard way. Anyway, the people in charge knew better all time with the result that the Zeichenfilm company, with a budget of RM 4.5 million, 100 employees plus 200 trainees, didn't achieve more than I did with a film of equal length but without any assistance.
>
> There was no evidence at all that any of the five chief animators of Zeichenfilm company were more skilled than others. They all were beginners compared to this artistic challenge and in some cases not artistically minded at all. If at all they were appreciated for political reasons and political disposition. Two were foreigners, one a true anti-fascist, the other unpleasant and pendant with occasional anti–Semitic statements. The 5th, however, the artist G. F., fraternized with the National Socialists. He sympathized with the respective ideas of the shop steward, shared deliberately all victory-focused propaganda foolery and spread these delusional ideas. In several copies he made caricatures showing Jews marked

with Jewish stars: a street scene populated by Stürmer types, the yellow star overemphasized, headline: "Es leuchten die Sterne [The Stars Shine]."[12]

Gerhard Fieber, *Bazillen* (Germs): DEFA 1945.

After the war, during 1948 and 1949, Fieber's EOS-Film G.m.b.H. created the first hand-drawn animated feature film in Germany, *Tobias Knopp, Abenteuer eines Junggesellen*, from an original by Wilhelm Busch, supported by 100 artists and technicians. "But when it was released it had no chance to compete with Disney's *Snow White* and other animated features that finally were shown in Germany as ours was only black and white, the American films, however, produced in Technicolor. It was like a dwarf fighting the giants!"

Fieber became a pioneer of German television. For Second Channel Television (ZDF), located in Mainz, he directed spots featuring the animated *Little Mainz Men* (*Mainzelmännchen*). In order to save money in animation in the early 1970s he even turned to Asia: "I went to Japan to meet with a cartoon director in Tokyo. He bowed and then, fluently, cited a poem by Heinrich Heine in German language. I couldn't have done that. He simply wanted to express that he would be honoured to contribute to the *Little Mainz Men* but the deal didn't come through. ZDF officials were afraid the German dwarf characters, once produced in Japan, might look too Asian!" Fieber even remembered the Japanese artist's name: Isao Takahata, the partner of Hayao Miyazaki. In 1988 Studio Ghibli released Takahata's stunning antiwar film *Hotaru no haka* (*Grave of the Fireflies*).

13

Snow Man and Weather-Beaten Melody: Hans Fischerkoesen and Horst von Möllendorff

There only was one studio that really delivered films of timeless quality to rival Disney. That, of course, was not the highly sponsored DZF but the small Fischerkoesen plant, founded by Hans Fischer who was born and raised in Bad Kösen. (Therefore he had named himself Fischerkoesen, as Fischer was too common a name in Germany.) A graduate of the Academy of Arts in Leipzig, Fischerkoesen came to Berlin in the 1920s, joined Ufa and later established his own studio in Potsdam (and also outsourced to a studio in the Netherlands). Before and after the war he produced successful animation, mainly advertising films. Goebbels let him do as he pleased. In the 1940s Fischerkoesen produced a trio of color animated shorts for German Newsreel that remain unparalleled in Germany for camerawork (in several scenes, instead of Multiplane, Fischerkoesen employed Max Fleischer's three-dimensional "stereo" animation stand, providing a combination of 2D and 3D) and lively animated characters.

By 1938 there were 5,000 cinemas in greater Germany. The cinema owners were obliged to run the German Newsreel before the main feature. To intersperse some funny shorts was not allowed. Audiences who showed up in time for only the main feature were sent away.

After Germany invaded Poland on September 1, 1939, Minister Dr. Goebbels controlled the progress of the newsreel as a daily routine, but also wanted some entertaining segments in the newsreel presentation. He asked Dr. Fritz Hippler to do some research. Hippler presented his boss with reports about soldiers' life at base, showing them reading, playing cards, fishing, playing sports and exercising and so on.

On June 20, 1940, Berlin opened the first cinema devoted entirely to newsreels. The Nazis planned to build 15–20 special newsreel cinemas in Germany where audiences could watch the recent political issues for little money (40 pfennig: 10:00 A.M.—4:00 P.M., 60 Pfennig: 4:00 P.M.—10:00 P.M.). On September 4, 1940, Goebbels discussed with Hippler the reorganization of the newsreel and put the different film magazines under a central roof. On September 4, 1940, Deutsche Wochenschau G.m.b.H. was founded under the supervision of the aforementioned Heinrich Roellenbleg.

Hans Fischerkoesen, Leipzig, 1920 (courtesy Dr. Hans Fischerkoesen).

For the newsreel cinemas, not only newsreels were needed but also shorts, funnies as well as cartoons. On July 7, 1942, the Propaganda Ministry wrote to the propaganda departments of the Supreme Military Commander in Belgium and northern France about programming for newsreel cinemas: "Currently we are at work, in association with Deutsche Wochenschau G.m.b.H. and in agreement with the Reich Ministry for Enlightenment and Propaganda, compiling programs and will provide, if possible, missing segments (cartoons, trickfilms, sketches and films recommended for the youth); particularly the last mentioned program segments are vital for loosening up a program of one hour length and necessary for attracting the respective audience."

For programming the newsreel cinemas, Roellenbleg found a qualified employee in Dr. Hans Alfred Christian Karbe, who was born to German parents in London on October 11, 1905. He had attended English schools until deportation in 1914, then visited gymnasiums in Lübeck, Berlin, Stettin and Berlin again. He left *Untersekunda* [tenth schoolyear] in 1922 to focus on agriculture. After his father's death he gave up an apprenticeship as export merchant, joined a bank and sat for his *Abitur*. Then he changed, took a different route and joined the theatre as assistant director at *Volksbühne*. In 1930 he directed at Deutsches Künstlertheater and studied theatrical sciences, art history, literature and archaeology in Berlin, Munich and Frankfurt. In 1935 he took his degree in Würzburg. From 1932 to 1936 he was married to state actress Gefion Helmke. In 1935–36 he went as director and dramatic adviser to Hagen in Westphalia where he also supervised the NS Kulturgemeinde (National Socialist Cultural Community). In 1936 he became dramaturge of the Dietrich Eckardt Bühnen, a theatrical platform that was located on the Olympic Field in Berlin. Two years later he started in films. Roellenbleg hired him on July 28, 1942, and assigned him the supervision of trickfilm production as well on August 2, 1942, for an additional monthly fee of RM 500.

Roellenbleg and Karbe found an ideal studio for their purposes in Fischerkoesen and signed him for five cartoons. Fischerkoesen-Film-Studio at that time mainly produced classified training and public advertising films (which had become a dilemma in itself) but the number of commercials was reduced by order of the Ministry of Enlightenment and

Fischerkoesen Studios in Potsdam, 1943 (courtesy Dr. Hans Fischerkoesen).

Propaganda. In 1941 Dr. Goebbels decided: "I have to discontinue propaganda for goods and merchandise, particularly food and clothes, which practically nobody can buy anymore and so it would draw blood."[1] Consequently, on October 14, 1941, the *Werberat* (advertising council) prohibited advertising for so-called *Mangelware* (scarce goods). Fischerkoesen had to look elsewhere as advertising wasn't big business anymore. This was no problem, as he was still immensely popular. *Film-Kurier* reported on Fischerkoesen under the headline "Gang durch ein Zeichenfilm-Atelier" (Walk through an Animation Studio):

> Above the roofs of Potsdam, near the cultured park of Sanssouci, there is the studio of animation film production, Fischerkoesen, which currently produces on behalf of Wochenschau-Sonderproduktion [Newsreel special production] cartoon films. The cartoon film is a form of filmic expression which now has become modern in Germany too. Special Newsreel production not only has cartoon films produced in Berlin but also in Amsterdam, The Hague, Paris, and Prague. [...]
>
> In spite of its extremely modern and attractive forms the animated film is not as new as one would assume, in any case it is older than sound films which, however, have contributed to its actual prestige. Hans Fischerkoesen, for instance, has started in 1917 to focus on animation film and has used it for many years in advertising. But only since August 1942 he makes animated films for the big audience in the fringe events of regular cinema programs.
>
> The uniqueness of animated film production is especially due to the fact that these films must completely grow out of the imagination and out of a versatile talent if they shall please. The animation producer employs writers, composers and artists but he must have himself a creative mind regarding writing, image and musical score and, if possible, should be himself an all-round artist in these fields.

Fischerkoesen Studios Potsdam in 1942 during production of *Der Schneemann* (courtesy Dr. Hans Fischerkoesen).

> The technical process of manufacturing a cartoon, for instance, starts with the determination of the musical score, the soundtrack already exists before the final drawing will be provided. Therefore the whole movie must be finished inside its creator before practical work will begin. [...]
>
> The ideas for the two films which were drawn by Fischerkoesen for the newsreel so far — Verwitterte Melodie and Der Schneemann — were conceived by Horst von Möllendorff [2].

Although in his own estimation, Möllendorff was no expert in animation, his writing services for DZF, Fischerkoesen and later Prague Film were outstanding, highly regarded and well paid. He had joined Fischerkoesen first for *Die verwitterte Melodie* (*Weather-Beaten Melody*) in 1942 after leaving DZF: "One morning in mid–1942 Dr. Karbe called me in my apartment. We knew each other from Ullstein. He told me about the idea to produce some entertaining cartoons with Fischerkoesen. Therefore he urgently needed a funny story. On ten pages, written in short sentences, I outlined *Die verwitterte Melodie.* Karbe was enthusiastic but insisted on a finished screenplay which I submitted too."

On a sunny summer day a wasp (some reviews erroneously spoke of a bee), reminiscent distantly Waldemar Bonsels' Maya, discovers an abandoned phonograph in a meadow. There is a technically rather complicated shot of the wasp flying down from the sky and entering the picture through 12 multiplane layers of grass and flowers and circling around the three-dimensional phonograph. Accidentally, she touches the record with her stinger and is surprised to hear some chords. Astonished, she checks her stinger. Then she runs along the record and produces more sound, using her stinger as a stylus to play the record. The weather-beaten phonograph starts to produce some jazz and swing music, which attracts more insects. But dust makes the wasp come to a standstill. The music sounds distorted. A stately caterpillar, which has watched curiously, comes to the rescue and cleans the record. On the now mirror-like surface the wasp, however, starts to slip and skid. Only with the support of two helpful beetles does she get onto her legs again. Pairs of beetles dance and sway to the music in the branches. Even the hedgehog, the snail and the frogs are in the best mood.

After awhile, from intense recording, the wasp's sting starts to glow. Beetles refresh with dewdrops from the cup of a bellflower. A stag beetle whirls the wasp around until the wasp is thrown out with a broken sting. The sting has to be sharpened and the show goes on.

The late animation historian and Fischerkoesen biographer Dr. William Moritz proved a good observer and even discovered some subtle "bit of forbidden information" in Fischerkoesen's little cartoon:

> The discovery of an abandoned phonograph takes on a new meaning, especially when the record on the turntable is a swing number with lyrics that say, "The week wouldn't be worthwhile without a weekend when we can get away to enjoy nature." Near the phonograph lies an "abandoned" clasp from a woman's garter belt (with a lucky four-leafed clover growing out of it!), which suggests that the interrupted picnic that left behind the musical instrument had also involved erotic play — something also strictly forbidden by the puritanical Nazi codes. So from beneath the charming surface of this cartoon emerges a subversive message: women, far from the unnatural Nazi-designated stereotype of "children, church and kitchen," can escape into Nature to be self-reliant and adventurous, erotic and free — they can discover or revitalize a suppressed world of forbidden joy in music and friendship between diverse creatures who may be brown or white, frog or caterpillar — or even a pair of ladybug beetles who may be a same-sex couple."[3]

***Verwitterte Melodie*: Dimensional model of phonograph used in 1942 short.**

***Verwitterte Melodie* (1942): Pencil drawing.**

According to Moritz, *Verwitterte Melodie* is "quite the opposite of the Nazi requirements for a dedicated Aryan citizen." One should remember, however, that later in the war the image of women had changed, as females were invited to work in the armament factories and take on the jobs of the men who were dying at the front.

Fischerkoesen transformed the idea with the support of 14 employees in his Potsdam studio. Colorization was outsourced to a studio in The Hague where another 17 employees were busy.

Möllendorff recalled: "Fischerkoesen and his studio worked effectively and very fast on the cartoon. He was in straight competition with Reich-owned Deutsche Zeichenfilm G.m.b.H. which for some time worked on *Hansi.* Based on his long experience with advertising films and commercials Fischerkoesen had developed his own style and as I was not experienced in manufacturing cartoons I only submitted the idea for him."[4]

As a reward for his writing services Möllendorff received a rare commendation during Reich Week of the German Culture Film Munich 1943:

> The color cartoon WEATHER-BEATEN MELODY by Fischerkoesen-Film-Production was awarded a prize.
>
> With this award the achievement of HORST VON MÖLLENDORFF as writer got recognition.
>
> Munich, 12 November 1943
> Der Reichsminister für Volksaufklärung und Propaganda
> Signed,
> Dr. Goebbels

The *Weather-Beaten Melody*, or *Scherzo*, as it was also called, received good reviews from foreign countries too. On January 17, 1944, Emil Reinegger, head of A.C.E. Paris Film Distributors, reported to Ufa Berlin:

> End of November 1943 the above mentioned cartoon film was started at Urban Theatre, Zurich, as supplement to the feature film, Der weisse Traum.
>
> For me this was a special event because — as is known to you — the whole American animation production (Walt Disney — Dave Fleischer) for years took a prominent place in the programming of American films.
>
> At that time I had the opportunity to participate in the premiere of Scherzo in Zurich. The audience response was surprisingly favorable and I can say better than the bulk of all American trickfilms. The audience followed enthusiastically and liked the excellent idea, the colours, the score and the supremely funny gags. Particularly surprised were audiences and press too by this German work because everybody actually believed that only Americans would be able to produce this kind of film.
>
> While the Americans work with mostly grotesque gags, Scherzo caught eyes particularly for the European view and the not excessive humour as well as the plain kind this film had its impact on the audience. When the movie finished the audience applauded frenetically as I never experienced it with a Walt Disney picture.
>
> During a trip to Berlin I got the opportunity to see another cartoon, Der Schneemann, which I regard on the same level and which should have the same impact as Scherzo.
>
> I believe that we cannot render a greater service to German filmmaking than to release these films as soon as possible.

As Reinegger mentioned, German Newsreel had asked Möllendorff for another funny story that could be turned into an animation short. There was one idea he had already offered DZF but was turned down. One evening Möllendorff sat in a Berlin beer garden hoping to find a suitable topic for a cartoon, and eventually he came up with the story of a snowman who has a warm spot in his heart. He wakes up under a full moon night in a quiet marketplace. After some adventures he creeps into a house to rest on a sofa. There he discovers a calendar. The calendar

REICHSWOCHE
FÜR DEN
DEUTSCHEN KULTURFILM
MÜNCHEN 1943
*
DER FARBIGE ZEICHENFILM
VERWITTERTE MELODIE
DER FISCHERKÖSEN-FILM-PRODUKTION
WURDE MIT EINEM PREISE AUSGEZEICHNET.
DAMIT HAT DIE LEISTUNG VON
HORST VON MOELLENDORFF
ALS AUTOR IHRE ANERKENNUNG GEFUNDEN.
MÜNCHEN, DEN 12 NOVEMBER
DER REICHSMINISTER FÜR VOLKSAUFKLÄRUNG UND PROPAGANDA

Commendation to Horst von Möllendorff (1943).

***Der Schneemann* (1943–44): Pencil drawing (courtesy Dr. Hans Fischerkoesen).**

page for January shows a snowman like himself in a winter landscape. He browses through February and March and stops in July. For the first time he learns about that loveliest of seasons: summer. He longs for to experience it. He gets himself frozen in the refrigerator, and emerges with the advent of summer. Everything looks exactly as the calendar picture promised. The snowman grins from ear to ear and is all smiles when he leaves the house. He enjoys the sun tremendously and welcomes "the summer of his lifetime."

The snowman picks flowers and spreads them around. He sticks a red rose into his cold breast. He surprises an excited hen with an egg made of ice and snow. The warm July sun begins to burn. Slowly the snowman starts to melt leaving only a top hat and his carrot nose which is picked up and eaten by a little rabbit.

Moritz wrote: "The snowman, an average person with some good and bad qualities, is trapped in a given environment, Winterland. Although it is functional, it is cold and in some ways inhospitable. He reads that there is another place, sunny and free, and arranges to escape there for some thrilling moments of warmth and freedom, even at the cost of his life, as we hear him gurgle in the death throes of song, twisting and melting in the hot sun."[5] The snowman's tragicomic death in some odd way also reflects the millionfold death that had become a firm part of German society. A number of German leaders seemed to belong to a suicide club themselves as, when the war was lost, they committed suicide: Joseph Goebbels (he and his wife took their children who had so much enjoyed the *Snowman* into death), Heinrich Himmler, Hermann Göring, Robert Ley and Adolf Hitler (with recently married wife) himself.

Möllendorff smeared the story onto A5 pages which he pinned and posted to Deutsche Wochenschau, not forgetting to ask for a sizable fee. Newsreel, in turn, asked for a typewritten manuscript which he immediately forwarded to get his money.

From Newsreel the manuscript went to Fischerkoesen, who was still busy finishing *Weather-Beaten Melody* for a budget of RM 148,650. In the beginning scenes, the master animator again used his Fleischer-type revolving miniature set left over from an earlier advertising film depicting a 2D snowman as he approached the house during a frozen winter night.

Notes of a Radio Broadcast (6):

Starts with the title melody from *Der Schneemann* (by Rudolf Perak).

Then Dr. J. Petersen is going to interview the writer, Horst von Möllendorff.

JP: Dear Listeners! The melody that you just heard has a special meaning: for to its rhythm there doesn't move a man but — a drawing. For the first time new animated cartoons have been closely linked with music and fine arts.

To this melody a snowman is dancing in a new cartoon that you will know very soon. With his first move he seems to look familiar; with almost affecting happiness he smiles all over his face and this is no miracle. For the father of the little smiling character that you all will know from the newspapers is nobody else than the artist Horst von Möllendorff who has contributed the idea for this film which was produced in the animaton studios of Fischerkoesen. We have asked Horst von Möllendorff to join us to tell us a little bit. Many of you will like to hear him once; for the Snow Man's sister in spirit many of you will already know. This is the wasp, the star of the animated cartoon *Weather-Beaten Melody*, which accidentally draws some sound out of an old phonograph record according to an idea by the same Horst von Möllendorff.

Melody from *Verwitterte Melodie* (by Lothar Brühne).

Herr von Möllendorff, we know that the artist's idea is a big secret but as you will know us laymen are always eager to learn more about. Please would you kindly tell how you came across the idea for the *Snow Man* film?

VM: To conceive an idea you need two things: open eyes to walk around the world and the imagination. With my very eyes I once have seen a snow man which was surrounded by snowdrops which meddle-

***Der Schneemann* (1943–44): Ultraphan cel (courtesy Dr. Hans Fischerkoesen).**

Fischerkoesen: *Der Schneemann* (1943) (courtesy Dr. Hans Fischerkoesen).

somely were watching out of the snow. And in my creative mind this image became an idea. In my mind I have transferred a snow man who never has seen the splendor blossoming in summer to summertime. In the cartoon the snow man really experiences the summer.

JP: How long did it take to transform the lovely idea into a cartoon?

vM: The animated cartoon *The Snow Man* was produced in 5 months work in the animation studio of Fischerkoesen Film Production. That is an extremely brief working period if one considers that each frame of the whole film strip has to be drawn separately. Before it will be drawn each frame has to be sketched. Besides that, in one frame often appear several characters so that again for each character an individual animation drawing is necessary. In this brief period in the studio of Fischerkoesen, for a single film that runs for approximately 15 minutes, 52,000 individual drawings were produced.

JP: One barely can grasp this surprisingly great and versatile work if one sees the color screen adventure of the snow man.

vM: That is a good proof for our work.

JP: We only can agree; for the strongest impact of the film was the great serenity which affects all of us, shining and liberating with every laugh that has been born of true humour.

How does it come, Herr von Möllendorff, that this cheerfulness is so outrageously affecting?

vM: Well, Herr Doktor Petersen, that is almost more difficult to explain than to do but I will try. As much as beauty has to be painted into a painting if it should reflect true beauty delight has to be drawn into a drawing if it should have a delightful effect. And I do my work with great joy and hope that our cartoon film will come off the screen radiant with joy onto you.

JP: Herr von Möllendorff, in the name of all listeners I assume I can assure that we will accept the cartoon with similar joy.

In a letter addressed to Cautio Treuhand, the Propaganda Ministry informed Dr. Winkler that the minister had viewed *The Snow Man* on November 20: "He liked the picture very much."

Karl Neumann of DZF saw Fischerkoesen's rising star with envy. He tried to convince Goebbels to assign Fischerkoesen to DZF. A September 29, 1943, entry in Dr. Goebbels' diary: "Oberregierungsrat Neumann whom I have entrusted with the preparation of a cartoon film production makes a report about his previous work. He has tackled with the problem efficiently and has already accomplished notable things. The first cartoon film which has been screened to me from his production still shows many weak points; but it is a good beginning. Besides there is another production from cartoon film producer Fischer-Kösen which Neumann would love to take over by force and integrate into his own production. I refuse temporarily. As long as a new film production is in its infancy it is good if there is competition." For *Der Schneemann* Möllendorff received by order of Goebbels a bonus of RM 500. When the *Snow Man* was released as supplementary film to Heinz Rühmann's *Der Engel mit dem Saitenspiel* Werner Fiedler, writing in *Deutsche Allgemeine Zeitung* (December 21, 1944), reviewed the short with more words than the Rühmann feature. An incensed Rühmann complained to Reich Film Intendant Hans Hinkel.

In spite of their success Fischerkoesen and Möllendorff split. Fischerkoesen disliked the promotion that Möllendorff received in the media. Möllendorff: "Although the success of our cartoons was very great, our working relationship changed. I was displeased to only receive a credit while Fischerkoesen believed that I was given too much credit as source of the idea. Anyway, after *Schneemann* it was over with Fischerkoesen." Fischerkoesen preferred to finish a third Agfacolor short on his own: *Das dumme Gänslein* (*The Dumb Goose*/*The Silly Goose*) in 1944: A stupid young goose almost falls victim to a fox. "The fox's sinister lair is run by slave labor—a weasel

Der Schneemann (1943–44): Ultraphan cel. (courtesy Dr. Hans Fischerkoesen)

***Das dumme Gänslein* (1944): Advertisement (courtesy Dr. Hans Fischerkoesen).**

cranking a spit, a cat on a treadmill that makes xylophone music with dangling bones—and a cage full of geese waits for slaughter."[7] It was the weakest in the trio of Fischerkoesen shorts. *Film-Kurier* wrote:

> In his most recent film which portrays a "silly little goose" that goes astray, Hans Fischerkoesen, for the first time in his short film career, will not only perform as his own chief animator, but also his own author. The fable of the "dumb goose"was written by himself and offers the possibility to open up a new field for the animated cartoon: the physiognomy. In the funny animal stories of this picture, maybe some patrons will recognize their own features. Haven't the animal fables of the ancient Greeks jeered at human weaknesses? And are there not many "dumb geese" around in the world?
>
> For Fischerkoesen this is a challenge. Already his whole studio is occupied with preproduction work for this newest and in its kind most modern cartoon topic.
>
> In a few months the picture will be finished. At any rate, it will contribute to increase and improve the technical and aestethic qualities of German animated films which, in recent times, have developed in a fast and happy way and so will give people something for which they will thank today with all their heart: the pure, carefree humour [8].

14

A Surprising Underwater Cartoon from Prague: Wedding at Coral Sea

Finally, Horst von Möllendorff, the hero of the two Fischerkoesen cartoons, was able to ask for an assignment on his own: "In mid–1943 Dr. Karbe showed me a cartoon film made by Dillenz in Prague. His *Zauberlehring* [*Sorcerer's Apprentice*] in human shape I found too sad. Disney's *Sorcerer's Apprentice* in *Fantasia* with Mickey Mouse was much more flexible, smooth and funnier. Dr. Karbe told me of the problems with Dillenz in Prague. They were looking for a creative person to supervise and run the artistic end of the enterprise. We then drove to Prague and visited the animation studio. They wanted me badly as creative director, however they wanted me to stay over there. I would have had to leave Berlin for a longer time but this I didn't want.

"Only provided that I wouldn't have to be over there all time I would agree. There was a solution for this problem and I agreed. The next day I met all supervising animators to have a brainstorming and find an idea for a cartoon film. They had already done some research on their own and thought of the adventures of some exotic fish in the ocean.

"Thus my idea for *Hochzeit im Korallenmeer* was born."[1]

On July 29, 1943, Möllendorff signed for two cartoons. The first (to be submitted by August 15, 1943), was titled *Hochzeit im Korallenmeer* (*Wedding at Coral Sea*), a tale of two fish falling in love until the bride is being kidnapped by an evil pirate octopus. He would receive a total fee RM 5,000 in two installments. The second script, still untitled, was to be finished by September 15, 1943. For his six-month services as creative director he would receive a monthly fee of RM 1,800.

He recalled, "My activities in Prague were a totally new task for me. Now I was creative director of more than one hundred artists. They worked, contrary to German animation, on a high, professional level. I always thought that there were some artists with Disney experience involved. To create the optical illusion of underwater life they clamped two panes of glass on top of each other under the camera lens. Between the panes of glass some drops of oil dissolved and, due to the heat and fast photography, left the impression of life in the sea. They have built even some kind of multiplane camera. On the floor there were 10 mtr. (30 feet) tracks and a camera moved towards the different layers to produce depth of focus."

Hochzeit im Korallenmeer **(1944).**

Möllendorff worked with the nucleus and cream of the future Czech animation industry: Jiří Brdečka, Eduard Hofman, Stanislav Latal, Josef Kandel and Jilis Kalaš.

The story left enough room for action and imagination: The pirate octopus kidnaps the fish bride and hides in the wreck of a sunken ship. To please her and win her over, he performs wild Cherkessian dances (that reveal him as aggressive Russian type) but this frightens the fish girl, who starts to cry. In the meantime the bride-groom isn't idle. He assembles auxiliaries and frees his beloved with the assistance of other fish, mostly swordfish and sawfish. Ufa acquired the release rights to the film for RM 337,134,28. To use it as a supplementary short for Martin Fric's *Dir zuliebe* (starring Hans Holt and Winnie Markus), they ordered 158 prints for a total cost of RM 61,569,68.

While the Czech animators finished the short, Möllendorff worked on the second script. On September 15, 1943, as required by contract, he submitted *Das Wetterhäuschen*, the story of a weather house and its residents, a couple of wooden puppets. It was apparently inspired by a Pinschewer puppet film of the same title released in 1929.

On May 25, 1944, Möllendorff's contract was renewed for a third short, *Das Fledermäuschen* (The Little Bat) for another RM 5,000 telling that the place of jurisdiction is Prague under German law: "*Gerichtsstand ist Prag. Es gilt deutsches Recht.*"

Again Möllendorff conceived a detailed sequence list. *Das Fledermäuschen*, was a charming spoof on the Johann Strauss operetta *Die Fledermaus* (The Bat), which at that time was to be filmed in color by Ufa in Barrandov Studios using the talents of Marte Harell and Johannes Heesters. (However, it was released after the war, in 1946.) The cartoon version was supposed to open in the ruins of a little rococo castle. In an alcove a couple of bats hang sleeping — Mr. Bat in black cloak, Mrs. Bat in nightgown. Mr. Bat wakes up, takes his top hat and a mask and tries to sneak away. As he does so Mrs. Bat wakes up too. When he realizes that, he hastily returns, taking off his top hat and mask. While she eyes him suspiciously he lulls and rocks her to sleep. Then he leaves again. Via a spiral staircase he enters — or, better, falls — into a banquet hall, with a bat-girl ballet on stage. He ends up in the lap of a bat lady. He kisses her and also flirts with the ballet dancers. At that moment Mrs. Bat turns up and sees what is going on. She dons a silver-grey spiderweb as a dress, then hides behind a mask. Mr. Bat doesn't recognize her. While he is inflamed with passion for the mysterious lady she flirts with four other cavaliers to make him jealous. He dons a crown of champagne foam. Finally she lets the cavaliers go and both start to waltz. While they dance he tries to remove her mask but she raps him over the knuckles. In the meantime the four cavaliers entertain themselves with a champagne firework. Mr. Bat and the unidentified inamorata retreat to a loge. Again he tries to unmask her. A red crown of foam froths on her head. A rococo clock beats. All participants unmask and throw their masks around the ballroom. With the final beats she takes off her mask and the spiderweb gown. With surprise Mr. Bat recognizes his wife. Then he smiles and they hug.

Möllendorff: "As I said, I didn't stay in Prague continuously. In Berlin there were rumors that due to the war animation companies would be evacuated or closed. So I had to reckon that Prague would be shut down too."

Möllendorff was right. None of his later short film projects were made. On October 2, 1944, Reichfilm Intendant Hinkel reported to Dr. Goebbels that according to recent activities in Prague all personnel of the animation studio was now employed at the Junkers factory: "The animators will remain in their previous workrooms and are put under the supervision of the responsible management of Junkers-Werke."

The Germans' funding and support of Czechoslovakian animation, however, would lead to the establishment of an important Czech animation industry in Zlín after the war. Hermina Týrlová and Karel Zeman (and Antonín Horák, who was forced to mediate between the two rivals as photographer) did puppet shorts in a former shoe factory founded by Jan Bata. From 1939 on, additional work for cartoons such as *Fritz and Fratz* was produced. Degeto-Kulturfilm G.m.b.H. continued to commission short films, for instance two puppet films, *Der brave Slim — Abenteuer eines niedlichen Käfers* (1943) and *Weihnachtstraum* (1944), which cost approximately RM 130,000,- and were released not only to home cinemas but also theatrically. (Zeman in the mid–1950s, started to direct fantasy and science fiction feature films as George Pál did in Hollywood, notably the highly acclaimed *Vynález Zkázy/Invention of Destruction*, released in the States as *The Fabulous World of Jules Verne*.) In Prague the outstanding Jiří Trnka founded the *Brothers in Trick* (and directed the anti-fascist *Federmann and the SS*). After some 2D work he turned to stop-motion as well and did some of the finest puppet film work ever.

15

*Deutsche Wochenschau and the "Collaborators" of the Europäischer Zeichenfilm Ring**

On February 17, 1943, Horst von Möllendorff had signed a contract with Joop Geesink, a former George Pál cohort, and Amsterdam animation company Toonder-Bouman to write a cartoon, *Das Steh-Auf-Männchen.* As in the case of *Luftikus,* Möllendorff wanted to devise a character that would be able to carry a whole series. He conceived a bon vivant, sort of a daredevil, who believes in the motto "Nothing is going to happen to me." He is very inventive but all his inventions at the end are of little avail. However, like some indefatigable Germans and convinced Nazis who decorated their ruins with banners reading "Our murals broke but our hearts didn't," this cartoon character doesn't lose his faith and optimism, so he was considered a worthwhile role model. Ufa bought the idea for release, advanced RM 91.350 (of the RM 175.000 budget) and retitled the project *Das musikalische Auto.*

Another project Möllendorff sold to Geesink in July 1943 was a puppet color film project, *Brummis Nachtmusik,* that dealt with the misadventures of a pianist. Ufa retitled, this, too, as: *Das verhinderte Klavierkonzert,* and advanced the bulk of the RM 58,000 budget (RM 50,000) to Geesink.

The dream of establishing a German animation industry (with the outrageous plan of setting up a European cartoon industry on Crimea Island) had almost come to an end. As Councillor Neumann was not able to deliver sufficient cartoon footage, his administration came up with the plan of usurping the forces of other European studios and put them under the roof and label of DZF.

In a letter signed by Undersecretary Dr. Gast and addressed to Mayor Dr. Winkler, Berlin NW 87, Brückenallee 3, regarding animation film it was stated "that after a screening of *The Snow Man* Mr. Roellenbleg has repeated his question if various groups of animation producers should be put under the roof of Deutsche Zeichenfilm G.m.b.H.. which would follow the request of Oberregierungsrat Neumann. The minister, however, expressed that he does NOT wish the subordination of various animation manufacturers under the roof of Deutsche Zeichenfilm G.m.b.H.. On the contrary, he regards the current

**Deutsche Wochenschau=German Newsreel; Europäischer Zeichenfilm Ring=European Animation Film Circle.*

state of independent development of these groups far better because it will create a healthy artistic competition." So Roellenbleg and Karbe, in charge of Sonderreferat Kulturfilm, had to try without DZF (although in the long run they had exactly that in mind). A paper dated February 7, 1944, was compiled with a suggestion to organize an animation film circle throughout Europe, a cluster now exclusively controlled by German Newsreel. The paper was signed by Heinrich Roellenbleg.[1]

> Proposal
> for combination of small animation film studios in Europe to raise artistic and economic achievement (efficiency)
> A year ago Deutsche Wochenschau [German Newsreel] got the assignment to organize a German animation film production which should be able to make up for the technical and artistic advance of Americans in shortest time. Therefore at suitable commercial film productions in Germany as well as in the occupied countries appropriate rearrangements have been taken and experts as well as equipment have been supplied. Furthermore, in the occupied countries some companies have been newly established and at last artistic and partly technical supervision of animation departments of the state-controlled companies

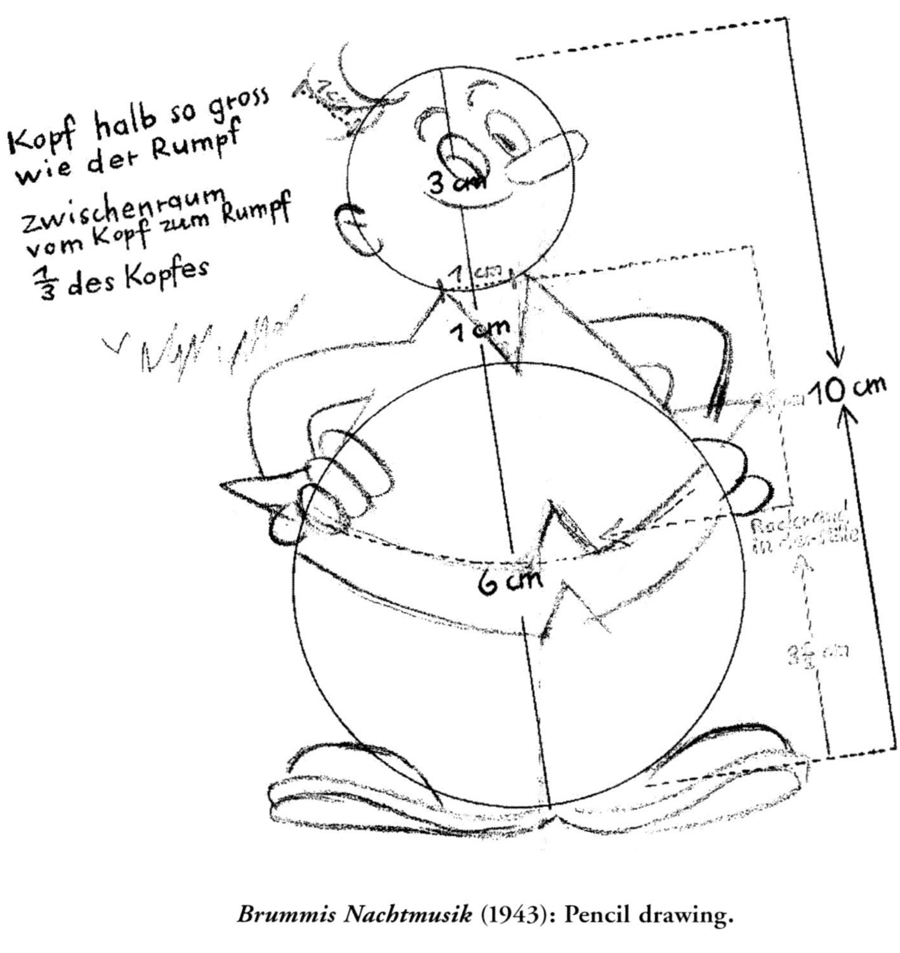

***Brummis Nachtmusik* (1943): Pencil drawing.**

was taken over. For all units and workgroups, in closest cooperation with the artists and new writers, suitable manuscripts were supplied and submitted to the studios for production.

In no less than 14 studios, spread all over Europe, different animation and puppet film artists are at work. 8 of them already have been signed by German Newsreel while deals with the rest will soon to be closed. (The 3 studios of Deutsche Zeichenfilm G.m.b.H. are not included.) These groups have different prerequisites and craftsmen unevenly distributed, with partly very inadequate technical equipment. All of them, in spite of one-sided experience, have started work. If they have accomplished till today relatively much nobody can deny that everywhere there are considerable drawbacks. In one group that might be technically superior much is left to be desired regarding artistic discipline while another group that might do splendid animation hasn't much story mind with a nod to the audience. A third group still has problems with colour but on the other hand has an exemplary working schedule which saves hundreds of man-hours while another group seems to have found the key to an ideal "Fahrplan" [exposure sheet], which is the heart of any well organized animation company.

From uneven beginnings the abilities of each respective studio have developed of course unequally. One has gained special abilities in this field, another in a different. It is natural that suddenly from all parties comes a desire to cooperate more closely, exchange experiences, support each other.

For this reason it is suggested to found a

ZEICHENFILM — RING

(circle or cluster of animation)

which will enclose all smaller companies with their individual background and ownership left untouched.

This "Zeichenfilm-Ring" shall not transform into a second Deutsche Zeichenfilm G.mb.H. but shall only and exclusively enhance and promote the artistic and technical development of German animation in Europe and in the interest of all involved parties and in our all interest to streamline methods [of production].

The studios of "Zeichenfilm-Ring"

"Zeichenfilm-Ring" might include the following studios:

1. Fischerkösenfilm, Potsdam and The Hague
2. Bavaria-Zeichenfilm, Munich and The Hague
3. Prag-Animation, Prague
4. Joop Geesink, Amsterdam
5. Toonder-Bouman, Amsterdam
6. Les Gemeaux, Paris
7. André Rigal, Paris
8. Raymond Jeannin, Paris
9. Dansk Favre ok Tegne Film, Copenhagen
10. Animation department of Descheg, Zlin
11. Philippart, Brussels
12. Former Bassoli Group, Rome

If Deutsche Zeichenfilm G.m.b.H. should participate in "Zeichenfilm-Ring" has to be decided at high places.

The Assignments of "Zeichenfilm-Ring"

A great number of assignments have arisen for German animation film in Europe which, if at all, only can be solved by a united advance of the various studios:

Exchange of artistic experiences

Development of technical facilities
Streamlining the whole process
Investigation on economical profitability
Solution of acute problems with color film stock
Foundation of the first Lehrstuhl [Professorship] in the world for humour
Establishment of a script department [dramaturgy]
Research on new possibilities in musical scoring
Standardization of animation material
Mutual support after air raids

Edition of humorous magazine, "Der bunte Ring" (The Colorful Ring)

1. Exchange of experiences
   a) On the field of film technique,
      In order to fastly develop a relatively uncomplicated multiplane stand
      And other new and flawless shooting methods
   b) On the field of special effects technique
      To achieve surprisingly new stunning effects;
   c) On the field of drawing
   To fastly achieve perfectly fluid movement without losing the own line by copying Disney pictures or losing characteristic charm of pure graphics in favour of merely naturalistic movements through rotoscoping ["Kinoxen" in German]
2. Investigation of economical profitability
   a) Small private studios as well as larger state-controlled animation studios need to investigate the best relation in number and skills of animation artists for each picture in order to avoid the always repeating and costly idel running.

***Das musikalische Auto* (1943): Ultraphan cels (collection NIAf).**

   b) Determination of adequate fees for the various working steps; elimination of antisocially low and of unjustifiably excessive fees.
3. Productive cooperation with Agfa and process laboratories to exploit all technical possibilities of color film stock to its full extent resp. assist the chemists of I.G. Farben in developing a special color film stock for animation films. Today's Agfacolor film stock was mainly created for the conditions of feature films. The animated films, however, have entirely different prerequisites.
4. Foundation of the world's first Lehrstuhl [Professorship] for humour. The Lehrstuhl for humour intends to make animators familiar with the essentials of humour which always should remain sympathetic. It is not intended to train humorists; this task would prove impossible. However, it has turned out that most humorists and almost all animators lack in mental tools. We must succeed in making them think disciplined and execute their ideas logically. The rules of a punch line et al have to be worked out. But as every gag has to be sympathetic-humorist the element of humour has to be introduced into the drawing itself, i.e. into the line. To contemporary animators these things are only a foggy term if not totally unknown.
5. Creation of a Script Department with the assignment of
   a) finding new qualified writers, creating unique ideas und having screenplays prepared "made to measure" for the various studios or in association with them,
   b) establishing an according Music Department to explore the novel effects of nowadays still too conventionally used scores. Film animation necessitates differently assembled orchestras (smaller) than feature film as well as different composition und especially a novel orchestration.
6. Standardization of animation material.
   The conditions of today's animation film are similar to those of feature films 40 years ago. Then there were dozens of various film formats, different perforation, cameras and projectors which made a standardized working process impossible.—Today each animation studio works on a different format which would make the cooperation of various studios on one assignment right now highly difficult. As then in feature films, it is time now in animation to prepare for a standardization of daily material and special equipment. The standardization would include an economical aspect: if for instance Ultraphan [cells] would be delivered not in ten different sizes but only one, the cheapest one, this would reduce costs considerably.
7. The most exclusive assignment of all animation studios remains the mutual help and support in case of damages by air terror. Temporary establishing of workplaces, exchange of equipment and material would reduce the breakdown.
8. As collective achievement "Zeichenfilm-Ring" can go public with an entirely new idea, with a periodically published film humour magazine that like magazines as "Simplizissimus" or "Lustige Blätter" successively presents a colourful sequel of drawn film gags titled

   "Der bunte Ring."

   This humorous magazine would gain artistic significance as entirely new writers with daring, also avant garde ideas could be used to explore what later be used in short films. Economically that would mean that idle running could be stopped if each studio would provide just half a dozen elaborated gags ready for drawing which would absorb freelancers as required. This aspect especially is extremely important for a streamlined workflow of studios.

Joint work of specialists

There are only a few and very simple organizational steps necessary to execute the mentioned tasks which would serve and maintain a high-standard of art as well as streamlined work process for the benefit of German animation film in Europe. The steadiness of the organization of "Zeichenfilm-Ring" will rest on the expertise and experience of a limited number of the most skilled specialists. These experts will take over one respective field and support, beyond their work in their own studios, the other units before start of production with valuable advice. In this way we will provide that every of our companies will have the best experts of all fields for each film.

The inner organization of "Zeichenfilm-Ring" is suggested as follows:

President	Roellenbleg
In Charge	Dr. Karbe
Specialist for Trickfilm Technique	Fischerkösen
Specialist for film technique	Dr. Boucek
Specialist for Color	Dr. Heymer
Specialist for Humour	von Möllendorff
Scenario department	Dr. Karbe
Press and Broadcast	Dr. Eckardt[2]
General Manager	von Hamm

Also it is suggested to commission

Financial controlling	Ernst Mosich.

Controlling would be executed in the offices of Reichsbeauftragter [commissioner] for the Deutsche Filmwirtschaft [German film industry] and should include all economical issues of "Zeichenfilm-Ring" as well as Deutsche Zeichenfilm G.m.b.H. and all further advertising or other studios working in the field of 2D and puppet animation.

As in the course of time it has proved unsuitable to execute European animation film matters under the label of Deutsche Wochenschau G.m.b.H. [German Newsreel] they should be summed up in the future under the new label "Zeichenfilm-Ring." The organization of "Zeichenfilm-Ring" remains under control of Sonderreferat Kulturfilm, Reichsfilmintendant.

The execution of this proposal is possible without high costs and offers an expert way to enhance the efforts of smaller 2D and puppet film studios considerably in quality. Forces, material and equipment will be used better, idle running will be avoided and budgets reduced. Particularly, however, the work of "Zeichenfilm-Ring" will contribute to further development of the characteristics of German animation whose basics have been founded so far and to establish a future, likewise important branch of German film industry with products that will be welcome and seen with joy in all countries as an expression of German character and German nature in a framework of European culture.

February 7, 1944.
Signed,
Roellenbleg

There was an attachment:

The relationship "Zeichenfilm-Ring"—Deutsche Zeichenfilm G.m.b.H.

If Deutsche Zeichenfilm G.m.b.H. should become part of "Zeichenfilm-Ring" or not has to be decided at higher places. Out of artistic reasons one should advise against that because at Deutsche Zeichenfilm G.m.b.H. they follow a completely different process unter closest dependence on the Americans than in the other studios in Germany and Europe.

> The attempts of Deutsche Zeichenfilm G.m.b.H., however, are absolutely legitimate and one day might contribute to general enhancement. One should change therefore neither the direction of the process of Deutsche Zeichenfilm G.m.b.H. after three years of work before the fruits of labor are within reach, nor water down the stylistic line of "Zeichenfilm-Ring" by integration of Deutsche Zeichenfilm G.m.b.H. To obtain an artistically independent chance of development of all attached studios "Zeichenfilm-Ring" must show to the outside the homogeneous face of a German resp. European character that is free of American "model" and headstrong. [...]

The paper was met with different reactions. On March 14, 1944, K. J. Fritzsche of Tobis House, answered Director F. Merten of Ufa-Film G.m.b.H.: "I return the draft by Mr. Roellenbleg re: "Zeichenfilm-Ring." I do not share your opinion that such a combination is necessary right now. I think that in free competition the problem will move faster than it would do in the intended combination. Heil Hitler!"

The heads of UFA-Film G.m.b.H. were more sympathetic to the idea of monitoring European animation and answered Dr. Karbe, saying that the comments have found their interest but that they would postpone it at the moment.

On November 15, 1944, Dr. Winkler held a critical review of the project in his hands: "Technically, the proposal brings new things only with edition of a humorous paper and the foundation of the world's first *Lehrstuhl* for humour. Instead of editing a new paper for which, in the war, there is obviously no urgent need, one would prefer, similarly to what happens in America, England and France, to deliver to the daily and illustrated press a series of topical caricatures and strips which consist of 4–6 drawings — concerning a figure of fun in which the sequel of a humorist incident is being portrayed in drawings. During war particularly, interesting would be characters of propaganda (*Kohlenklau, Liese-Miese* etc.).

The establishment of a central dramaturgy maybe would eliminate the artistic competition of the various companies to a large degree.

All other things, exchange of experiences, investigation of economical profitability, above all standardization of drawing material is already in the hands of the newsreel management.

Apparently it is intended to put Deutsche Zeichenfilm G.m.b.H. under the control of the Newsreel.

Against the obvious intent to distribute all films under the new label, nothing is to object, provided one would properly credit additionally the individual companies resp. studios which are involved in the respective animated film."

Der Reichsfilmintendant Sonderdezernat Kulturfilm (Dr. K) addressed a memo dated March 31, 1944, to mayor Dr. Winkler and general manager Kaelber:

> Re: Animation film studio "Les Gemeaux," Paris.
>
> In fulfillment of the Minister's request to create an efficient animation film production in Europe which under all circumstances must be qualified to compete with transatlantic competitors in quality and to some degree also in quantity currently smaller and bigger studios in Berlin, Potsdam, Neubabelsberg, Munich, Vienna, Prague, Zlin, Amsterdam, The Hague and Copenhagen have been commissioned.
>
> One extraordinarily efficient animation studio sill stands aside. This is the group LES GEMEAUX in Paris. About three years ago this studio was commissioned by the Ministry

of Propaganda through Continental Films to execute a color short Der Notenhändler.[3] This film was, regarding the artwork and drawings, in each respect remarkable. It reflects a high standard in art, good movements, unusually refined backgrounds, austerity in color and form, limitation and concentration of each frame onto the essential and for the first time in Europe a completely un–American style of drawing. Unfortunately, scenario-wise the film was misguided. Although the basic idea was excellent an abundance of (unnecessary!) lacks was admitted, which render the film unintelligible.

In other work which was undertaken with financial support of the French state on their own account the drawing style was even more improved and removed further from Disney. Scenario deficits only count to a lesser degree; however, the French still are not pleased with their own scripts what they let us candidly know. They vividly would welcome cooperation.

This results in the following situation:

1. Political:

We are not interested to raise some productions in Paris but in this case it involves a company that produces anyway and that — when Agfacolor stock was blocked — turned to the simple Trichrom process to produce their films in a way that some day they might be transferred to Technicolor.

If animation films are produced in Paris we should care that they are marketed internationally in Agfacolor and not Technicolor. Equally the spiritual line of this production should be dictated by us and not by completely French offices. Artistic quality of said group is that high that we should use it as an important ally in our fight against all American.

If in fall of this year we will be ready to compile a feature-length program from a series of our first 6 — 8 animation films it might leave (with regard to the political effects in all foreign territories, namely countries like Sweden, Switzerland, Portugal, Spain, Turkey) an unlikely stronger impression if in this actually "European collaboration" the French are included. A series of good color animation films that don't originate from America will gain without doubt some attention. This attention can be enhanced into a political event for the new Europe if today the French are integrated.

2. Production-wise:

The enhancement of production as required by the Ministry would be met as annually we could expect about 3 good color shorts more.

3. Economically:

One should note particularly that the French work on incredibly low budgets. For the next two films sums are called for of ffrs. 1.700.000 that is RM 85.000 and ffrs. 2.025.000 that is about RM 100.000. For an annual production of 3 films only RM 300.000 would be requested in French francs. We therefore would profit from the grosses in France and the other countries in foreign currency.

The integration of this French production would serve as well to make the program of our other short films more attractive for foreign territories because it would be better received including French films than without — and therefore have longer runs.

[...]

Here must be mentioned that LES GEMEAUX is not some small animation film company but an artistically serious group which in spite of its scenario deficits will make its way. Above all political, production and economical aspects for us it should be a matter of cultural responsibility to have this group under German leadership and working in a European spirit that is dictated by us.

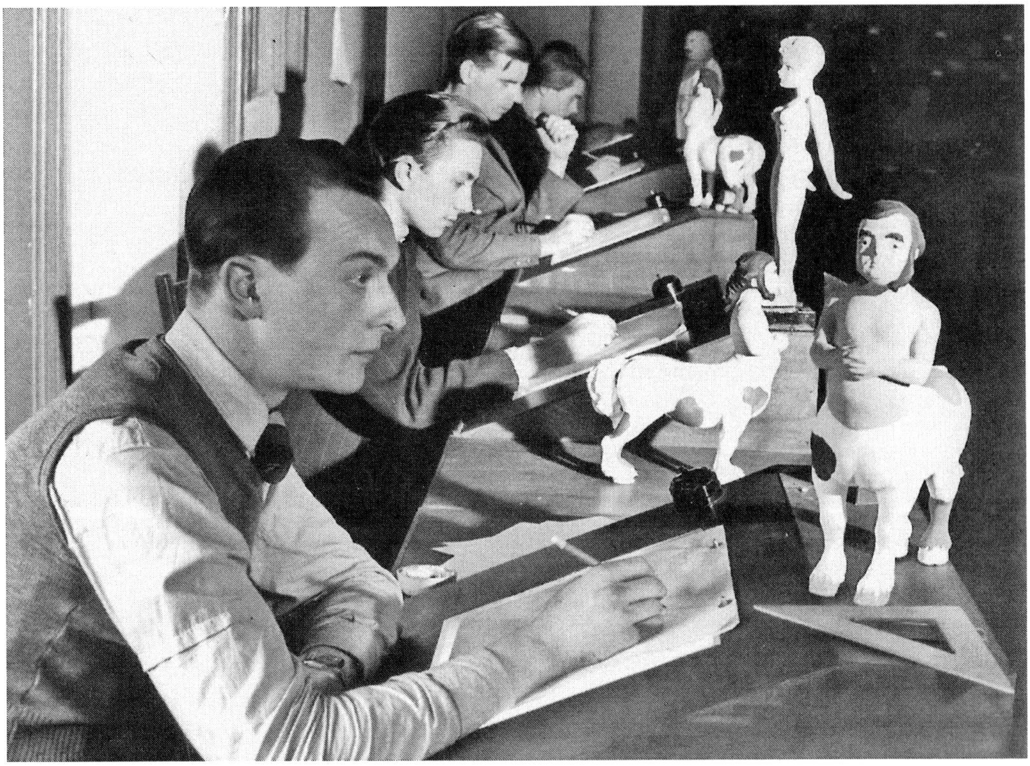

Der Zentaur: **Hans Held project, Studios The Hague (courtesy Erika Held).**

In a way the Ministry of Enlightenment and Propaganda saw the need for more animation. In a letter dated April 5, 1944, we read:

> The animation film companies founded by us or inspired by us, such as Deutsche Zeichenfilm G.m.b.H., are not able to manufacture as many cartoon films as the many European cinemas need. Particularly German and foreign newsreel theatres which due to their concentrated propaganda in a fast changing program of supporting features and short films reach an extraordinary big number of patrons need annually about 50 cartoons which will animate audiences — especially the youth — to attend theatres.

This spring Dr. Hans Karbe was busy traveling. He visited all branches of DZF and Bavaria in Munich as well as animation studios in Amsterdam and The Hague, Prague and Paris. Sometimes he was accompanied by his friend von Möllendorff, who had become an employee of Sonderreferat Kulturfilm on April 1, 1944, for a monthly salary of RM 2,500. He then conceived a detailed report about production commissioned by UFA subsidiaries and forwarded it to Dr. Max Winkler. The business-minded Möllendorff offered his services overseeing the foreign operation for a gross monthly fee of RM 2,000. In Winkler's office they even discussed the closing of DZF, which seemed to be highly ineffective, but Dr. Karbe and even competitor Fischerkoesen vetoed this idea as Fischerkoesen still saw some value in it to recruit young talent from DZF Nachwuchsstudio. They were still convinced of the plan to subsume European animation studios under one label, and it was suggested to integrate DZF in Europa Zeichenfilm G.m.b.H.. Möllendorff, specialist in humor, immediately took advantage and submitted a script, *Klapperstorch im Sommernest,* to Europa.

But, of course, there would never be 50 cartoons annually. Now the Reich had more complex problems than those of the fledgling cartoon industry. The Germans even had to allow Disney cartoons for screenings in certain territories.

On July 20, 1944, the Foreign Department of the Ministry recorded:

> Dr. Schmidt vividly inists not to comply with the repeatedly uttered requests to completely withdraw American cartoons from the program of Greek newsreel cinemas.
>
> One cannot object that German short films which would take their place would NOT substitute American shorts in Greece. The screenings of Mickey Mouse films are (as everybody knows) controlled by our Greek branch in accordance with the Propaganda.

16

Bavaria, Munchausen and the Town Musicians of Bremen

With fierce competition from DZF and Fischerkoesen Hans Held continued at Bavaria. In September 1941 Bavaria had moved its animation operation from Friedrichstrasse to a large old villa at Griebnitzsee, an idyllic lake area not far away from Ufastadt Babelsberg. There the company occupied three floors. Held was allowed to live there, Strasse der S.A. No. 32, while all the others had to get in from Berlin very early. Train tickets (*S-Bahn*), however, were repaid. (For some time, *Reichsmarine* [the German navy] was interested in the property, too, but Bavaria couldn't change quarters and was allowed to stay.)

On October 14, 1941, production manager Ernst Mosich and Held were invited by letter to meet Dr. Hellmuth Keil, Bavaria's authorized representative, at Bavaria's Berlin offices, now located at Lützowufer 38. Dr. Keil was upset about the working conditions and lax discipline: too much overtime, too lavish sums granted for lunch and dinner and so on. Mosich appeared on time; Held was the one who didn't show up. Weeks later, confronted by Dr. Keil in the studio at Griebnitzsee, Held apologized and claimed that he never had received the letter.

By mid–January 1942, Bavaria had decided to expand its animation operation. But there was not enough talent in the German capital. Everyone who could hold a pencil was drafted by DZF. To get its *Munchausen* short film finished, Bavaria approached Bassoli Studios in Rome. Hans Held voted against a joint venture with Bassoli and offered to find the necessary artists in bordering countries.

On March 24, 1942, he had renewed his enrolment declaration to Reichsfilmkammer Fachschaft [department] Film (section: actors and directors). Six days later, on March 30, he flew to Copenhagen and on his return on April 11 he had hired some good (unemployed) Danish animators, Erik Rus, Borge Hamburg and Erik Christensen. Later Arne Jørgensen and Otto Jacobsen would follow.

In a way Held behaved like an artist and did what pleased him. In his spare time, together with cameraman Hans Robert Bonsack and animator Horst Günther Koch, he built and rigged up model airplanes. He didn't put stress on punctuality other than in the timing of his animation. If funds weren't sufficient he didn't care for budget. He didn't care for schedule if at least he could achieve what he had in mind. If it came to quality,

Hans Held: Sketches Babelsberg (1940) (courtesy Erika Held).

he wasn't able and willing to compromise. In case of lack of quality he simply would restart work.

Anyway, Held and his wife began to enjoy their new life style in a villa at Griebnitzsee. They had horses and what else. Held didn't give a damn about what Bavaria said. But then, however, an executive and proxy of Ufa-Film G.m.b.H., a Mr. Mielke, approached Dr. Winkler's office and reported about the scandalous conditions in Held's villa. There were not only male but female employees as well. 18 women working there. Rumours spread about the little whorehouse. Mr. Pfennig, a lawyer of Winkler's office, got in touch with director Erich Walter Herbell of Bavaria Filmkunst. There were rumours that Bavaria might close its animation department but they were denied. Actually, work there should continue at least until mid 1943, with the completion of an animation short titled *Sommerballade* (*Summer Ballad*). Then everything should be decided. Director Herbell didn't care for Babelsberg gossip: "As typical for gossip in the beginning it will be broadcast effusively and exuberantly, but at the end it will dissolve with the excuse: Maybe there was nothing! It is not true that in the only restaurant where our staff members have their lunch tensions arose. Against that, the truth is that the host of *Bürgerhof* sets great value upon the regular visits of our staff members."

In a board meeting on December 4, 1941, Ufa decided to announce as its next big color production, on the occasion of the 25th anniversary of the company, *Munchausen*, a feature film starring Hans Albers and featuring a cast of Germany's leading actors (Ilse Werner, Brigitte Horney, Wilhelm Bendow, Leo Slezak, Marianne Simson, and Ferdinand Marian, the original *Jew Suss*). There was some animation to do during

Hans Held at Studios The Hague, 1943 (courtesy Erika Held).

the ride on the cannonball sequence of Munchausen circling around a minaret at the siege of Otchakov fortress. A portrait of Hans Albers blinked. And end credits form out of candle smoke blown by Albers. So Ufa approached Bavaria and asked to borrow out their chief animator, Hans Held. Held asked for a fee of RM 25.000 for his services. Finally, before the movie was released in March 1943, Ufa and Bavaria settled for RM 10.000. In December 1942 Held had received a new contract from Bavaria with a monthly fee of RM 2.500.

On two pages, Erich Kästner's original screenplay for the Ufa version had suggested to tie Munchausen's horse on a pole that stuck out of high snow which, after melting down, turned out to be a church spire with the animal now helplessly hanging on it. Most likely, the described sequence was never shot but it became part of Held's animated *Munchausen* version for Bavaria.

On November 26, 1942, Hans Held traveled to Holland to meet a German-Dutch, Egbert van Putten, and discuss with him the takeover of an animation studio in The Hague. By agreement with Fischerkoesen (December 29, 1942), this studio would become part of both operations, but when Held, accompanied by Dr. Keil, returned to The Hague in late January 1943 to inspect the studio he observed severe faults. On February 1, 1943, Dr. Keil noted:

> Re: Contract with Mr. van Putten
>
> 1. A staff that would consist of about 45 persons as listed in contract does not exist. For there are 13 other persons in our staff while some other employees simply do

> not exist. Finally an additional number of employees were newly signed to start on January 11.
> 2. The fees of the staff members are much lower than stated in the basic estimate by Mr. van Putten.
> 3. Equipment, especially both tables, colors and brushes, doesn't exist at all or in a quality that is not sufficient.
>
> Mr. Held stated that he has tried to maintain the working capability of the unit by hiring additional talent at Mr. van Putten's charge and procurement of new equipment at Mr. van Putten's charge as well. He always had his doubts if the performance could be guaranteed as required in the contract. Also Mr. Held pointed out to me that Mr. van Putten has said to him repeatedly that he thinks the whole contract would have to be revised, as it has proved unusable for instance re: quality control, the monthly output, with Mr. van Putten claiming that he hadn't found the time to study the contract carefully before signing it. Then I discussed all complaints made by Mr. Held with Mr. van Putten. He tried to explain every issue evasively.

Because some artists would be hired no sooner than January 11, Held assumed that van Putten apparently wanted to take advantage of Bavaria and Fischerkoesen. Eventually, three months after signing, on March 29, 1943, all parties withdrew from the contract. For his previous efforts, van Putten received RM 18.630 and was out. Bavaria and Fischerkoesen took over the studio on May 1, 1943. Van Putten (1899–1996) had come to Germany in 1934 and worked on a number of German films before he became involved in animation. With Thea von Harbou of *Metropolis* fame he co-wrote the screenplay for Heinz Rühmann's *Lauter Liebe* (1940). His name, however, is also linked with one of the most infamous cartoons, *Van den vos Reynaerde* (1942–43), made from a children's story by Dutch-Belgian writer Robert van Genechten, which turned a medieval poem into an anti–Semitic animal fable with the rhinoceroses substituting for the Jews. Rhinoceros, *Neushoorn* (nosehorn) in Dutch and *Nashorn* in German, referred to the stereotypical Jewish nose as did the name of a central rhinoceros character, Jodocus, meaning Jew. The film was never shown publicly and only later was discovered in film archives.

Hans Held: *Die gestohlene Krone* (1943) (courtesy Erika Held).

Held became art supervisor in

The Hague. Fischerkoesen used the studio only for coloring while Held traveled back and forth between Babelsberg and The Hague. In January 1943 he had begun pre-production on another short, *Das Gespenst* (*The Ghost*), from an original idea by Horst von Möllendorff. For his collaborative work on the treatment he received RM 1,500. RM 2,000 were due for outlining with Hans Krüger the idea for *Der Zentaur* (*The Centaur*), RM 2,500, for *Jägerlatein—Mein kluger Waidmann*, and in July 1943 another RM 2,500,—for *Die gestohlene Krone* (*The Stolen Crown*). Few of these pictures were made. Other ideas went unrealized too: *Aussenseiter*, *Tanzbar*, *Star*, *Falstaff*.

In the meantime, the ministry was highly dissatisfied with cartoon achievements. While *Armer Hansi*, *Verwitterte Melodie* and *Der Schneemann* were well received, the annual target of 50 shorts was in far distance. And Bavaria had not presented any since *Der Störenfried* but amassed overheads of RM 733.682.

In December 1943, Bavaria received a note from *Reichsfilmintendant* saying that if animation production exceeded RM 750.000 all efforts would be halted and investigated before they could continue.

On June 6, 1944, while Allied troops invaded Normandy, Held still worked on his *Munchausen*, at least as a short film. Although Held's contract as head of production had been canceled, nobody else was available, so he remained as a consultant. Finally, he got drafted, but of course was not the least interested in waiting for marching orders to the Eastern Front. As he had a visa valid for the Netherlands, he boarded a train to Amsterdam on August 26. Thus he escaped, with the result that in Germany he was sought as a deserter. His wife, Waltraude, claimed to know nothing of his whereabouts. In the Netherlands, apparently, a female animator at The Hague studio had hid him. After Allied troops had marched in he was arrested and thus survived the war.

Die gestohlene Krone: Sketches and conceptual art by Hans Held (1943) (courtesy Erika Held).

"My husband was no realist," recalls Erika Held, his second wife, in a telephone conversation. "Much of what he told me was not made up but — he lived like in a fairy tale. He lived in those dreams. He lived in his characters. His first wife didn't know him. I didn't. He has carried around too many problems and not [dealt with them]. He preferred to withdraw into his snail shell. I knew that this man had gold in his fingers. I would compare him with Leonardo da Vinci. But in all his life he never has provided a golden threat, a guideline to follow, and gloated at journalists who would ask him if there was anything he didn't do. But he wasn't interested in selling himself. He didn't get along with Goebbels. Goebbels showed all films to his children, the fox [i.e., the rabbit in *Der Störenfried*], however, was a *Hinkefuss* [walking with a limp]. In spite of kidney cancer he faced a benevolent death: a last wheeze at home."

Illustration by Hans Held (courtesy Erika Held).

Even after animation film activities of Bavaria were shut down by the Ministry of Propaganda and Enlightenment, there was some hope they would continue. In September 1944 Margrith Helena Karbe and Horst von Möllendorff proposed a cartoon series with characters that were new neither to international nor German cartoons.[3]

> Their lasting success in cartoons Americans have reached by creating series. Mickey Mouse, Donald Duck, Silly Symphonies etc. are examples how popular singular cartoon characters resp. groups of characters might become. Only after Mickey Mouse had become a household name the audience longed all the more for more humorist films with this main character.
>
> Until now Germany hasn't found a topic which would suit very well for the production of cartoon series. The following proposal for the first German cartoon series to my estimate brings all prerequisites which are necessary for a series.
>
> The series bears a title which is well known from the German treasure trove of fairy tales among our people and abroad.
>
> *Die Bremer Stadtmusikanten*
>
> [The Town Musicians of Bremen].
>
> The characters (appearing separately, by two, three or four) are sympathetic in nature and well to animate: a dog, a cat, a donkey, and a rooster.
>
> The first film of the series Bremen Town Musicians will feature the original fairy tale,

i.e. the four musicians meeting on the country road and forming a quartet. On their trip the four prankster musicians have 4 to 5 funny adventures, the last being the famous expulsion of the robbers from the lonely forest hut.

Of course, the four Town Musicians of Bremen are equipped with all possible and impossible instruments, from tuba, piccolo, and violin to mere imaginary instruments with novel clang colors. Each of the animals will command all instruments and all gags will be musically conceived.

The second film, under the headline Bremen Town Musicians, would show the adventures of the funny quartet *Im Strandbad* [On the beach]. All different animals basking in the sun. It is hot, the mood is tired. The four funny musicians arrive and turn the whole beach upside down. Out of a scene on the water slide a crazy splashing develops which mounts into the blown fountains of elephant and walrus. Later the four guys ride on the back of the walrus through the water; and when it dives all is continued under water, with the music of the four now gurgling and producing water bubble effects. The fantasy under water world will play a lively part and so on and so on.

The third film could show the adventures of the Bremen Town Musicians—*In Vienna Prater*. Dog, cat, donkey and rooster perform with and against each other funny musical nonsense on the giant wheel, in the swing, in the ghost train, on the merry-go-round and in the Aunt Sally.

The fourth film could show the fate of the Bremen Town Musicians—*On Board the Flying Dutchman*. The four guys would row on water leaving the Free Hanseatic City of Bremen and reaching the sea. At sunset they would encounter a big five-master which moves around rudderlessly on the sea. They would row alongside, the ship would turn out to be the Flying Dutchman, and the film would show the fantasy adventures the four musicians would have as only crew by storm and at calm sea aboard that ghost ship.

The fifth film could show the adventures of the Bremen Town Musicians—In the Alps. The colourful cattle drive. The four funny musicians would join in singing and playing, riding and marching and inbetween performing in the villages and on the steep bridges all kind of musical allotria [monkey business]. Performed by the animals we would see the life in the hay barns and on the chalet and watch the cows and calves which would yodel to each other. An extremely odd kind of milk and cheese production as well as a final climbing tour with the four Bremen Town Musicians equipped with pickle, rope and mountain boots on the steep slope of a north face upwards would provide many options for funny cartoon gags.

A sixth film could show the adventures of the Bremen Town Musicians—*As Fishermen*. In a harbor bar they will make a bet. There shall be contest between the four musicians and the fishing animals, the herons, sea gulls etc., which are trained to go out fishing in boats and with nets like the humans do. The Bremen Town Musicians would bet to be able to fish as well as them. All would set out in their boats from Bremen the Weser River down the sea. Fast sailing and pulling are the experts; miserably and not highly skilled left behind the four musicians. Many accidents occur. Alternatingly they fall into the water, and the boat gets socked wet. But with a good musically performed idea they set afloat again. Long since outside the others tow in their nets full of floundering fish; only then the Bremen Town Musicians, above the brim of the boat, start to grab fish with their paws. The animals of the sea want to play a trick on them and let the boat capsize. They [the four musicians] are so enthusiastic about the fantasy world under water that they forget to get out of danger. One flirts with a mermaid (flute duel). And Father Neptune is so ecstatic about the big trumpet that he exchanges it for a dyad of six mighty fish which finally draw

> the boat with the four funny Bremen Town Musicians set afloat with the help of the king of the ocean and brimfully filled with baked fish from Neptune's ice cellar. They return in triumph towards the harbour and pass the remaining fishing fleet.
>
> Topics of that kind for the four funny animals of the Bremen Town Musicians are countless in number. One could show the Bremen Town Musicians On a Trip to the Stratosphere, On a Persian Market, With the Devil in Hell, At a Soccer Game, On a bicycling tour, Among Polar Bears, Among Zulu twerps, At Billiards, At the Races, In a Movie Studio and on and on. Such a series starring these well-known, sympathetic and easily to draw characters from German fairy tale treasure trove should be quite useful for a German animation film production.

On September 29, 1944, Bavaria Filmkunst accepted the proposal and commissioned Mrs. Karbe to write a screenplay for the first episode with Möllendorff. They were prepared to pay RM 1,500 for the idea and RM 3,500 for the first script but nothing was heard about it again. By that time animation production had stopped all over the country.

17

Animated Maps to Hail German Victories: Svend Noldan

Of course there wasn't solely humor and innocent naivité in German animation. There also was Svend Noldan.

Heinrich August [Svend] Noldan was raised in Marburg where he became friendly with Erwin Piscator. In 1911 he accompanied his friend to Munich where he studied painting at Königlich Bayerische Akademie der Künste [the painting class of Becker-Gundahl/von Marr]. He funded his studies by painting churches. In January 1915, both, Noldan and Piscator were drafted for infantry at Flanders. Noldan became an observer and draughtsman commissioned to outline enemy positions.

Right after World War I, in January 1919, the two friends went to Berlin. Piscator became a theatrical legend willing to hire his friend to do scenic designs. In the meantime Noldan had become involved in the Dada circle of George Grosz, Wieland Herzfelde, and John Heartfield. It was Heartfield who invited him to join him at Ufa's animation department. When Heartfield left Noldan participated in medical educational films (*Geschlechtskrankheiten und ihre Folgen*, *Die weisse Seuche*) and cultural films (*Der Rhein in Vergangenheit und Gegenwart*) and eventually specialized in living (animated) maps.

In 1922, while still employed by Ufa, Noldan founded his own studio. In spring 1925 he began work on a two-part compilation film: *Der Weltkrieg* (*The World War*). He was not the first one to do animated maps and ordnance maps and move pointed arrows frame by frame. French animation pioneer Emile Cohl had done it already in the early days of animation. In between, Noldan devised film projections for Piscator's stagings *Konjunktur* and *Des Kaisers Kulis*. Noldan's most important work, however, was a venture in natural science: *Was ist die Welt?* (*What Is the World?*). For five years he worked on this ambitious project with Fritz Brunsch. After its premiere under the patronage of *Reichsverband Deutsche Bühne* in early 1934 the film was released by the Film Department of Reich Propaganda Leitung of NSDAP. At that time Noldan's friend Piscator had already left the country. A writer commented, "Noldan shows us a lot about the life of plants, the life of animals, the origins of the earth, the origins of the mountains, of the development of the plant world in thousands of years, about the origins of coal, glaciers — in short — such an abundance of knowledge that man, understanding the interaction of origin, will stay respectful in front of the eternal laws which cause and determine all these origins and all these developments."[1] In 1937 the film was awarded the Paris Grand Prix at German Art Week during World Expo.

From then on Noldan became heavily exposed to National Socialism and supplied graphic art in motion pictures. In 1937 he was commissioned by NS Cultural Community and German Research Community with finishing an expedition film, *Das grosse Eis*. In 1937, at the Biennale in Venice, his reportage film *Deutschland* premiered, which was made in the Berthon Siemens Color Pro-cess: "It shows [Germany's] lands-capes and countrysides, its people and its achievements, festivals and conduct of life. The daily life in city and country is being recorded, on acres and in factories, on streets, highways, in the high mountains and at sea. Clever photographic effects demonstrate the rebuilding of the Reich, the *Arbeitsdienst* [National Labour Service], the fight against unemployment, the education of the youth and images of the May Day festivities."[2]

Noldan, together with Fritz Brunsch and cameraman Hans Noack, was involved in photographing effects for Leni Riefenstahl's party rally film of 1934, *Triumph des Willens* (*Triumph of the Will*), and her two-part Olympics film (Olympic torch relay footage). His last independent production was commissioned by Deutsche Arbeitsfront DAF: *Deutsche Arbeitsstätten*.

Then came the war, and with it the return of animated maps on a big scale. Noldan animated attack and defense maps, as well as battle action for Nazi Germany's first big war documentary, *Feldzug in Polen*. A year later he was part of Fritz Hippler's unit for the infamous *Der ewige Jude* for which he detailed the perceived expansion of Jewry over Eastern Europe.

After these pictures Noldan got drafted and served as technical sergeant, then a lieutenant on cinematic war efforts like *Sieg im Westen*, a war documentary of Oberkommando der Wehrmacht: "It didn't matter to record and show a sequel of exciting, thrilling sensations. The authenticity and reality which speaks out of these images is more powerful and vivid than all studio footage. The faces of soldiers, who progress in attack, the silence which surrounds a young officer who gives orders, the pace in which an attack unreels, the smoking ruins of a village, the embarrassed faces of the victims of Dunkirk, the power and the force and nonpersonal greatness of the whole events capture the viewer."[3]

All Noldan tried after this production, however, failed. A sequel to *Was ist die Welt?* was announced in 1941 as *Der Erde Lebensraum*. There was also a project about Europe, which was stopped after the rough cut. The last two years of the war Noldan spent as a civilian living in Berlin.

After the war he was banned from employment, but some time later he rejoined BASF, making industrial films. He made short films like *Kleine Laus—ganz gross* (1953) and *Ungräser—Geisseln des Ackerbaus* (1963). After retiring Noldan focused on painting until his death in 1978.

18

Classified Animation: Training the Military

As in America, animation had to serve the needs of the military. One of the main suppliers of military training films was Mars-Film G.m.b.H. in Berlin, which commissioned the talent. Mars-Film emerged as part of the Ufi concern, the umbrella of German film, with an authorized capital of RM 20,000. Its task was to supply films for the Wehrmacht. Two separate offices, Heeresfilmstelle (Army Film Office) and Marine-Hauptfilmstelle (Navy Film Office), had been disbanded already to make room for a central office. In 1941 both offices had inserted in trade papers looking for animators who were able to handle paint spray technique too. Some films, like *Geheime Kommandosache* (Secret Command Documents), were still commissioned by the Reichsluftfahrt Ministry (Luftwaffe) but then transferred to Mars-Film. So Mars-Film became a *kriegswichtiger Betrieb* [enterprise relevant to the war]. Mars-Film even kept an SS Production Group. No wonder that the Ministry of Enlightenment and Propaganda confirmed the monopoly of Mars-Film.

In January 1945 Mars-Film employed a staff of 183, 153 of them in production: 19 directors and dramaturges, 21 cameramen and assistants and 11 trick experts. All employees were "skilled film workers who had proven themselves as soldiers at the front." Kurt Parbel, Deputy Reichsfilm Intendant, reported to the minister that they employed only persons who were at no risk of being drafted and who were usable for the armament industry only with reservations. The company was funded by Filmkreditbank G.m.b.H., another brainchild of Dr. Max Winkler. The accountants, however, reported that the company made no profit.

By special contracts the company "owned" the most important German animation producers. There were seven companies, including Boehner-Film Dresden, Fischerkoesen-Film-Studio, Curt Schumann and Major Hans Ewald. After 1944 Wolfgang Kaskeline and Paul Lieberenz signed too. For a studio like Fischerkoesen, sometimes it was not easy to keep the teams apart that worked on family entertainment and those involved in training films for the army.

Live action usually was shot on the Wehrmacht backlot, at military training areas, air bases and in naval ports. The animated segments were made in the Mars-Film studios in Berlin-Spandau and later in a turnout in Zehdenick near Berlin. The prints were supplied by a lab owned by Mars-Film.

Schiessen im Hochgebirge (1943): Army training.

Schiesslehre (1942): Military training.

The former advertising filmmakers used their talents and experience to animate technical processes (motors and drives), ballistic (projectiles), maps and chemical (fog generating) mechanisms.From December 1944, seven films with 300 prints each produced by Mars-Film G.m.b.H. were released to train the Volksturm.

Mars-Film was strictly secret, temporarily "protected" by SD with a confidential informant. There was no shortage of film footage, including color film stock, gas and coals. Some films are known only by title: *Überwinden von Minensperren (Break Through Mine Obstacles), Hemmungen am MG (Block of Machine Guns), Lufttorpedo-Schiesslehre (Air Torpedo Shooting Guide), Kampfstoffe (Chemical Weapons)* and *Artillerie-Munition (Artillery Ammuniton).* There were no credits, of course. It is unknown, therefore, who actually made the films: "The filmmaker involved in military training films has to be a soldier. His moral maturity, his consciously soldier-like approving view guarantees the direction of the films." And: "There is no director's name above the title. No title names a director. Modestly and soldierly the title opens: The Oberkommando des Heeres [High Command of the Army] presents..."[1]

With the capitulation of Berlin, Mars-Film Studios fell into the hands of the Red Army. Here they started to dub Russian films. In 1949 Mars-Film began to produce advertising and industrial films for clients like Farbwerke Hoechst, Christliches Wohlfahrtswerk Stuttgart, Agfa, marketing boards, and trade associations. Even the West-German Bundeskanzleramt (Chancellor Adenauer's office) in Bonn asked for military training films for the planned Bundeswehr. Later Mars-Film, however, was liquidated, with parts of the capacities transferred to the Rhine Valley.

19

The Aftermath: The Postwar Era of German Animation

Most German animators were able to continue after the war. Only a few had got some problems that didn't last long. For instance, Fischerkoesen was arrested by Soviet troops. They assumed that he was a Nazi collaborator, so he was kept in Sachsenhausen concentration camp for three years before he was exonerated. While in Sachsenhausen, working in the kitchen, he painted ironic, allegorical wall murals with anthropomorphic, walking vegetables. Having been released, in 1948 Fischerkoesen fled East Germany at nighttime. In West Germany he settled in Bad Godesberg and remained a successful producer of advertising films and commercials, but never returned to short film production.

Horst von Möllendorff had some trouble too. On December 11, 1945, the Magistrat of the City of Berlin, Department for Volksbildung — Presseamt — informed the Political Examination Committee that in September they had received a letter: "Recently I read in the *Tägliche Rundschau* or *Deutsche Volkszeitung* some articles about Käthe Kollwitz, Heinrich Zille and Otto Nagel. In this issue I also read reports about the caricaturist Herbert Sandberg, a former K.Z. convict, and about the cartoonist Penguin who was a disciple of both, Käthe Kollwitz and Otto Nagel. Now one sees regularly in the Berliner Zeitung which is published by the city cartoons drawn by a Mr. von Möllendorff. Pg. [party member] or not. Same Möllendorff during the Nazi time published the *herrlichsten* Nazi propaganda drawings in the weekly Saxonian magazine, *Lustige Welt.* He glorified Nazism and ridiculed everything that was anti-fascist; he glorified the war and agitated against all enemies of the Nazis. Was this Möllendorff ever a soldier? No, because the Nazis needed him. Just read the old issues of *Lustige Welt* and you will find Möllendorff again as an extremely active Nazi propagandist. The City of Berlin, however, insists to make this *Mantelträger* [shabby coat] its in-house cartoonist. With this you render the *Antifa* [anti-fascist movement] powerless. Ask M. himself or his colleagues and you will have my remark confirmed."

Kaskeline teamed up with his sons and did, among other commercials, the *Sarotti Mohr*, a black child who promoted chocolate.

Hans Held illustrated popular magazines and books and remade the *Störenfried* for West German military propaganda, substituting a Russian bear for the fox.

Gerhard Fieber, later joined by Heinz Tischmeyer, went into a joint venture with producer Franz Thies and animated the *Little Mainz Men [Mainzelmännchen]* for Second Channel Television.

Ernst J. Schienke, who worked on advertising films in the 1930s and ended drawing animation for the war effort illustrating sabotage operations, destroyed the footage before the Soviets occupied Babelsberg Ufa studios. Later he designed the elaborate German title cards for MGM releases, then created *Tele-Bärchen* (a little teddy bear) for Berlin Television.

The Diehl brothers, who produced two more feature films and a number of shorts, survived by licensing their Mecki puppet character to *Hör Zu* magazines and Steiff toys. Later their lifetime work was sold to Deutsches Filmmuseum in Frankfurt am Main.

In Dresden, East Germany, by then called German Democratic Republic, state-controlled DEFA founded its own animation studio in 1955. But more successful than their many shorts and occasional feature-length puppet films was the puppet character of the Sandman created by Gerhard Behrendt and introduced to television in 1959 (and even after reunification still going strong).

Most animators continued in television. Only sporadically did they try an animated feature, as Curt Linda did in Munich with Erich Kästner's *Konferenz der Tiere* (*Animal Congress*). It was re-made [as *Animals United*] in 3D stereoscopic animation by Constantin Film and Holger Tappe's Ambient Entertainment in 2009–10. Back then animated features were scarce but became more common with the success of French-German co-productions [*Asterix and the Big Fight*], later with the work of Berlin-based producers Gerhard Hahn and Thilo Rothkirch. Rothkirch did two *Little Polar Bears*, *Laura's Star* and *Laura's Star and the Mysterious Dragon Nian,* the first Sino-German 3D co-production (25 years earlier the producer Manfred Durniok, an honorary citizen of the City of Beijing, had made already two puppet films and 2D features in cooperation with the Shanghai Animation Studios). In January 2011, Dr. Michael Schoemann of Benchmark Entertainment followed with a second co-production that was released in China with a big promotional campaign: *Little Big Panda.*

In 1982 the International Trickfilm Festival was launched in Stuttgart. From time to time some innovative shorts were released, including two stop-motion entries and Academy Award winners, *Balance* (1989) by Christoph and Wolfgang Lauenstein and *Quest* (1996) by Tyron Montgomery and Thomas Stellmach.

But Hitler is still alive on many screens. A 3D short cartoon spoof, originally intended as a feature film titled: *Der Bonker* (*The Bunker*), starring a silly caricature of Adolf Hitler singing in the bathtub during air raids in his bunker has had some eight million downloads. The cartoon was created by Walter Moers and animated by Felix Gönnert, a graduate of the animation classes of Hochschule für Film und Fernsehen in Potsdam Babelsberg.

20
The Filmmakers: Biographies

Alexandre Alexandrovitch Alexeieff

Born on April 18, 1901, in Kazan, Russia. Spent early childhood in Istanbul where his father was military attaché. In Paris designed and painted sets for the Pioteff Theater. In 1931, using a large pinscreen, made famous experimental short, *Night on Bald Mountain*, an adaptation of the symphony of Modest Mussorgsky. In 1936 was invited to Berlin, where he maintained a small studio until spring 1938 to produce some advertising films for Gasparcolor (*Aroma, mehr Aroma*). Then returned to Paris. In 1940 he and his family fled to Bordeaux to apply for visas at the U.S. Embassy. Died on August 9, 1982, in Paris.

Jürgen Clausen

Born on February 24, 1905, in Eisenach. Trader, newspaper publisher, journalist and advertising expert with a keen interest in films. In 1935 focused exclusively on advertising and particularly animated films. Joined Gasparcolor as business and production manager. Later was hired by Tobis as color film expert and promoted the establishment of a color puppet film production along the lines of Georg Pál. He even secured the services of former Pál employees, but his ambitious plans didn't materialize. Clausen was forced to leave Tobis in 1942. In March 1944 he died in action as a combat newsreel cameraman (*Kriegsberichterstatter*).

Werner Bernhardy (Ufa Werbefilm) drawn by Egon von Tresckow, 1940.

Ferdinand Diehl

Born on May 20, 1901, in Unterwössen, Traunstein. Son of a painter. Trained as violin maker. (His

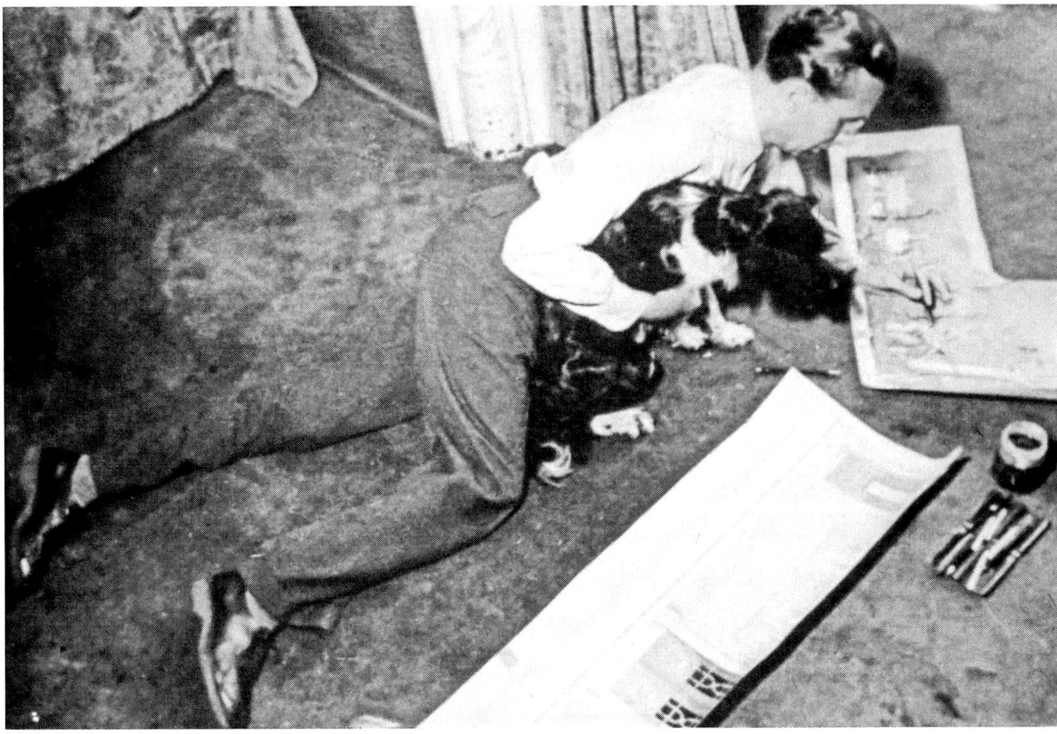

Ufa, unknown illustrator (c. 1940).

grandfather was a violin maker in Darmstadt.) Then attended Kunstgewerbeschule (art academy) in Munich. After seeing an Italian version of *Quo Vadis?* starring Emil Jannings as Nero, became interested in the technical aspects of the movies. In 1925 joined Emelka Studios in Munich Geiselgasteig as painter, then with the help of cameraman Otto Martine landed a job at the short film department and worked at the animation stand. When Emelka folded in 1928 Diehl and two brothers (Hermann and Paul) became independent and, in the period 1929–30, did a 20-minute silhouette short, *Kalif Storch (Caliph Stork),* following in the footsteps of Lotte Reiniger and *The Adventures of Prince Achmed,* then started to do puppet films like Starevich did, shorts and feature-length. For *Zwischpaduri, der Strolch* (1931) Diehl used wooden armatures. A series of *Wupp* films featuring a moon-faced boy with big eyes and turned-up nose that was released by Bavaria-Filmverleih and Leo-Film A.G. between 1931 and 1933 turned to articulated ball-and-socket armatures. Also tried advertising film (*Kohlweisslings Töchter*, a spoof on *Kohlhiesels Töchter*, 1932). In 1935 signed long-term contract with Reichsstelle für den Unterrichtsfilm, which in 1940 was renamed Reichsanstalt für Film und Bild in Wissenschaft und Unterricht. For this institution the Diehls mainly produced fairy tales. In 1937 the Diehls' first puppet feature, *Die sieben Raben*, premiered with poor box-office returns. In 1938 for the first time he animated a hedgehog character for *Der Wettlauf zwischen dem Hasen und dem Igel* that after the war became well known as Mecki. Died on August 27, 1992, in Gräfelfing/Munich near his studio. His puppets became part of the collection of Deutsches Filmmuseum in Frankfurt am Main.

Hermann Diehl

Born on December 5, 1906, in Gräfelfing/Munich. Studied painting and sculpting at Munich Academy of Art. Joined his brother Ferdinand and created hundreds of stop-motion puppets for Diehl films, including Mecki the hedgehog. Died on December 20, 1983, in Grünwald.

Paul Diehl

Born in 1886 in Munich. Grammar school teacher (*Gymnasiallehrer*) until 1951. Joined his brothers as scriptwriter and also wrote some articles on silhouette and puppet films. Claimed in one of his articles, *Der Puppenfilm als Kunstwerk*, that puppet films are high art compared to ordinary feature films. Died in 1976 in Gräfelfing/Munich.

Gerhard Fieber

Born on October 20, 1916, in Berlin-Treptow as Gerhard Willi Otto Fieber. Attended Rütli School in Berlin-Neukölln. Between 1930 and 1936 attended art school and the Academy of Arts in Berlin, a graphic design school and *Volkshochschule* (community college). In 1930 started work at the publicity department of Ufa and began to do humor for the press. Until 1937 also worked in a department store of Rudolf Karstadt chain. In the 1930s became associated with Wolfgang Kaskeline animation. One-year contract with Epoche-Werbefilm A.G. In 1938 became illustrator for Berlin Lewilbo Advertising. In late 1940 changed to Ufa and assisted Kurt Stordel on Ufa's animation project *Quick macht Hochzeit* (*Quick Marries*). On August 20, 1941, signed with Deutsche Zeichenfilm G.m.b.H. For a brief time worked for DEFA. In 1948 founded EOS-Film in Bad Sachsa, did a feature-length Wilhelm Busch cartoon, *Tobias Knopp—Abenteuer eines Junggesellen* in the period 1948–49. Later, after joining forces with producer Franz Thies, was involved in television and *Mainzelmännchen (Little Mainz Men)* spots for Second Channel TV. Wolfgang Dresler interviewed Fieber for a DVD titled *Trickfilm-Fieber—Der Zeichentrick-Pionier Gerhard Fieber.*

Hans Fischerkoesen

Born on May 18, 1896, Hans Fischer in Bad Kösen, near Naumburg, at the River Saale in Saxonia. Later renamed himself after his birth town. The son of an entrepreneur dealing in building material, began to draw while still a child, plagued by asthma. Later, for three years, he and his equally gifted sister Leni attended the Academy of Graphic Arts in Leipzig. During World War I worked in army hospitals near the front line. First experiments in animation, since about 1916 or 1917, resulted in a short, *Das Loch im Westen* (*The Hole in the West*), which identified the war profiteer as the true cause of war. A few years later in 1921, he made his first animated commercial, *Bummel-Petrus (Strolling Peter)*, for a Leipzig shoe factory, Nordheimer. This was followed by *Die Entführung* (1921), *König Grogs Löwenabenteuer* (1921, both Transocean-Film), *Professor Sprit* (Dux-Film). In 1922 made *Seemannsliebe* for leading Berlin advertising company Werbefilm G.m.b.H. Pinschewer. Signed a joint venture with producer Julius Pinschewer in 1923. As a result of this collaboration, produced *Die Besteigung des Himalaja* (1923), *Abbau auch im Harem* (1924), *Brand im Wolkenkratzer* (1924), *Glück auf!* (1924), *Der Glücksvogel* (1924), *Im Urwald* (1924), *Nunak, die Eskima* (1924), *Der Pfennig muss es bringen* (1924), *Sonnenersatz* (1924), *Die Prinzessin von Honolulu* (1924, Dux-Film), *Das Zauberpferd* (1924), *Der kluge*

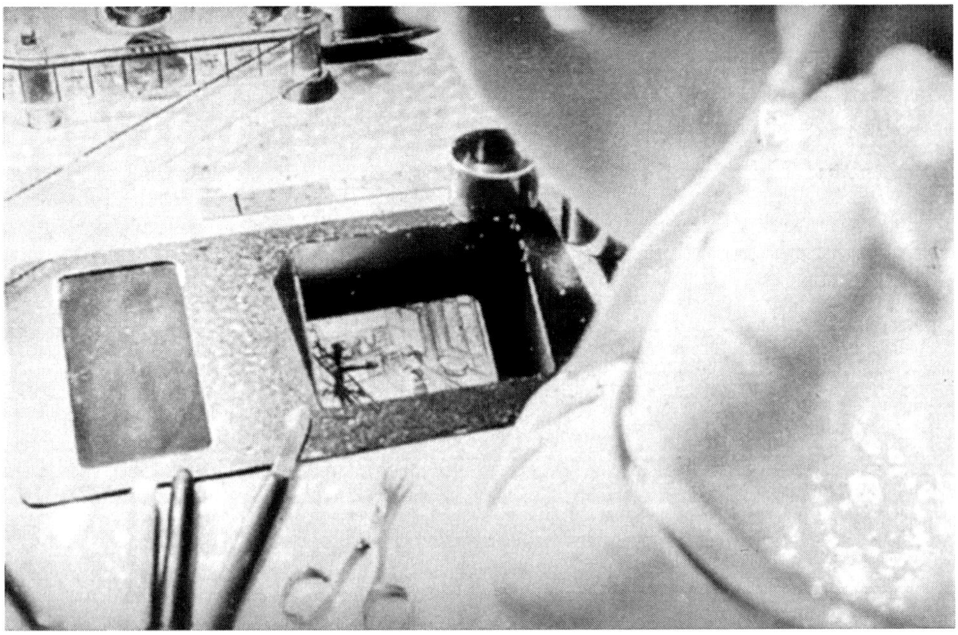

Fischerkoesen Studios Potsdam, 1942 (courtesy Dr. Hans Fischerkoesen).

Dackel (1925), *Jette's Ausgang* (1925), *Meier glüht* (1925), *Der kluge Einfall* (1925), *Das Seegespenst* (1925), *Die Geschichte vom Scholokadenkasper* (1926), *Auf der Skitour* (1926) and others. In 1927 Fischer-Kösen-Film released its output to Ufa through Epoche Reklamegesellschaft m.b.H. (Werbekunst Epoche G.m.b.H.) and finally moved its activities to Berlin Charlottenburg: *Herr Meyer geht schon wieder aus* (1927), *Alltagsgeschichten* (1927), *Das glückliche Heim!* (1927), *Die Hausfrau in Nöten* (1927), *Der rettende Kahn* (1927), *Die richtige Adresse* (1927), *So ändern sich die Zeiten* (1927), *Wege zu Kraft und Schönheit* (1927), *Das Wichtigste* (1927), *Wünscht Deine Frau* (1927), *Die Freundin* (1928), *Eine Hausfrau sagt's der zweiten* (1928), *Herr Jedermann ist wissensdurstig* (1928), *In Köln um Mitternacht* (1928), *Unerschütterlich* (1928), *Unglaublich, aber wahr!* (1928), *Der unvollendete Schiller* (1928), *Von der Stirne heiss* (1928), *Menchliches Vorrecht!* (1928), *Zur gefälligen Beachtung* (1928), *Dem verwöhnten Ohr* (1929). In the early 1930s, after doing some work for Tolirag (Ton-Lichtbild-Reklame A.G.), became established at Ufa Werbefilm: *Selbsthilfe* (1930), *Tanztee* (1930), *Das Stehaufmännchen* (1930), *Das ideale Auto* (1930, Tolirag), *Zurück zur Natur* (1930, Tolirag), *Die andere Seite* (1931), *Grosse Wäsche* (1931), *Melodie der Wellen* (1931), *Der Überriese* (1931), *Der gläserne Motor* (1931), *Die Krönung* (1932, Muratti commercial), *Wettkampf der Sender* (1932), *Getrennt marschieren, vereint schlagen!* (1932), *Wohnung zu vermieten* (1933), *Schall und Rauch* (1933), *Taler, Taler, du musst wandern* (1933), *Der Wegweiser* (1934), *Sichtbare Gedanken* (1934), *Vertrag mit der Hölle* (1935), *Das blaue Wunder* (1935), *... dann hast Du in der Not* (1935), *Fernsehen* (1935), *Gesang des Kragenknopfes* (1936), *Aufregung in der Speisekammer* (1937), *Überfall am Finkenhof* (1937), *Spuk im Walde* (1937, in cooperation with Egon von Tresckow), *Der Fortschrittler* (1938), *Dicke Luft* (1938), *Unter der Haube* (1938), *Im Glückshimmel* (1940), *Goldenes Mainz* (1940), *Der Bach Vo* (1940). In 1939 became independent, founded his own company, Fischerkoesen-Film-Studio, and

Fischerkoesen: *Verwitterte Melodie* (1943); Camera: Kurt Schleicher (courtesy Dr. Hans Fischerkoesen).

moved to Potsdam, near Ufa Studios Babelsberg. Besides commercials and advertising films, contributed animated sequences to culture films as well as doing military training films for OKW (Army High Command) and Mars-Film G.m.b.H. Famous for his technically superior trio of Agfacolor shorts: *Verwitterte Melodie, Der Schneemann, Das dumme Gänslein—Weather-Beaten Melody* (1942–43), *The Snowman* and *The Silly Goose* (both 1944), which Dr. Goebbels (and his children) liked so much. In 1945 his studio was confiscated by the Red Army. Fischerkoesen was arrested and imprisoned at Sachsenhausen concentration camp for three years as a suspected Nazi collaborator. When released in 1949, moved his operations to the French zone, first to Castle Marienfels near Remagen, then to Bad Godesberg-Mehlem, where he established himself as Germany's leading producer of animated commercials with Der Spiegel devoting to him a cover story (August 29, 1956). For West German television (Hessischer Rundfunk) he created the popular character of Onkel Otto. By 1956 had won major prizes at various commercial film festivals: Rome, Milan (three times), Venice, Monte Carlo, and Cannes. Fischerkoesen died in 1973. His original studio had closed a year earlier, but his son, Dr. Hans Fischerkoesen, reorganized it and ran a new company.

Hans Fischinger

Younger brother of Oskar Fischinger. Born on September 15, 1909, in Gelnhausen. For some time worked jointly with his brother. Later made own abstract short film, *Tanz der Farben* (1939), which was purchased but not released by Tobis. Drafted. Missing in August 20, 1944, in Serbia.

Oskar Wilhelm Fischinger

Born on June 22, 1900, in Gelnhausen. Theater critic Bernhard Diebold introduced him to the abstract film work of Walter Ruttmann. Fischinger started experiments on his own, then was hired by veteran Luis Seel to produce satirical cartoons. In Berlin opened trickfilm studio in Friedrichstrasse. Did commercials, advertising films, titles, special effects (*Der Weltkrieg* in 1926–27, *Der Unüberwindliche* in 1928, Fritz Lang's *Frau im Mond* in 1928–29, *Die Försterchristel* in 1930, *Das Blaue vom Himmel* in 1932, *Annette im Paradies* in 1933–34 as well as the logo for Europa Distribution Company) and abstract *Studies Numbers 1 through 12*, assisted by his wife Elfriede and his brother Hans. In the early Nazi years did a very successful Gasparcolor short with marching cigarettes, *Muratti greift ein* (*Muratti Marches On*/*Muratti Gets Into the Act*, 1934). Also did *Kreise* (*Circles*, 1934) and *Komposition in Blau* (*Composition in Blue*, 1935). It was Ernst Lubitsch who in 1936 brought him to Hollywood and, briefly, to Paramount Pictures. His Gasparcolor *Allegretto* was originally envisioned as part of *The Big Broadcast of 1937*. Fischinger even did some work for Disney, on *Fantasia* and *Pinocchio*, the titles for *Jane Eyre* (1944) and the dream sequence for Fritz Lang's *Secret Beyond the Door* (1947), but mainly continued in painting and experiment. Died on January 31, 1967, in Los Angeles.

Joop (Johan Luis) Geesink

Born on April 28, 1913, in The Hague. Career started as set dresser for stage revues. In the 1930s, turned to comics and, in 1939, with Marten Toonder founded Geesink-Toonder Studios which produced comics as well as 2D animation. In 1943 Geesink and Toonder split as Geesink became more interested in puppet animation. After the war, with former members of the George Pál team, founded Dollywood Studios. His most famous creation was *Loeki de Leeuw*, the Lion mascot of Dutch television. Geesink died on May 13, 1984, in Amsterdam.

Hans Held

Born on May 23, 1914, in Holzminden. Career as scenic artist and actor began in Hanover. Came to Berlin and had some bit parts in movies, then teamed up with Dr. Kurt Maetzig's studio designing film posters and doing animation. In 1938 joined Bavaria Film as trickfilm animator. For Bavaria made Agfacolor short films, *Der Störenfried* and *Die Abenteuer des Freiherrn von Münchhausen (Eine Winterreise)*. After World War II became a successful and versatile graphic artist in West Germany (and occasionally made a cartoon film, like *Kalif Storch* in 1949). Beginning 1949 designed *Darbohne* books for coffee roasters Darboven and also worked for another one, Eduscho. He created Meister Knispel for the magazine *Für Sie*, Susi the dog for *Revue*, QuickU the Ape for *Quick*, Chief Bravo for *Bravo*. Notably, his longtime association with publisher Axel Caesar Springer resulted in work for newspapers (Hamburger Abendblatt) and TV magazines (*Hör Zu!* offered his *Mecki* comic strip). Held was also active in rocket engineering, aviation, and sculpting. After a long illness he died in Haid on March 15, 1995.

Bernhard Huth

Born on October 28, 1905. Finished three semesters at Technische Hochschule (Technical University) Berlin, then quit studies. Internship with Berlin Streetcar and other enterprises. In 1927 started a film career as animator and effects technician at Ufa. In the mid–1930s focused mainly on advertising films. For a few years was in charge of Ufa Werbefilm division: *Onkel Theodor amüsiert sich* (1934), *Das Lied von der Mühle* (1934), *Warmbad überall?* (1935), *Fussball-Matsch* (1936), *Sonnenzauber* (1937), *Der Sache auf den Grund gegangen* (1937), *Das alte Haus* (1938), *Eine rührende Geschichte* (1941, with Egon von Tresckow), *Afro auf Reisen!* (1941, with Werner Bernhardy), *Saubere Arbeit* (1941), *Süsse Geheimnisse* (1942, with Egon von Tresckow). Although an NSDAP member since April 1933, after the war, in a questionnaire (dated May 3, 1948), claimed that his membership must have been sort of a gift (of which he had learned in 1937).

Wolfgang Kaskeline

Born on September 23, 1892, in Frankfurt am Main. While a young man he developed an interest in painting and drawing. War volunteer. In October 1914 was severely wounded. Two years hospitalized, invalid thereafter. Drawing instructor and art teacher in Berlin middle school. Developed an interest in film animation. Later, as a graphic artist, started work in animation and was joined by a former pupil, Gerhard Huttula, who became his cameraman and later one of Germany's most accomplished optical and process cinematographers. First both men worked in Kaskeline's home in Berlin-Tempelhof. In the beginning, released his animated commercials through Mendelfilm and Epoche-Film (Werbekunst Epoche G.m.b.H.) in Frankfurt am Main. Epoche went into partnership with Ufa for some time. In 1927 was able to negotiate a distribution agreement with Ufa: *Das Wunderei* (1927), *Acis und Galathea im Vogelreich* (1927), *Die Geburt der Ly.* (1927), *Das neue Paradies*

***Afro auf Reisen!* (1941): Ufa Werbefilm Ultraphan cel.**

(1927), *Der Schwerenöter* (1927), *Welt-Spar-Tag* (1927), *Nur für Herren* (1927), *Kennst Du das Land?* (1928), *Soll und Haben* (1928), *Von der Petrix-Batterie* (1928), *Spare Silber* (1928), *Ach hätt' ich doch* (1928), *Gegensätze* (1929). He produced some of the first color advertising films, including a spot for Meierei C. Bolle, in 1928 and established himself at Ufa as their no. 1 animator. The signet Ufa Kaskeline became famous with clients and audiences as well: *Eine kleine Teufelei* (1930), *Der Schlüssel zur Freude* (1930?), *Eine wichtige Mission* (1930), *Die Kunst aller Länder* (1930), *Die kluge Hausfrau* (1930), *Guten Appetit* (1931), *Denke daran!* (1932), *Endlich mal was Neues* (1932), *Greif zu!* (1932), *Wandlung* (1932), *Palmenzauber* (1933), *Die Schönste von allen* (1933), *Und jetzt die ganze Welt* (1933), *Zwei Farben* (1933), *Für Sie!* (1933), *Der Schwarzwald* (1934), *Märchen vom Orient* (1934), *Noch ist es Zeit* (1934), *Quellenwunder* (1935), *Alles* (1935), *Feuer* (1935), *Stoffmärchen* (1935), *Zauber der Schönheit* (1935), *Ein bunter Tag* (1935–36), *Der blaue Punkt* (1936), *Die Kette* (1936), *Meine Herren, ein Film für Sie!* (1936), *Sieg* (1936), *Huiii!* (1936), *Ungetrübter Genuss* (1936), *Dreifach* (1937), *... so appetitlich frisch* (1937). In later years he was neutralized for his partly Jewish background (denounced as "Quarter Jew"). When finally forced out of Ufa in 1937, continued making advertising films for Epoche Gasparcolor-Film AG: *Heute abend hab' ich Gäste* (1938), *Erträumtes Glück* (1938), *Gesundes Leben — Frohes Schaffen* (1938), *Meister Zwirn marschiert* (1938), *Der praktische Geist* (1938), *Trari-Trara!* (1938), *IA-33* (1938), *Wie sag' ich's dem Berliner?* (1938), *Passen Sie, bitte, genau auf!* (1939), *Perlen* (1940), *Hinter den Kulissen* (1941), *... lau bis badewarm* (1943), *Nach zwei Stunden* (1943), *Nur zum Einweichen* (1943), then returned to do some work for Deutsche Zeichenfilm G.m.b.H. In 1944 signed with Mars-Film G.m.b.H. to animate secret training films for the *Wehrmacht*. After the war, continued to make advertising films and commercials in a studio located in Berlin at Knesebeckstrasse 50, such as *Asbach Uralt* (1951), *Wäsche geflügelt* (1951), *Seid doch gescheit* (1952), *Bama Neuschritt* (1953), *Pril* (1955), and particularly the popular character Sarotti Mohr, a black boy in Arabian dress who appeared in the shorts *Gavotte* (1962), *Die traurige Prinzessin* (1963), and *Serenade* (1963). In 1949 opened first private film school which after his death one of his sons, Heinz, turned into Kaskeline-Film-Akademie. Wolfgang Kaskeline died in Berlin in 1973.

Bernhard Klein

Born in 1888. Younger brother of famous artist-designer César Klein (1876–1954) who designed the Marmorhaus film theater in Berlin. In 1920 Bernhard assisted him in painting the Expressionist sets for *Genuine*, another Expressionist movie by *Caligari* director Robert Wiene. While César's paintings in the Third Reich were defamed as Entartete Kunst (Degenerate Art), Bernhard found a niche for himself in animation. Independently he produced an animated short, *Sonntagsabenteuer*, that was purchased for release by Tobis-Filmkunst in 1941. He then was hired as co-writer and animator for Tobis' ill-fated *Rübezahl* project and finally was delegated to Deutsche Zeichenfilm G.m.b.H. where, in his own words, he suffered due to incompetence of the people in charge. Married to a Jewish woman. After the war worked for Fischerkoesen. Klein died in 1967.

Rudi (Rudolf) Klemm

Born in 1904 in Stuttgart. Studied architecture and interior decoration. In 1925 moved to Berlin where, a year later, he became acquainted with animation. For Pinschewer animated famous silhouette sound film *Die chinesische Nachtigall* in 1928 and *Ein Lämmchen* in 1930. In 1936 and 1938 animated puppet Nivea spots *Die blaue Dose* and *Katharine.* War camerman. After war imprisonment returned to Stuttgart and did colored silhouettes for children's books. Also worked as cameraman on documentaries for Ottomar Domnick until his death in 1955.

Erwin Kramp

German animation cameraman who worked as an independent. In 1928 he adapted one of Grimm's fairy tales for home movie release: *Hans im Glück.* Later with Kurt Stordel and Ufa. Studied and scrutinized Disney's multiplane technology and registered a simplified German version which was rejected, however, by Deutsche Zeichenfilm G.m.b.H.

Gerhard Krüger

Born on November 14, 1904 in Waldenburg (Silesia). Studied painting. In Berlin first worked as advertising graphic designer for the department stores of Hermann Tietz, then assisted Paul Peroff. In September 1933 began to work as a full-fledged animator for various Berlin studios. In 1938 did *Hansemanns Traumfahrt.* In 1940 producer Hubert Schonger assigned him to adapt *Die Wiesenzwerge*, a 1902 picture book by Cologne illustrator Ernst Kreidolf, for a Gasparcolor short. The story is about the feud of two dwarves.

Dr. Werner Kruse

Born in 1904. Trained in the studio of famous poster designer Julius Gipkens. Attended evening classes at various art schools, then studied economy. To finance his studies he worked for a number of advertising film companies. Assisted, for instance, Curt Schumann: *Geheimnis des Tempels* (1928), *Meisterdieb & Co.* (1928), *Das Vielbegehrte!* (1928), *Wahre Geschichten* (1928), *Herr und Hund* (1929). In 1930 animated *Fräulein Hurtig—die Kanone.* Not only an artist but also a qualified organizer. In 1934 opened his own animation studio in Berlin and signed a contract with Tolirag (Ton-Lichtbild-Reklame) to produce advertising films, such as *Was die Eiche rauscht* (1935) for Deutsche Reichsbahn. In 1937 started cooperation with Ufa Werbefilm: *Mit dem D-Zug um die Wette* (1938), *Die Morgenstunde* (1938), *Wintermärchen* (1938), *Zwergenland in Not* (1939). Beginning in 1940 also made documentaries and training films. In 1941, for one year, joined Deutsche Zeichenfilm G.m.b.H. In the period 1946–48 made educational films for East-German DEFA. In 1949 restarted production of advertising films with old (Bernhard Huth) and new talent (Werner Klemke). In 1957 started popular HB Männchen (Little HB Man) series designed by Roland Töpfer to promote HB cigarettes. In 1959 the company Kruse-Film Industrie- und Werbefilme moved to Munich and continued there with clients like Maggi, Henkel, Telefunken and Philips. Date of death unknown.

Horst Heinrich Wichard von Möllendorff

Born on April 26, 1906, in Frankfurt am Oder. Interviewed by J.P. Storm in Berlin on July 30, 1988, he had to admit that he never drew a trickfilm. Nevertheless, he inspired some of the finest German cartoons and invented sentimental stories for animation. In his youth Möllendorff attended cadet school but had to quit following a tragic riding accident. During a hospital stay, he developed a keen interest in drawing cartoons. In the late 1920s and 1930s most of the prominent German magazines published his comic strips and cartoons, including *Scherl-Magazin, Uhu, Die Dame, Gute Laune.* In 1930 created the original face that later won fame as "Smiley": "Didn't think then to have it copyrighted," he recalled. Commissioned by the leading publishing houses like Ullstein, Scherl, and Mosse, which guaranteed him a steady income. On January 1, 1935, a Berlin publishing house, Drei Masken Verlag, published August Hinrich's popular novel, *Das Volksbuch von Jolanthe*, with illustrations by Möllendorff. In 1937 Ullstein was renamed Deutscher Verlag. Möllendorff continued to work for their *Berliner Illustrirte Zeitung*. Simultaneously, for *Nachtausgabe* of August Scherl Verlag, he developed a new character, Onkel Bohne (Uncle Bean), which also appeared in *Gartenlaube* magazine. In 1938, illustrated Friedrich Böer's book *Sport macht Spass*. *Das kleine Schmunzelbuch: Herrliche Karikaturen in Hülle und Fülle*, published in 1939 by Verlag Lothar Blanvalet, was an extensive anthology of his cartoon work. In 1940 Möllendorff started to contribute to some new magazines published by Deutscher Verlag: *Signal* and *Erika, eine frohe Zeitung für Front und Heimat*. When Deutsche Zeichenfilm G.m.b.H. was founded a number of press cartoonists were recruited to invent characters and stories. Möllendorff happened to be one of them. He submitted scripts for short films like *Luftikus im siebten Himmel* and *Frosch-Sinfonie*, but finally scenario supervisor Frank Leberecht decided in favor of another project, *Armer Hansi*. Möllendorff was involved in the initial stages of that project but then Deutsche Zeichenfilm G.m.b.H. terminated his contract. Some time later, however, his writing services were needed for two of the finest Fischerkoesen cartoons, *Verwitterte Melodie* and *Der Schneemann*, which surpassed anything Deutsche Zeichenfilm G.m.b.H. had produced. Eventually Möllendorff was made head of Prague Animation and supervised the execution of another Agfacolor short, *Hochzeit im Korallenmeer*. Until the end of the war he submitted scripts and ideas for projects that mostly remained unfinished. In the 1950s published a weekly column in *Stern* magazine. Died on December 17, 1992, in Berlin.

Karl Neumann

Although Neumann was no artist and not even a production professional, for a few years he was a seminal force in German cartoon manufacture. Karl Albrecht Wolfgang Neumann was born on June 14, 1900, in Koeslin, the son of teacher Karl Neumann. In 1907 he attended primary and middle school in Koeslin, then from 1911 to 1919 gymnasium. In the following decade he worked as clerk and proxy, mainly for sausage and meat factories. In spring 1931 joined NSDAP, membership no. 567 908. On October 31, 1931, having lost his job, he worked on a voluntary basis for Gau administration, Pomerania. On

Alfons Ley (Ufa Werbefilm) drawn by Werner Bernhardy, 1941.

January 20, 1932, was promoted to deputy Gau propaganda chief, then Gau propaganda and news service head, on June 1, 1932, and to full-time Gau propaganda chief. On October 15, 1934, became referee in Reich Ministry for Enlightenment and Propaganda: "*Ich gelobe: Ich werde dem Führer des Deutschen Reiches und Volkes, Adolf Hitler, treu und gehorsam sein und meine Dienstobliegenheiten gewissenhaft und uneigennützig erfüllen.*" On April 12, 1938, Neumann was promoted to *Oberregierungsrat* (Councillor). One year later, Leopold Gutterer suggested to promote Neumann to deputy and *Ministerialrat* (undersecretary). On October 1, 1939, Neumann changed to a position in Deutsche Propagandaatelier G.m.b.H. Goebbels took notice of him and assigned Neumann to the reorganization of cultural film production. Pleased with Neumann's work, Goebbels eventually put him in charge of Deutsche Zeichenfilm G.m.b.H. In June 1945, the former Nazi functionary was found in a Soviet camp, hanged in a toilet.

Kurt Neumann (c. 1920).

Svend Noldan

Born Heinrich August Noldan on April 25, 1893, in Bad Nauheim, son of station assistant Konrad Noldan and wife Auguste Dorothea Christine née Bornscheuer. Raised in Marburg. Studied painting in Munich. As painter and artist in postwar Berlin, was a supporter of the Dada movement and a lifelong friend of theatrical legend Erwin Piscator. Entered film animation in 1920 when John Heartfield and George Grosz opened a trick and experimental film department at Ufa. A short time later, Heartfield and Grosz left what they considered a reactionary company after the murder of Rosa Luxemburg and Karl Liebknecht, but before they did so secured Noldan a supervising job with the animation department. Noldan made cartoons and worked with experimental filmmakers Viking Eggeling and Hans Richter. In 1927 and 1928, did map animation for two-part documentary on World War I, *Der Weltkrieg*, that foreshadowed his later work. In 1922, while still employed by Ufa, opened his own animation studio. It is little known that it was Noldan who animated Hein Priembacke, a cartoon sailor, for I.G. Farben and Agfa. In Ozaphan 16mm series, Priembacke became a perennial home movie. In 1933 *Was ist die Welt?* was released to some critical acclaim. During the Nazi era, was involved in map animation, special sequences and effects animation for several propaganda efforts of the regime: Leni Riefenstahl's *Triumph des Willens* (*Triumph of the Will*, 1934–35) and *Olympia—Fest der Völker* (1936–38), Fritz Hippler's *Feldzug in Polen* (*Campaign in Poland*, 1939) and *Der ewige Jude* (*The Eternal Jew*, 1939–40), and *Sieg im Westen* (*Victory in the West*, 1940–41), for Oberkommando der Wehrmacht (OKW). After the war for some time was under an employment ban, then became active again in industrial films for BASF. Retired in 1969, focused on painting. After the death of his second wife in 1977, moved from Ludwigshafen to Darmstadt where he died on May 1, 1978.

Georg Pál

Born Györgi Pál Marczincsák in Cegled, Austria-Hungary, on February 1, 1908. Studied architecture at the Budapest Academy of Art, then developed an interest in animation. Started as an animator in Budapest. As Hungary was lacking in animation facilities back then Pál came to Berlin and in 1929 assumed a post with Ufa Werbefilm: *Um die Erde* (1930–31, with Wolfgang Kaskeline), *Wer den Pfennig nicht ehrt* (1930–31, with Wolfgang Kaskeline), *Der Bazillenschlucker* (1931), *Sauberkeit ist keine Hexerei* (1931). Also created a comic strip character named Habakuk for Scherl Publishing House. Around that time, switched from hand-drawn animation to stop-motion: *Jeder weiss* (1931), *Zum Wohle* (1931). In a letter to Paul Kohner, then with MGM, dated July 15, 1936 (filed in the Berlin Cinematheque), Pál wrote: "I produced a great number of animated cartoons, and was able to improve my technique considerably. Although these films were very favorably commented upon by the press and the leading critics, I personally was really never satisfied with the work I turned out, because I felt that with the enormous resources the American trick film production could put behind their films, I would never be able to successfully compete with such productions. Plans, therefore, ripened in my mind to produce cartoons in the third dimension. Being an architect and interior decorator, it was not difficult for me to design suitable décors and figures for such a film." Patented Pál Doll Process in Natural Color (Naturfarbiger Pál-Doll-Trick) end of 1931. With Paul Wittke, Jr., a Berlin entrepreneur, founded Trickfilm-Studio-Gesellschaft Pál und Wittke (*Herr Kollege*, 1932), but some time later they split. For a Cologne company, Levante Film, did two advertising shorts for Oberst Tobacco which starred marching cigarette formations in

Hanna Ziemens (Ufa Werbefilm) drawn by Werner Bernhardy, 1941.

replacement animation technique. Both were released in 1933. By that time Pál had left Germany. First went to Prague to do some film work for the Schicht Margarine Concern in Aussig, then with the support of the Gasparcolor company, which had developed a new color film process, established himself in Eindhoven, Holland, and mainly worked for client Philips Radio: "The UFA several times tried to engage me again and get the exclusive rights for my process." Pal's replacement puppet films became the founding stone for his Hollywood career, which started in 1940 with two Paramount series, *Puppetoons* and *Madcap Models*. In 1943 the Academy of Motion Picture Arts and Sciences acknowledged Pál with a Special Award (plaque) for the development of novel methods and techniques in the production of his Puppetoons. When Paramount withdrew from Pal's short subjects, the producer turned to feature films and specialized mainly in science fiction *(Destination Moon, When Worlds Collide, War of the Worlds,* and *Conquest of Space* for Paramount, *The Time Machine* and *The Power* for MGM*)* and fantasy *(Tom Thumb, Atlantis the Lost Continent, The Wonderful World of the Brothers Grimm* with locations shot in Germany, *7 Faces of Dr. Lao).* Pál died on May 2, 1980, in Beverly Hills, Los Angeles.

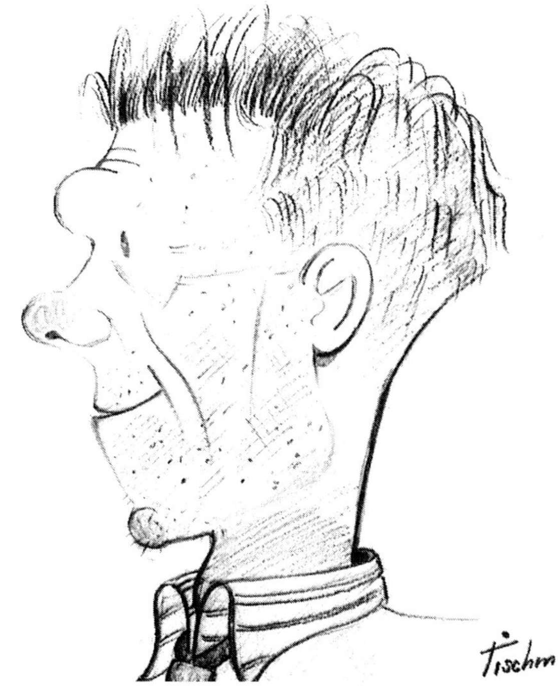

Unknown Ufa Werbefilm artist drawn by Heinz Tischmeyer, 1940.

Paul (Pawel) Nikolaus Peroff

Born on March 18, 1886, in St. Petersburg. Before World War 1 immigrated to the United States and studied at Art Students League (1914–16 and 1918–19). American citizenship since 1918. Joined America's military Siberian Expedition 1918–20 and fought the Red Army. In the 1920s began as a cartoon designer. In 1927 founded Peroff Pictures in New York City. During the depression, left America and returned to Europe. Offered his services as cartoonist in Barcelona as well as Paris. Eventually went to Germany where he was involved in making advertising films for Ufa Werbefilm and other companies. Among his first German short films were *Die Hauptsache* (1928), *Die Abenteuer des Herrn Baron Münchhausen oder Die Wahrheit über alles* (1928–29), and *Willis Zukunftstraum* (1929) which starred Willi Schmierfink (*Schmierfink* is a dirty fellow), a new cartoon character introduced by Peroff. For Ufa did three program pictures or supporting films in 1930: *Der quäkende [quakende] Narr, Die Meistersinger* (assisted by Leo von Malachowski), *Russische Symphonie*. In 1931 Peroff animated *Träume sind keine Schäume, Die Froschprinzessin, Der gläserne Motor* and *Geisterschänke*. Although he was promoted to supervising animator by Ufa, Peroff preferred to stay independent and the same year founded his own studio, Atelier Peroff, in Berlin-Wilmersdorf, Düsseldorfer Strasse 74, where he finished his short *Die Froschprinzessin*. In 1929 a Wiesbaden company, KALLE, offered 16mm home movies on Ozaphan safety film stock and partly was associated with Agfa (and Kinagfa). Peroff became a frequent contributor. *Afrika lacht* (1931) and *Die geknipste Jungfrau* (1931) were printed on 16mm Ozaphan and sold to the public cut into several parts. Releases after 1933 included *Des Kindes Traum* (in 1935), *Ein astronomisches Abenteuer, Ein lustiges Autorennen, Die Streiche von Fritz und Franz,* and *Der versunkene Schatz* (all in 1936). Later Peroff returned as drawing instructor to Ufa. During World War II made propaganda films for the Eastern Front while his old films were rereleased to newsreel cinemas in Paris or Brussels. After World War II animated 52 episodes of pioneering animated TV series *Jim and Judy in Teleland* (1949–50). Died in 1980 in Connecticut.

Günter Schilling

Born in 1926 in Berlin. Trained at Deutsche Zeichenfilm G.m.b.H. and Kunstakademie Berlin. After the war he continued to work for Gerhard Fieber on the feature *Tobias Knopp* and shorts like *Die kleine Lok* (camera: Gerhard Huttula) for which he animated and built models. Remained with Fieber and EOS-Film Göttingen until 1972. Then worked independently for various studios (Manfred Schmidt, Loriot) from Starnberg/Percha.

Hubert Schonger

Born on April 19, 1897, in Bachhagel/Danubia. In 1923 founded Naturfilm Hubert Schonger, which specialized in documentaries (German towns, nature and film expeditions). Schonger also released Robert Flaherty's *Nanook of the North* in Germany. Thanks to a long-term distribution contract with Willy Wohlrabe's Jugendfilm Company, Schonger started to adapt fairy tales in 1938. In 1939, when it became clear that Disney's *Snow White* wouldn't be screened in the German Reich, he rushed into production with his own live-action version of the Grimm Brothers' fairy tale *Schneewittchen und die sieben Zwerge* directed by Carl Heinz Wolff. Occassionally produced animation shorts: *Die Wiesenzwerge*, the anti-Semitic

Animation trainee Günter Schilling, 1943.

Vom Bäumlein, das andere Blätter hat gewollt and *Die Bremer Stadtmusikanten*. In 1947 moved his operations from Berlin to studio facilities in Inning/Ammersee near Munich and renamed his company Schongerfilm. Schonger continued to produce fairy tales and feature films and, with Jugendfilm and Heinz Tischmeyer, for a while revived his animation production in a small studio located in Tutzing: *Zirkus Humsti Bumsti*. Also produced puppet shorts by Gerda Otto [*Die wandelnde Glocke, Das Wunderfenster*], imported and dubbed American International horror pictures, made some sex films and promoted young filmmakers Marran Gosov and Peter Fleischmann (*Herbst der Gammler*). According to Dr. William Moritz (*Optical Poetry: The Life and Work of Oskar Fischinger*), in the early 1950s Schonger volunteered to rerelease some of Fischinger's animation shorts but apparently never paid for it. Schonger who ceased active production in 1972 died on February 21, 1978, in Inning.

Curt Schumann

Old-time animator. Born in 1894 in Köthen/Anhalt. Lithography trainee at renowned Leipzig publishing house Brockhaus. Studied at Academy of Graphic Arts and Book Trade, interrupted for a brief time by World War I, during which (Schumann served as cartographer). Like his lifelong friend Hans Fischerkoesen, started in advertising films with Hermann Grau's company in Leipzig: *Die Geschichte des bösen Rasselmann* (lost), then *Die Bürgschaft* (1922). In 1922 and 1923 worked for Fischerkoesen and Fischerkoesen's company Dux-Film. Then moved to Berlin where he was put in charge of advertising film studio of Heinrich-Heine-Werbefilm. In 1927 became independent. Credits include *Heinzelmännchen von heute* (1923, Ufa), *Tobias Ohneschwung* (1924), *Die Heinzelmännchen* (1925), *Felita, die Katze* (1926), *Kleine Ursachen—große Wirkung* (1926), *Glück im Unglück* (1926, Ufa), *Kultur* (1926), *Adam und Eva* (1927, Epoche), *Familienglück* (1927, Epoche), *Der Glücksjäger* (1927, Epoche), *Zwei Helden* (1927), *Ein Forscher am Nordpol* (1928, Epoche), *Geheimnis des Tempels* (1928, with Werner Kruse), *Hausfrau sei modern* (1928),

Curt Schumann, 1942.

Katzenjammer (1928), *Meisterdieb & Co.* (1928, Epoche, with Werner Kruse), *Herr und Hund* (1929, with Werner Kruse), *Die moderne Henne* (1928), *Das Vielbegehrte!* (1928, with Werner Kruse), *Das Attentat* (1929, Epoche), *Gertrud Ederle, die Kanalschwimmerin* (1929), *Bildfilm [Wäscherei]* (1930), *Moment-Aufnahme* (1930), *Zu Hilfe* (1931, Dux-Film), and the independently produced short *Bimbo und der Autodieb*. In the early 1930s joined Ufa Werbefilm studios and occasionally worked with Wolfgang Kaskeline: *Vom Deutschtum im Ausland* (animated segments for 1935 short), Guido Seeber (who since 1935 had been in charge of Ufa process and trick studio in Neubabelsberg), directors Dr. Johannes Guter or Dr. Martin Rikli (*Unendlicher Weltenraum*). When Kaskeline was forced out Schumann gradually took over his duties: *Die Feuerprobe* (1935), *Eine feuchte Geschichte* (1936), *Der gute Eindruck* (1936), *Das Geld, das man im Topf vergräbt ...* (1937), *Hauptrollen* (1937), *Das Herz auf dem rechten Fleck* (1937), *Die Mäuse nagen alles* (1937), *Leistungs-Sonder-Wettbewerb* (1937), *Ein vergnügter Abend* (1937), *Die Brücke zum Wohlstand* (1938), *Die Einladung* (1938), *Die Erholungskur* (1938), *Jedem das seine* (1938), *Herr Ober, bitte!* (1938), *Mode und Gesundheit* (1938), *B.B.C.* (1939), *Am Kreuzweg* (1940), *Es regnet ...* (1941), *Du und die Drei* (1942), *Vereint ist mehr* (1942). Later did secret military training films for Mars-Film G.m.b.H. After the war joined Fischerkoesen. Schumann died in 1975.

Louis (Luis/Ludwig) Seel

Born in 1881 in Wiesbaden (according to other sources on March 15, 1889, in Deidesheim). In 1915, while in the United States, joined Bud Fisher on the Mutt and Jeff series. In 1918 produced own *Screen Novelties*. In 1919 returned to Germany and was one of the founding fathers of German animation. For Moeve Film designed art titles and between 1921 and 1926 produced satirical *Münchner Film-Bilderbogen* (later *Louis Seel Filmbilderbogen*) which consisted of episodes running 3–5 minutes published every second week. In 1922 Seel left Moeve Film and, with his wife Olivette Thomas, set up his own company Seel-Thomas-Film and cooperated with Oskar Fischinger. In 1924 opened an office in New York. In 1925 started production in Britain. From 1927 until 1939 established himself in Rio de Janeiro to create animated films for South and North America. In 1939 was summoned from Rio and returned to Germany where he supervised the establishment of Tobis animation film studio in Berlin-Dahlem which failed as did his brief association with Deutsche Zeichenfilm G.m.b.H. Later Seel tried his luck in Prague. He died in Wiesbaden in 1958.

Herbert Seggelke

Born in 1905 or 1906 in Hanover. Studied in Munich and Paris. Seggelke produced more than 40 short films for cinema and television. In 1943, in *Strich-Punkt-Ballett* (*Semi-Colon Ballet*), he painted images directly onto the film strip like Norman McLaren would do in Canada. After World War II first German employee of Radio Munich. In 1954 cofounder of Deutsches Institut für Film und Fernsehen (DIFF).

Sergei Sesin

Born on September 18, 1909, in Moscow. Originally sculptor. In 1928 left Soviet Union. Started career as an animator with Döring-Film-Werke and Ufa in Berlin. In

1941 joined Deutsche Zeichenfilm G.m.b.H. and worked on *Armer Hansi*. After the war did another short, *Dob, der Stallhase*, but, as exiled Russian, decided to leave Berlin. According to reports he might have gone to Australia.

Sergei Sesin DZF 1943.

Paul Simmel

Born in 1887. Attended Berlin Art Academy from 1906 to 1908. Studied in Paris and Munich. From 1918 on regular cartoonist for *Berliner Illustrirte Zeitung* as well as other journals like *Lustige Blätter*. Liked to draw Berlin original characters like *Raffke, Kümmerling, Suffke*. Turned to animated films and worked for Deulig, Erich-Stoecker-Lichtbild AG and Ufa. Ufa announced his work in the credits as "A Paul Simmel film of Ufa." Simmel was mentor to Egon von Tresckow. Committed suicide in 1933.

Vladislav (Ladislas) Starevich

Born on August 8, 1882, in Moscow, to Polish parents, as Wladyslaw Starewicz. By 1910, Starevich had become director of a museum of natural history in Kaunas. There he started to do live-action documentaries. After having seen animated matches in *Les allumettes animees* (1908) by French animation pioneer Emile Cohl, decided to try his hand at stop-motion photography and transformed two beetle carcasses into articulated puppets: *Valka zukov rogacki*. A year later, in 1911, he moved to Moscow and worked in animation starring insects and animals. The same year, the czar decorated Starevich for his short *The Grasshopper and the Ants*. In 1912 he adapted Nikolai Gogol's *The Night Before Christmas* for the screen. After October Revolution, fled from Russia and ended in Paris. With other Russian émigrés took over Georges Méliès' old studio. Starevich's major opus, supported by his daughters, was the feature-length *Le Roman de Renard* (*The Tale of the Fox*) which became highly popular in Germany as *Reineke Fuchs*. Married to a German wife, Starevich lived and worked for a while in Nazi Germany. Passed away on February 26, 1965, in Fontenay-sous-Bois, Seine (today Val-de-Marne), while working on *Comme chien et chat*.

Ursula Steneberg

Born Ursula Harms on July 19, 1920, in Hamburg. Married to Eberhard Steneberg. Three years' training in painting and graphic art at Norddeutsche Fachschule für Mode in Hamburg. For eight months joined Alsterhaus, a famous Hamburg department store, as graphic artist. Then came to Berlin and for seven months was animator in Kurt Stordel's unit at Ufa. On February 1, 1941, joined Tobis for the *Rübezahl* project. Eventually was recruited by Deutsche Zeichenfilm G.m.b.H.

Carla Stephanie Steuer

Born on October 25, 1917, in Berlin-Wilmersdorf. Attended Vereinigte Staatsschulen für freie und angewandte Kunst. Joined Deutsche Filmgesellschaft as animator for advertising films: *Panik durch Ping-Pong, Minimax* (object animation), *Philips-Radio Wort und Ton, Blaupunkt, Hier fehlt etwas, B 35.* Other studios she worked for included Atelier Walter Born, Boehner-Film, Gasparcolor, and Tobis-Filmkunst (on the *Rübezahl* project). After Tobis closed its animation studio Steuer became a unit member of Deutsche Zeichenfilm G.m.b.H. After the war worked at Freie Universität (Free University) in Berlin-Dahlem as scientific illustrator.

Kurt Stordel

Born on July 30, 1901, in Morgenroth district, Beuthen. Attended Realgymnasium up to Obersekunda (11th school year). At age 18 started to study at Kunstgewerbeschule (art academy) in Danzig, then for some semesters at *Hochschule für freie und angewandte Kunst* in Hamburg. Finished his studies at art academy in Berlin-Charlottenburg. Painter, graphic artist, book illustrator and cartoonist. For some time was hailed as the German Walt Disney. In 1931 compiled *Das Trickfilm-Magazin* to promote his animation skills to potential clients. In 1936 he animated for Hansa-Film-Produktion *Graf Habenichts* (Puss in Boots) which was the first entry in a series of *Deutscher Märchen Kranz* for Tobis-Europa. Became more famous for two Gasparcolor shorts starring the dwarf Purzel released by Terra Filmkunst. Ufa was going to use him for an animated feature, *Quick macht Hochzeit* (*Quick Marries*), in 1940, but after the project failed Stordel returned to unimportant advertising films like *Ferien im Sonnensee* (1942) for Döring-Film-Werke. In 1944 and from 1949 to 1951 worked for Schonger Film (*Zirkus Humsti Bumsti*). Then did mostly information and promo-

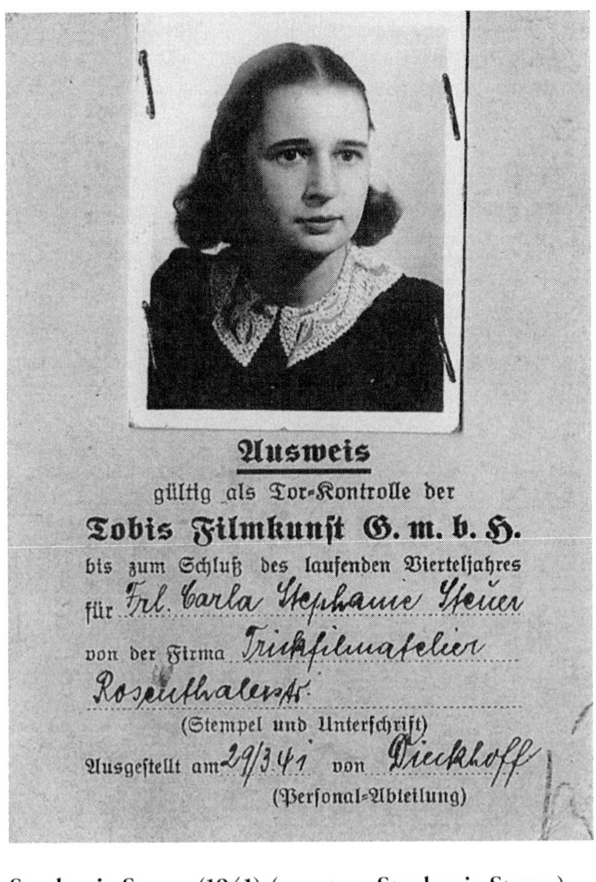

Stephanie Steuer (1941) (courtesy Stephanie Steuer).

Kurt Stordel (left) and unknown person at DZF.

tional films: *Hansestadt Hamburg* (1949–50), *Laterna Magica Hamburgensis* (1959), *Hänschen klein* (1959), *Der Preis der Freiheit* (1961), *Das neue Haus* (1961–62), *... sie bewegt sich doch* (about Deutsche Mark—1965). In the 1950s Stordel moved to Taiwan to do animation. Died in Hamburg on November 19, 1993.

Anna-Luise Subatzus (Subatczus)

Born on November 7, 1913, in Hamburg. Her father was a painter. After finishing Lyceum she attended *Kunstgewerbeschule* (art school) to become a graphic artist. Animator with Kurt Stordel and Ufa, then joined Deutsche Zeichenfilm G.m.b.H. After the war worked for Gerhard Fieber's EOS Film on feature-length *Tobias Knopp*, then for Fischerkoesen and Ufa in Dusseldorf until she rejoined Fieber and EOS. Died in 1994 in Bremen.

Heinz Wolfgang Tischmeyer

Born on January 20, 1913. Gifted illustrator and cartoonist. A school drawing instructor admired his skills and suggested to Tischmeyer's parents to find the boy a job with a trickfilm company. At the age of 16, Tischmeyer started at animation film studio Otto Waechter in Berlin. At the same time attended art school and arts college (evening classes). In the period 1931–33, worked for George Pál. When Pál's studio was liquidated, Tischmeyer (on Pal's recommendation) joined Ufa's animation studio and Wolfgang Kaskeline (with a brief sojurn to Switzerland where he hoped to land a job with Julius Pinschewer). In 1936 started freelance work. Did numerous commercials, for instance *Die süsse Insel* in association with Ernst Joachim Schienke and Karl Sonntag. The commissioner, Stoecker-Film, however, became dissatisfied with delays, resulting in some unfriendly acts. Apparently Tischmeyer did some work for the SS, and for Naturfilm Hubert Schonger animated the anti–Semitic, *Stürmer*-like caricature of a bearded Jew who is after the golden leaves of an innocent little tree in *Vom Bäumlein, das andere Blätter hat gewollt*, an illustration of a poem by Friedrich Rückert (1813): "*... ging der Jude durch den Wald mit grossem Sack und grossem Bart/Der sieht die goldnen Blätter bald;/Er steckt sie ein, geht eilends fort/und lässt das leere Bäumlein dort.*" (The Jew came through the woods with a big bag and a big beard/ Soon he sees the golden leaves/He pockets them and goes away/and leaves the little tree empty.") On Kurfürstendamm in Berlin, Tischmeyer met animation artist Stephanie Steuer, who told him that Tobis was looking for animation personnel to do *Rübezahl.* Tischmeyer applied for a job and was signed on September 16, 1940, on one-month probation, for a monthly salary of RM 700. In the studio he met two former colleagues, Karl Sonntag and Klaus Markus. Then rejoined producer Schonger for *Die Bremer Stadtmusikanten.* Poor health prevented him from being drafted. In September 1942 met Dr. Werner Kruse, who hired him as animator for Deutsche Zeichenfilm G.m.b.H. After the war, he was recruited by Theo Nischwitz, in charge of visual effects at Bavaria Studios, and did some effects animation for Bavaria productions, *Der Apfel ist ab* and Heinz Rühmann's *Der Mann vom andern Stern*. In 1947 resumed his association with producer Hubert Schonger and opened Schonger/Jugendfilm animation studio in Tutzing. Later did some work for Fischerkoesen and then rejoined Gerhard Fieber on TV's *Little Mainz Men*. Also provided titles for TV cartoons, *Ein verrücktes Paar* and *Drei Damen vom Grill.*

Heinz Tischmeyer in 1940.

Marten Toonder

Born on May 2, 1912, in Rotterdam. The brother of writer Jan Gerhard Toonder was the Netherlands' most successful comic artist, who created the characters Tom Poes (Tom Puss) and Olivier B. Bommel (Oliver B. Bumble). His father, a sea captain, had brought young Marten comic strips from America that inspired the boy to become a comic book artist himself. In 1939, with Joop Geesink, formed Geesink Toonder Studios to produce animated films, partly for German release. When the team split, Toonder continued as Toonder-Bouman Studios. Died on July 27, 2005, in Laren.

Egon von Tresckow

Born on February 27, 1907, in Montigny-lès-Metz. Was raised in Bielwies near Steinau. Studied music, then tried different jobs. Paul Simmel, a German animation pioneer, was the first to discover von Tresckow's talent for trickfilm. Tresckow finally went to Berlin in 1927 and became a press cartoonist. Signed his work with abbreviation "Tres." Worked for Ufa Werbefilm beginning in 1930: *Parole!* (1933), *Ablösung vor!* (1937), *Der Sache auf den Grund gegangen* (1937, animation with Bernhard Huth), *Herr Kolossal und wir* (1941). Scheduled to do a color short *Tilo Voss* from original designs by Otto Waffenschmied which eventually was cancelled for budgetary reasons. Occasionally while at Ufa was associated with Hans Fischerkoesen as with *Spuk im Walde* (1937), and later often with Bernhard Huth. In 1943 rejoined Fischerkoesen's company and was involved in the classic *Verwitterte Melodie*. Some filmographies refer to him erroneously as Ewald von Tresckow. After the war worked as a cartoonist for *Hessische Nachrichten* in Kassel and published comics he called *Märchenbuchfilme* (fairy-tale films]. Died on March 25, 1952, in Kassel.

Johann Weichberger

Artist's name: H. W. Eichberger. Born on February 19, 1910, in Trieste, Austria-Hungary. Studied graphic arts with Professor Paul Kirnig at art school Vienna Kunstgewerbeschule (today Universität für angewandte Kunst). In 1933 joined Julius Pinschewer, émigré producer of advertising films, in Bern, Switzerland. After his return to Vienna worked for Robert Müller. In April 1939 moved to Berlin to animate advertising films for Ufa, Döring-Film and Commerz-Film A.G. Also signed with Tobis-Degeto

Egon von Tresckow, 1942.

Kulturfilm G.m.b.H. which offered *Degeto Schmalfilmschrank* home films in 8, 9.5 and 16mm. Tobis commissioned him to do a series about cheeky twin brothers *Fritz und Fratz, die beiden Rangen,* complete from script to answer print, with each episode running three minutes, for a monthly fee of RM 1,500. In 1942 he followed this with another series, *Peterle's Abenteuer,* although drafted in October 1941. Nevertheless was allowed to continue in animation in his spare time. Presumably was also employed by Mars-Film G.m.b.H. and/or Deutsche Zeichenfilm G.m.b.H., In 1943 he negotiated a cartoon film with Ufa Sonderproduktion and on May 31 signed a contract for a project called *Knax, das törichte Zwerglein* which on Ufa's request was revised by Horst von Möllendorff. After the war Weichberger returned to Austria to resume production in Vienna under his own company banner, Herold Film. Died in 1992.

Susi Weigel

Born on January 19, 1914, in Prossnitz (Prostejov), Moravia. Studied at Hochschule für angewandte Kunst and Akademie für bildende Kunst in Vienna, then moved to Berlin where she did animation for trickfilm series like *Peterle's Abenteuer* in 1941 and 1942. After the war re-joined Peterle's co-animator Johann Weichberger in Vienna, then focused on children's book illustrations, for instance books written by Mira Lobe. Died in 1990 in Bludenz.

Ingeborg Wichert

Born on February 20, 1922, in Berlin. As animator for Epoche Color-Film Aktiengesellschaft worked on a number of advertising films: *Reichsgartenschau, Hamburger Gas, Dyckerhoff Zementwerke, Die Betörung, Lodix,* and *Mercedes Benz.* Staff member of Deutsche Zeichenfilm G.m.b.H.

Bruno Wozak

Born on September 9, 1903, in Vienna. Studied sculpture, then did poster design and cartoons. Joined forces with Karl Thomas (born on June 14, 1903) and founded, around 1935, a small trickfilm studio in Vienna's Neubaugasse. Besides advertising films (*Die Geisterstunde* and *Ihr Geheimnis,* 1938) the studio also did some short films like the opera spoof *Carmen* (1937–38). In 1941 both partners were drafted. Wozak died on September 25, 1944, in Montenegro.

21

Select Filmography

Die Abenteuer des Freiherrn von Münchhausen — Eine Winterreise (The Adventures of Baron Munchausen: A Winter Journey)

Agfacolor, 1943; *Director/Supervising Animator:* Hans Held; *Production Manager:* Ernst Mosich; *Camera:* Hans Robert Bonsack; *Music:* Hansom Milde-Meissner; Bavaria-Filmkunst G.m.b.H., Berlin and Munich; 9 min.— 209 m

Ablösung vor! (Detachment Ahead)

1937; *Animator:* Egon von Tresckow; Ufa Werbefilm [Universum-Film A.G.], Berlin; Advertising film for household appliances

Ach hätt' ich doch... (If I Had Only...)

1936; *Director/Supervising Animator:* Wolfgang Kaskeline; Ufa Kaskeline [Universum-Film A.G.], Berlin; 100 m; Advertising film for clients Agfa Cameras, Isochrom and Isopan film

Achtung, Frau'n!— wählt gelb-rot-braun (Attention, Women — Elect Yellow-Red-Brown)

Color, 1942; Boehner-Film Fritz Boehner, Dresden; c. 1¾ min.— 50 m; Advertising film for Königs Surrogate Coffee, Dresden

Adi, der Waschbär (Adi the Raccoon)

1938; *Animator:* Georg Woetz; Tiller-Film; Advertising film for client Radion Washing Powder

Afro auf Reisen! (Afro Travels)

Color, 1941; *Directors:* Werner Bernhardy, Bernhard Huth; Ufa Werbefilm, Berlin; 61 m; Advertising film [puppet and 2D animation] for client Afro-Minz Bonbon

Alarm

Color, 1938; Commerz-Film; 57 m; Advertising film for client Raiffeisen-Genossenschaft

Alle Kreise erfasst Tolirag (All Circles Captured by Tolirag)

Gasparcolor, 1933; *Director/Animator:* Oskar Fischinger; Ton-Lichtbild-Reklame A.G. (Tolirag), Berlin; c. 2 min.

***Afro auf Reisen!* (1941): Ufa Ultraphan cel.**

Alles (Everything)

1935; *Director/Supervising Animator:* Wolfgang Kaskeline; Ufa Kaskeline [Universum-Film A.G.], Berlin; Advertising film for client Volksstimme

Alle Wege... (All Roads...)

1938; *Producer:* Otto Waechter; Trickfilm-Atelier Waechter, Berlin; Advertising film for client shoe shop Dessau

Das alte Haus (The Old House)

1938; *Animators:* Egon von Tresckow, Bernhard Huth; Ufa Werbefilm (Universum-Film A.G.), Berlin; Advertising film for client Kessler Champagne

Die alte — und die neue! (The Old One — and the New One!)

1940; *Producer:* Otto Waechter; Trickfilm-Atelier Waechter, Berlin

Am Kreuzweg

1939–40; *Animator:* Curt Schumann; Ufa Werbefilm, Berlin; 40 m; Advertising film for sedative Olbas

Anzügliche Belehrungen

1939; *Director:* Dahme; Boehner-Film Fritz Boehner, Dresden; 58 m; Advertising film for client Esders-Bekleidungshaus, Dresden

Top: Werner Bernhardy Ufa, 1941. ***Above:*** Walter Born with wife and Milly Pfützner in 1943.

Armer Hansi (Poor Hansi) (working title: Die Geschichte vom kleinen Kanarienhahn, der in die Freiheit flog)

Agfacolor, 1943; *Director/Script Supervisor:* Frank Leberecht; *Production:* Kurt Neumann; *Story:* Hermann Krause; *Script:* Hermann Krause, Manfred Schmidt, Libertas Schulze-Boysen; *Supervising Animator and Character Design:* Gerhard Fieber; *Animation:* Sergei Sesin, Heinz Wolfgang Tischmeyer, Gustav Tolle, Anna-Luise Subatzus, Ane Melitta Meinhardt, Jan Coolen, Robert Salvagnac, Carla Stephanie Steuer, Jacobus Schadee, Miklos von Körnendy, Hermann Preuss, Ingeborg Weber; *Background Artists:* Kurt Blümel, E. Amadeus-Dier, Bernhard Klein, H. Olberts; *Color Department Head:* Brigitte Quass; *Colorists:* Eveline Fischer, Gertrud Bratfisch, Doris Triebel, Fritz Winkler and others; *Camera:* Franz Hendrix, Hendrik S. van Manen; *Assistant Camera:* Joanna-Maria Hendrix; *Musical Score:* Friedrich Schröder; *Conductor:* Willy Mattes; Deutsche Zeichenfilm G.m.b.H., Berlin; 18 min.—483 m—

Aroma, mehr Aroma (Flavor, More Flavor)

1939; *Director/Animator:* Alexander Alexeieff; Epoche Gasparcolor-Film; Advertising film for client Coffee Franck

Artillerie-Munition (Artillery Ammunition)

Mars-Film G.m.b.H., Berlin; Military training film

***Rübezahl* project (1940): Ultraphan cel.**

Ein astronomisches Abenteuer (An Astronomical Adventure)

1935–36; *Director-Animator:* Paul N. Peroff; Atelier Peroff, Berlin/Kinagfa; 39 m; Released by KALLE on 16mm Ozaphan safety film stock (1st part of home movie Die Tierwelt lacht)

Aufregung in der Speisekammer (Uproar in the Pantry)

1937; *Director/Supervising Animator:* Hans Fischerkoesen; Ufa Werbefilm (Universum-Film A.G.), Berlin; Advertising film for Libby's Condensed Milk

B 3 1934

Director/Animator: Oskar Fischinger; Ton-Lichtbild-Reklame A.G. (Tolirag), Berlin; c. 2 ¾ min.; Advertising film for B 3 cigarettes

B 35

1939; *Director:* Walter Born; *Animation:* Carla Stephanie Steuer; Atelier Walter Born, Berlin; Advertising film for client Blaupunkt radios

Ufa Werbefilm Ultraphan cel (c. 1941).

Der Bach Vo (The Creek Vo)

1940; *Director/Supervising Animator:* Hans Fischerkoesen; Ufa Werbefilm (Universum-Film A.G.), Berlin; Advertising film for client Vobach magazines

BBC

Ufacolor (2-color process), 1939; *Animator:* Curt Schumann; Ufa Werbefilm (Universum-Film A.G.), Berlin; 36 m; Advertising film for client B.B.C.—Sigma-Elektro-Kühlschränke(refrigerators)

Bekämpfung britischer Brandbomben (Firefighting British Incendiary Bomb Containers)

Filmstudio der Friedrich Krupp A.G., Essen; Training film series which includes animated drawings

Der Berggeist Rübezahl (Rübezahl the Mountain Spirit)

Color, 1941–42; *Supervising Director:* Louis Seel; *Script:* Frank Leberecht, Bernhard Klein; *Animators:* Friedrich Brunner, Stephanie Steuer, Bernhard Klein, Klaus Markus, Karl Sonntag, Heinz Tischmeyer, Hildegard Sascha Czekanyki, Ane Melitta Meinhardt, Herta Schiller, Ursula Schönherr, Ursula Steneberg (Harms), Hildegard Greiser; Tobis-Filmkunst G.m.b.H., Berlin; Project was announced but not finished

Bilder aus den Stickstoffwerken der I. G. Farben-Industrie A.G. (Images from the Nitrogen Plant of I. G. Farben-Industrie A.G.)

1936; *Animator:* Svend Noldan; Industrial film with animated segments

Die blaue Dose (The Blue Can)

1936; *Animator:* Rudi Klemm; *Script:* Elly Heuss-Knapp; *KO:* Armin Lang; Epoche Gasparcolor-Film A.G., Berlin; Advertising film (puppet animation) for client Nivea

Der blaue Punkt (The Blue Dot)

Ufacolor, 1936; *Director/Supervising Animator:* Wolfgang Kaskeline; Ufa Kaskeline (Universum-Film A.G.), Berlin; 30 m; Advertising film for client Blaupunkt-Radiogeräte

Das blaue Wunder (The Blue Miracle)

Ufacolor, 1935; *Director/Supervising Animator:* Hans Fischerkoesen; Ufa Werbefilm (Universum-Film A.G.), Berlin; 71 m; Advertising film for client Muratti privat (cigarettes)

Bleistiftstudie (Pencil Study)

Gasparcolor, 1934; *Director/Chief Animator:* Dr. Werner Kruse; Ton-Lichtbild-Reklame A.G. (Tolirag), Berlin; Advertising film for client Faber-Castell, Nuremberg

Ein Blick genügt (One Glimpse Enough)

1938; Ufa Werbefilm (Universum-Film A.G.), Berlin; 40 m; Advertising film for shoes

Der brave Slim—Abenteuer eines niedlichen Käfers (Ferda Mravenec)

1942–43; *Directors:* Hermína Týrlová, Vladimir Zastéra; Written by Ondřej Sekora based on his book (first published in 1936); *Stop-Motion Animation:* Hermína Týrlová; *Camera:* Antonín Horák; Puppet Film Studio Zlín; Degeto-Kulturfilm G.m.b.H.; c. 10½ min.—291 m printed on 35mm film stock; Passed the Board of Censors on November 2, 1943; Released as 4-episode home movie (Degeto Schmalfilmschrank): Part 1: Ein hilfreicher Freund (A Helpful Friend); Part 2: Das schöne Fräulein Silvia (Beautiful Miss Silvia); Part 3: In der Falle (Trapped); Part 4: Feind Spinne gefangen (Enemy Spider Arrested)

Heinz Tischmeyer at DZF.

Die Bremer Stadtmusikanten (The Bremen Town Musicians)

1935; *Director/Animator:* Ferdinand Diehl; *Script:* Paul Diehl; Adapted from a fairy tale by the Brothers Grimm; *Puppets:* Hermann Diehl; Gebrüder Diehl Filmproduktion, Munich; 31 min.; Puppet animation

Die Bremer Stadtmusikanten (The Bremen Town Musicians)

1936; *Director/Animator:* Kurt Stordel; Adapted from a fairy tale by the Brothers Grimm; Deutscher Märchenkranz; Tobis-Europa, Berlin

Die Bremer Stadtmusikanten (The Bremen Town Musicians)

Color, 1942; *Animator:* Heinz Wolfgang Tischmeyer; Adapted from a fairy tale by the Brothers Grimm; *Music:* Fritz Wenneis; Naturfilm Hubert Schonger, Berlin; Distributed by Jugendfilm Verleih, Berlin/Rolandfilm, Dusseldorf and Frankfurt am Main/Czernyfilm, Vienna; 277 (259) m

Eine brennende Frage (A Burning Question)

Gasparcolor, 1936; Epoche-Gasparcolor, Berlin; 40 m; Advertising film for client Minimax fire extinguisher

Die Brücke zum Wohlstand (The Bridge to Fortune)

1938; *Animator:* Curt Schumann; Ufa Werbefilm (Universum-Film A.G.), Berlin; 65 m; Advertising film for client Dresdner Bank

Brummi's Nachtmusik (Brummi's Night Music)

1944; *Director/Animation Supervisor:* Joop Geesink; *Story:* Horst von Möllendorff; Joop Geesink's Filmproduktion, Amsterdam as commissioned by Deutsche Wochenschau G.m.b.H. (German Newsreel); Puppet animation

Der bunte Tag (The Color Day)

Ufacolor, 1935–36; *Director/Supervising Animator:* Wolfgang Kaskeline; *Music:* Rudolf Perak, Wolfgang Kaskeline; Ufa Kaskeline (Universum-Film A.G.), Berlin; 134 m; Puppet animation and live-action; Advertising film for Indathren

Carmen

1929 and 1934; *Puppets:* Gerda Otto, Hedwig Otto; *Stop-motion animation:* Hedwig Otto; Puppet animation

Dicke Luft (Thick Air)

Color, 1937–38; *Director/Supervising Animator:* Hans Fischerkoesen; Ufa Werbefilm (Universum-Film A.G.), Berlin; 104 m; Advertising film for client Fewa cleanser

Dob, der Stallhase (Dob the Domestic Rabbit)

1945; *Director/Animator:* Sergei Sesin; *Music:* Michael Jary; Produced by Werner Hochbaum, Alf Teichs, Franz Graf Treuberg; *Production Manager:* Wolfgang Brüning; 5 min.; Released after the war

Dornröschen (Sleeping Beauty)

1936; *Director/Animator:* Kurt Stordel; Adapted from a fairy tale by the Brothers Grimm; Deutscher Märchenkranz, episode 2; *Assistant:* Elli Stordel; *Camera:* Erwin Kramp; *Music:* Fritz Wenneis; Tobis-Europa/Tobis-Melofilm, Berlin (16mm: Gemeinnütziger Kulturfilm-Vertrieb); 310 m

Dornröschen (Sleeping Beauty)

1943; *Director/Animator:* Ferdinand Diehl; *Script:* Dr. Paul Diehl; Adapted from a fairy tale by the Brothers Grimm; *Puppets:* Hermann Diehl; Gebrüder Diehl Filmproduktion, Munich; 8 min.; Puppet animation

Dreifach (Triple)

Ufacolor, 1937; *Director/Supervising Animator:* Wolfgang Kaskeline; Ufa Werbefilm (Universum-Film A.G.), Berlin; 48 m; Advertising film for client Bemberg stockings

3 Kameraden (3 Mates)

1941; *Director/Supervising Animator:* Dr. Werner Kruse; Ufa Werbefilm, Berlin; 113 m; Advertising film for client ATA (Henkel)

Die Druckluftbremse

1941; *Animator:* Erwin Huschert; Ewald-Film, Berlin; 1441 m; Part of "Der Motorwagen"

Das dumme Gänslein (The Silly Goose)

Agfacolor, 1944; *Director/Supervising Animator:* Hans Fischerkoesen; *Animators:* Leni Fischer and others; *Music:* Adolf Steimel; Fischerkoesen-Film-Produktion, Potsdam, for Deutsche Wochenschau G.m.b.H., Berlin SW 68; c. 14 min.—376 m

Ein edler Wettstreit (A Fair Competition)

1940; *Director:* Piper; Ufa Werbefilm (Universum-Film A.G.), Berlin; Advertising film for client Perfume Chiffon

Einigkeit macht stark *see* Der Störenfried

Einladung (Invitation)

Color, 1938; *Animator:* Curt Schumann; *Idea:* W. Schmidt; Ufa Werbefilm (Universum-Film A.G.), Berlin; 65 m; Advertising film for client Sigma (BBC) (Stotz automatic fuse)

Emsig wie die Bienen (Busy Like the Bees)

1941; *Director:* Ernst Kochel; Ufa Werbefilm (Universum-Film A.G.), Berlin

Engeltje

1944; *Director:* A. C. J. Holla; Bavaria Filmkunst G.m.b.H., Berlion-Munich/Studio The Hague

Die erfrischende Pause (A Sprinkling Break)

Color, 1939; *Director/Supervising Animator:* Hans Fischerkoe-

Fischerkoesen: *Das dumme Gänslein* (1943): Ultraphan cel (courtesy Dr. Hans Fischerkoesen).

Ufa Werbefilm (c. 1941): Ultraphan cel.

sen; 6 min.; Advertising film for client Coca-Cola (German branch); Reissued after the war

Erstürmung einer mittelalterlichen Stadt um das Jahr 1350 (Storming of a Medieval Town around 1350)

1942–44; *Director/Animator:* Ferdinand Diehl; *Puppets:* Hermann Diehl; Gebrüder Diehl Filmproduktion, Munich; 12 min.; *Consultants:* Historical Museum Dresden, The Curator of the City of Cologne; Puppet animation

Erträumtes Glück (Dreamed Luck)

1938; *Director/Supervising Animator:* Wolfgang Kaskeline; Epoche Gasparcolor-Film A.G., Berlin; Advertising film for client Leiser (shoes)

Es kommt Besuch (Cold Call)

1937; *Director/Supervising Animator:* Wolfgang Kaskeline; Ufa Werbefilm (Universum-Film A.G.), Berlin

Es regnet... (It Rains...)

Color, 1941; *Director/Animator:* Curt Schumann; Ufa Werbefilm (Universum-Film A.G.), Berlin; 4 min.—102 m; Advertising film for client Henkel (Henko)

Es wächst das Korn, es wächst das Kind (The Corn Grows Like the Child)
Color, 1941; *Producer/Director:* Walter Born; *Script:* Elly Heuss-Knapp; c. 3 ¼ min.—90 (88) m; Advertising film for client Milupa (baby food)

Es war einmal... (Once Upon a Time...)
1935; *Director/Animator:* Ferdinand Diehl; *Puppets:* Hermann Diehl; Gebrüder Diehl-Filmproduktion, Munich; 58 m; Puppet animation; Advertising film for client Körting Radios

Etwas Besonderes (Something Special)
1941; *Director:* Ernst Kochel; Ufa Werbefilm (Universum-Film A.G.), Berlin; Advertising film for client Dom Pils (Brewery)

Der ewige Jude (The Eternal Jew)
1939–40; *Director:* Dr. Fritz Hippler; *Script:* Dr. Eberhard Taubert; *Map Animation:* Svend Noldan; Commentary narrated by Harry Giese; Deutsche Filmherstellungs- und Verwertungs-G.m.b.H. (DFG), Berlin

Fahrt ins Blaue (Trip into the Blue)
1939; Döring-Film-Werke, Berlin; 51 m; Animation and live action; Advertising film for client Nora Radios

Fahrt ins Grüne (Trip into the Countryside)
1937; *Camera:* Piper; *Music:* Dr. Giuseppe Becce; Döring-Film-Werke, Berlin; 53 m; Advertising film for client Rewe

Falsche Sparsamkeit (Wrong Parsimony)
1933; *Director:* Svend Noldan; Atelier Svend Noldan, Berlin; Advertising film for potash fertilizer

Fan-Tai-Tip
1941; *Director/Animator:* Louis Seel; Epoche-Color-Film, Berlin

Fantasien am Schreibtisch (Fantasies at the Desk)
1938–39; *Director/Animator:* Ferdinand Diehl; *Script:* Dr. Paul Diehl; *Puppets:* Hermann Diehl; Gebrüder Diehl Filmproduktion, Munich, for Bavaria Filmkunst G.m.b.H.; 390 m; Live action and puppet animation

Ferien in Sonnensee (Holiday in Sun Lake)
1942; *Animator:* Kurt Stordel; Döring-Film-Werke, Berlin; Advertising film for client Mipax mosquito repellent

Fernsehen (Television)
Color, 1935; *Director/Supervising Animator:* Hans Fischerkoesen; Ufa Werbefilm (Universum-Film A.G.), Berlin; 78 m; Advertising film for client Grude stoves

Eine feuchte Geschichte (A Humid Story)

1936; *Animator:* Curt Schumann; *Music:* Rudolf Perak; Ufa Werbefilm (Universum-Film A.G.), Berlin; 148 (112) m; Advertising film for client AEG boilers

Feuer (Fire)

1935; *Director/Supervising Animator:* Wolfgang Kaskeline; Ufa Kaskeline (Universum-Film A.G.), Berlin; Advertising film for client Deutsche öffentlich-rechtliche Feuerversicherungsanstalt (fire insurance)

Die Feuerprobe (Trial By Fire)

Color, 1935; *Animator:* Curt Schumann; *Script:* Horst Tiller; *Music:* W. Schütze; Ufa Werbefilm (Universum-Film A.G.), Berlin; 60 m; Advertising film for client Schott, Jena (fireproof glass tableware)

Das Feuerzeug (The Tinder Box)

1943–44; Adapted from the fairy tale by Hans Christian Andersen; Dansk Farve—og Tegne Film A.S., Copenhagen, for Ufa (Universum-Film A.G.), Berlin; Originally planned as animated feature film

Fewa

1942; Advertising film for client Fewa cleanser

Die Fledermaus (The Bat)

1937; Animated art titles produced by IMAGOTON Film G.m.b.H.; Tobis Filmkunst G.m.b.H., Berlin; (Animated Art Titles apparently were designed by Wolfgang Kaskeline under the name of one of his animators, Miss Jacobi, as a front.); Dancing shoes animation executed by Tobis trick expert Ernst Kunstmann

Der Fortschrittler (The Progressive Man)

Color, 1938; *Director/Supervising Animator:* Hans Fischerkoesen; Ufa Werbefilm (Universum-Film A.G.), Berlin; c. 2½ min.—68 m; Advertising film for client Mey (Mey Collars)

Eine Frau spricht zu den Frauen (A Woman Talks to the Women)

1942; Epoche Color Film, Berlin

Freudiges Ereignis (Happy Event)

1936; *Producer-Director:* Dr. Werner Kruse; Advertising film for client Ariston-Cabinet (cigarettes)

Fritz & Fratz

1940–41; Animation series in 12 parts (some possibly executed in Zlín); *Writer-Director:* Johann Weichberger; *Animation:* Johann Weichberger and others; *Episodes:* Die blinden Passagiere; Der Spuk an Bord; Die wilde Jagd; Die kleinen Helden; In Seenot/Onkel Steffen in Seenot; Ein Hai greift an; Onkel bei den Menschenfressern; Dem Tode entron-

Fritz + Fratz (1942): Advertisement.

nen; Jumbo als Retter; Die Landung im Wunderland; Tobis-Degeto Kulturfilm G.m.b.H. (Tobis-Filmkunst G.m.b.H./Degeto-Kulturfilm G.m.b.H.), Berlin; c. 30 m each; Released in 16mm prints by Degeto Schmalfilmschrank; episodes 1–4 on 35mm (280 m)

Fritz & Fratz

Episodes: Der geheimnisvolle Tempel; Auf Tigerjagd; 1943–44; *Writer-Director, Animation:* Johann Weichberger; Tobis-Degeto Kulturfilm G.m.b.H., Berlin; Released in 16mm by Degeto Schmalfilmschrank

5-Pfennig-Serenade (5 Penny Serenade)

1941; *Producer/Director:* Dr. Werner Kruse; Ufa Werbefilm (Universum-Film A.G.), Berlin; 2½ min.—70 m; Advertising film for client Ariston Gold (Muratti Ariston Gold cigarettes)

Für Sie! (For You!)

1933; *Director/Supervising Animator:* Wolfgang Kaskeline; Ufa Kaskeline (Universum-Film A.G.), Berlin; Advertising film for client Michels (textile)

Fussball-Matsch (Soccer Mud)

1936; *Animators:* Egon von Tresckow, Bernhard Huth; *Music:* W. Schütze; Ufa Werbefilm (Universum-Film A.G.), Berlin; 110 m; Advertising film for client Henkel (Persil washing powder)

Galathea (*Additional title in 1938:* Das lebende Marmorbild)

1935; *Animator:* Lotte Reiniger; *Musical Score:* Max Janzen; *Production Manager:* Carl Koch; *Assistant:* Arthur Neher; Charlotte Koch-Reiniger, Berlin; 308 m; Silhouette animation

Ganz einfach! (As Simple as That)

1940; *Producer:* Otto Waechter; Trickfilm-Atelier Waechter, Berlin

Gedankenleser Pfiffikus (Mind Reader Pfiffikus)

1943; *Director:* Gerd (Gerhard) Krüger; Heinefilm; Advertising film for client fashion house Passmann, Koblenz

Die Geisterstunde (The Witching Hour)

1938; *Director:* Bruno Wozak; Ufa Werbefilm (Universum-Film A.G.), Berlin; Advertising film for client Radio Center Alexander Prohaska, Berlin

Die gekränkte Sparbüchse (The Resentful Coin Bank)

1937; *Director:* Friedrich Wollangk; Boehner-Film Fritz Boehner, Dresden; 49 m; Advertising film for client Schlesische Krankenversicherungsanstalt für Handwerk und Gewerbe, Breslau (health insurance)

Das Geld, das man im Topf vergräbt... (The Money That You Bury in a Pot...)

1937; *Animator:* Curt Schumann; Ufa Werbefilm (Universum-Film A.G.), Berlin; Advertising film for client Sparkasse (savings bank)

Ufa Werbefilm (c. 1941): Ultraphan cel.

Gesang des Kragenknopfes (Song of a Collar Button)

1936; *Director/Supervising Animator:* Hans Fischerkoesen; Ufa Werbefilm (Universum-Film A.G.), Berlin; c. 2½ min.; Advertising film

Die Geschichte vom kleinen Kanarienhahn, der in die Freiheit flog *see* Armer Hansi

Geschichten aus dem deutschen Wald (Tales from the German Forest)

1935; *Director:* Friedrich Wollangk; *Music:* Clemens Schmalstich; Boehner-Film Fritz Boehner, Dresden; 132 m; Advertising film for client GEG (matches manufacturer)

Das Gespenst (The Ghost)

1943; *Director/Supervising Animator:* Hans Held; Bavaria Filmkunst G.m.b.H., Berlin and Munich, Studio The Hague

Der gestiefelte Kater *see* Graf Habenichts

Der gestiefelte Kater (Puss in Boots)

1939–40; *Director/Animator/Camera:* Ferdinand Diehl; *Script:* Dr. Paul Diehl; from the fairy tale by the Brothers Grimm; *Puppets:* Hermann Diehl; Gebrüder Diehl Filmproduktion, Munich, for client RWU; 24 min.; Puppet animation

Hans Held: *Das Gespenst* (1943) (courtesy Erika Held).

Das gestohlene Herz (The Stolen Heart)

1934; *Animator:* Lotte Reiniger; *Director:* Carl Koch; Fable: Ernst Keienburg; *Music:* Willi Geister; *Production Supervisor:* Herbert Just; Charlotte Koch-Reiniger Production in cooperation with Arbeitsgemeinschaft Hausmusik der Reichskulturkammer Berlin; 337 m; Silhouette animation

Die gestohlene Krone (The Stolen Crown)

1943; *Director/Supervising Animator:* Hans Held; Bavaria Filmkunst G.m.b.H., Berlin and Munich, Studio The Hague

Gesundes Leben — Frohes Schaffen (Healthy Life — Joyful Working)

1938; *Director/Supervising Animator:* Wolfgang Kaskeline; Epoche Gasparcolor Film, Berlin Advertising film for Exhibition at Messegelände Funkturm (radio tower), Berlin

Die goldene Gans (The Golden Goose)

Begun at the end, finished after the war; *Animator:* Lotte Reiniger; Adapted from a fairy tale by the Brothers Grimm; Reichsanstalt für Film und Bild in Wissenschaft und Unterricht (RWU); Silhouette animation

Goldenes Mainz (Golden Mainz)

Color, 1940; *Director/Supervising Animator:* Hans Fischerkoesen; Ufa Werbefilm (Universum-Film A.G.), Berlin; 52 m; Advertising film for client Kupferberg Gold

Hans Held: *Die gestohlene Krone* (1943) (courtesy Erika Held).

Goldregen (Gold Rain)

Color, 1939; *Animator:* Johann Weichberger; *Music:* Rudolf Perak; Döring-Film-Werke, Berlin; c. 4¾ min.—129 m; Advertising film for client Sparkasse (savings bank)

Graf Habenichts (Count Have-not)

1935–36; *Producer/Director/Animator:* Kurt Stordel; Adapted from the fairy tale "Der gestiefelte Kater" by the Brothers Grimm; Deutscher Märchenkranz, episode 1; *Assistant:* Elli Stordel; *Music:* Fritz Wenneis; Hansa-Film-Produktion, Stordel & Schürmann, Hamburg; 400 m; Distributed by Europa Filmverleih, Berlin

Das grosse Wunder (The Big Miracle)

1938; *Producer:* Otto Waechter; Trickfilm-Atelier Waechter, Berlin; Advertising film for Klasse-Kleidung (fashion)

Grosskampftage (Labor Days)

1938; *Producer:* Otto Waechter; Trickfilm-Atelier Waechter, Berlin; Advertising film for bedspring cleaning

Gut betreut (Well Served)

1939–40; *Directors:* Ernst Kochel, Hübel; Ufa Werbefilm (Universum-Film A.G.), Berlin 65 m; Advertising film for client Sparkasse der Stadt Berlin (savings bank)

Der gute Eindruck (The Good Impression)

1936; *Animation:* Curt Schumann; Ufa Werbefilm (Universum-Film A.G.), Berlin; Advertising film for client Ligel

Eine gute Lehre (A Good Lesson)

1942–43; *Animator:* Kurt Stordel; Döring-Film-Werke, Berlin; c. 2¼ min.— 62 (60) m; Advertising film for linseed cultivation in Silesia

Ein guter Einfall (A Good Idea)

Color, 1939–40; *Animator:* Egon von Tresckow; *Design:* W. Götze; Ufa Werbefilm (Universum-Film A.G.), Berlin; 46 m; Advertising film for client Haus Bergmann (cigarettes)

Ein guter Entschluss (A Good Decision)

1935; *Director/Animator:* Ferdinand Diehl; *Puppets:* Hermann Diehl; Gebrüder Diehl Filmproduktion, Munich; Puppet animation; Advertising film for client Kübler attire

Haben Sie schon daran gedacht? (Did You Think About It?)

1941; *Producer:* Otto Waechter; Trickfilm-Atelier Waechter, Berlin; Advertising film for client J. D. Müller (shoes), Stendal

Halali (Death-Haloo)

1935; *Director:* Georg Pál; Produced in the Netherlands for Ufa Werbefilm (Universum-Film A.G.), Berlin; Advertising film for client Wilhelm Horn (liquor), Leipzig

Der Handschuh (The Glove)

1938–39; *Director/Supervising Animator:* Hans Held; *Producers:* Hans Held, Max Wüstemann, Berlin; Film was finished and later sold to Bavaria-Filmkunst G.m.b.H. but not released

Hans Held: *Der Handschuh* (1938–39) (courtesy Erika Held).

Hänsel und Gretel (Hansel and Gretel)

193?; *Director/Animator:* Kurt Stordel; Adapted from a fairy tale of the Brothers Grimm Deutscher Märchenkranz; Tobis-Europa, Berlin; 16mm version: 38 m

Hansemanns Traumfahrt (Hansemann's Dream Journey)

1938; *Directors:* Georg Woetz, Gerd (Gerhard) Krüger; Commerz-Film

Hauptrollen (Leading Parts)

1937; *Animator:* Curt Schumann; Ufa Werbefilm (Universum-Film A.G.), Berlin; Advertising film for client Teppich- und Gardinenhaus Tega (carpets and curtains), Berlin

Der Hausfreund (The Gallant)

1938; *Directors:* Egon von Tresckow, Ernst Kochel; Ufa Werbefilm (Universum-Film A.G.), Berlin; 39 m; Animation and Live-Action; Advertising film for client Böhme, Dresden (fabrics and linen)

Hemden unter sich (Shirts Among Themselves)

Color, 1937; *Director/Supervising Animator:* Hans Fischerkoesen; Ufa Werbefilm (Universum-Film A.G.), Berlin; c. 2½ min.—70 (73) m; Advertising film for client Mey (Mey collars)

Hemmungen am MG (Block of Machine Guns)

Mars-Film G.m.b.H., Berlin; Military training film

Herbstfreuden (Autumn Joys)

1938; *Animator:* Curt Schumann; Ufa Werbefilm (Universum-Film A.G.), Berlin; Advertising film for client Kaufhof (textiles)

Herr Kolossal und wir (Mr. Colossal and Us)

1941; *Animator:* Egon von Tresckow; Ufa Werbefilm (Universum-Film A.G.), Berlin; Advertising film for client Pinofluol Bath Oil

Herr Ober, bitte! (Waiter, please!)

1938; *Animator:* Curt Schumann; Ufa Werbefilm; Advertising film for client Calisay (beverage)

Das Herz auf dem rechten Fleck (The Heart on the Right Spot)

Color, 1937; *Animator:* Curt Schumann; *Manuscript:* Horst Tiller; Ufa Werbefilm (Universum-Film A.G.), Berlin; 65 m; Advertising film for client Immerglatt-Einlage (anti-crease fabrics)

Heute abend hab' ich Gäste (Tonight I Will Have Guests)

1938; *Director:* Wolfgang Kaskeline; *Actor:* Georg Alexander; Epoche-Gasparcolor-Film G.m.b.H., Berlin; 111 m; Animation and live action; Advertising film for client Attika cigarettes

Hexona

1941; Started by Kruse Film-Produktion and finished by Deutsche Zeichenfilm G.m.b.H., Berlin; Advertising film for washing powder

Hiawatha der Indianer (Hiawatha the Indian)

1935; Märchenfilm-Produktion Alfons Zengerling

Jim + Plim in: Hilfe ein Löwe (Help, a Lion)—Ein Plastischer Trickfilm—

1933; *Director/Animator:* Alexander von Gontscharoff-Mussalewsky; *Musical Score:* Michael Buchstab; Terra-Film A.-G., Berlin; 296 m

Hinter den Kulissen (Behind the Curtain)

Color, 1941; *Director/Supervising Animator:* Wolfgang Kaskeline; Epoche Color-Film; Advertising film for client Frankfurter Illustrierte

Hochzeit im Korallenmeer (Svatha v karálovem mari) (Wedding at Coral Sea)

Agfacolor, 1944; *Production Supervisor/Story:* Horst von Möllendorff; *Supervising Animator:* Jiří Brdečka; *Animators:* Eduard Hofman, Stanislav Latal, Josef Kandel, Jilis Kalaš, Vácha; *Camera:* Vladimir Novotný; ; *Musical Score:* Julius Kalaš; Sound System: Tobis Klangfilm; Prag Film AG, Animation Department, Prague-Barrandov; c. 11 min.—303 (297) m

Hoera, "Het Tweede Front," Hoera (Hooray, "The Second Front," Hooray)

1943; Netherlands; 3:50 min.

Hokuspokus (Hocus-Pocus)

1933; *Director/Animation Supervisor:* Georg Pal; *Camera:* H(ugo) O(tto) Schulze; Levante-Film G.m.b.H., Cologne; Advertising film (stop-motion) for client Oberst Cigarettes, Cologne

Huiii!

1936; *Director/Supervising Animator:* Wolfgang Kaskeline; Ufa Werbefilm (Universum-Film A.G.), Berlin; Advertising film for client Kaiser's

Ein Hundewetter

1938; *Director/Supervising Animator:* Dr. Werner Kruse; Ufa Werbefilm (Universum-Film A.G.), Berlin; 65 m; Advertising film for client Bücking (loden coats)

IA-33

1938; *Director/Supervising Animator:* Wolfgang Kaskeline; Epoche Gasparcolor-Film A.G.; Advertising film for client IA-33 Perfume

Ihr Geheimnis (Her Secret)

1938; *Animator:* Bruno Wozak; Mayer's Filmbüro, Vienna; Advertising film for client Braun's Fabric Colors

Der Imbert-Generator (The Imbert Generator)

1941; *Director:* Hasso Preis; Gasparcolor Werbefilm; Advertising film for fuel

Im Blickpunkt (In the Spot)

1941; *Director:* Kurt Stephan; Ufa Werbefilm (Universum-Film A.G.), Berlin; Advertising film for fashion

Im Glückshimmel (Heaven of Luck)

Color, 1940; *Director/Supervising Animator:* Hans Fischerkoesen; Ufa Werbefilm (Universum-Film A.G.), Berlin; 60 m; Advertising film for client Deutsche Reichslotterie

Im Himmel ist Hochbetrieb (High Season in Heaven)

1942; *Director:* Gert (Gerhard) Krüger; Heinefilm; Avertising film for client Pommersche Bank

In einer Nacht... (In One Night...)

Color, 1938; *Directors:* Egon von Tresckow, Hübel; Ufa Werbefilm (Universum-Film A.G.), Berlin; 103 m; Advertising film for client Gütermann's silk thread

Innen beleuchten—nach Aussen verdunkeln!

1940; *Animator:* Svend Noldan; Atelier Svend Noldan, Berlin; Training film for blackouts

Ja, da kann man nur staunen (Yes, One Can Only Wonder)

1936; *Director:* Lumi (Lutz Michaelis); Tolirag; 102 m; Advertising film for client Reichsbahn

Die Jagd nach dem Glück (Hunt for Luck)

1935; *Directors:* Lotte Reiniger, Berthold Bartosch; *Animation:* Lotte Reiniger; I.G. Farbenindustrie A.G./Deutscher Werbefilm G.m.b.H.; Silhouette animation

Jedem das seine (To Each His Own)

1938; *Animator:* Curt Schumann; Ufa Werbefilm (Universum-Film A.G.), Berlin; Advertising film for client U6 (cigarettes)

John Bull in Nöten (John Bull in Trouble)

Gasparcolor, 1942; *Supervisor:* Jürgen Clausen (?); Tobis-Filmkunst G.m.b.H., Berlin; 5 min.—141 m; Puppet animation

Kabarett (Cabaret)

1938; *Director/Supervising Animator:* Wolfgang Kaskeline; Epoche Gasparcolor-Film A.G., Berlin; Advertising film for client fashion house Enders & Dyckhoff

Der Kaffeeonkel kommt (The Coffee Uncle Comes)

Gasparcolor, 1937; Gasparcolor Werbefilme G.m.b.H., Berlin; Advertising film for client Pfeiffer and Diller (coffee)

Kalif Storch (Caliph Stork)

1935; *Animator:* Walter Cornblum; Adapted from a fairy tale by Wilhelm Hauff; I.G. Farbenindustrie A.G.

Kalif Storch (Caliph Stork)

1935; *Director/Animator:* Lotte Reiniger; Adapted from a fairy tale by Wilhelm Hauff; 383 m; Silhouette animation

Kalif Storch (Caliph Stork)

1940?; *Director/Supervising Animator:* Luis Seel; Adapted from a fairy tale by Wilhelm Hauff

Kampfstoffe (Chemical Weapons/Combat Agent)

Mars-Film G.m.b.H., Berlin; Military training film

Kasperl und die Zauberdose (Punch and the Magic Can)

1936; Ton-Lichtbild-Reklame A.G. (Tolirag), Berlin
Advertising film for client Erdal shoe polish

Katharine

Gasparcolor, 1938; *Director/Animator:* Rudi Klemm; *Manuscript:* Elly Heuss-Knapp; Epoche-Gasparcolor-Werbefilme A.G., Berlin; 50 m; Puppet animation; Advertising film for client Nivea Creme

Kaufmann nicht Händler (Merchant Not Dealer)

1935–36; *Director:* Ernst Kochel; *Idea:* Joachim Walter; *Camera:* Conrad Wienecke; *Sound:* Erich Dölle; *Animation:* Bernhard Huth; *Music:* from compositions by Carl Maria von Weber; Appearances by: Theodor Adrian von Renteln, Robert Ley, Adolf Hitler; Ufa (Universum-Film A.G.), Berlin, for Hauptamt für Handwerk und Handel der NSDAP; 23 min., 8 secs.—633 m; Propaganda film (Deutscher Handelstag in Braunschweig, November 19, 1933) that includes animated segments

Die Kette (The Chain)

1936; *Director/Supervising Animator:* Wolfgang Kaskeline; Ufa Werbefilm (Universum-Film A.G.), Berlin; Advertising film for client Aspirin

Kinder-Varieté (Children Vaudeville)

1939 or 1940; *Director/Supervising Animator:* Luis Seel; Includes characters copied from Disney short Donald's Cousin

Des Kindes Traum (Santa Claus)

1931 and 1935; *Director/Animator:* Paul N. Peroff; I.G. Farbenindustrie A.G.

Der kleine Däumling (Tom Thumb)

1944; Adapted from the fairy tale by the Brothers Grimm; *Music:* Fritz Wenneis; Naturfilm Hubert Schonger, Berlin; 521 m; Puppet animation

Der kleine Häwelmann (Little Häwelmann)

1941; *Director:* E. Dautert; Naturfilm Hubert Schonger, Berlin; Live action with object animation

Eine kleine Königstragödie (A Little King Tragedy)

1934–35 (9.5mm amateur film), 1935–36 (new version filmed in 35mm); *Director/Cameraman/Animator/Editor:* Richard Groschopp; *Music:* Fritz Wenneis; Boehner-Film Fritz Boehner, Dresden; 191 m (35mm version)

Komposition in Blau (Composition in Blue) Additional Title: Lichtkonzert Nr. 1 (Light-Concert No. 1)

Gasparcolor, 1935; *Director/Animator:* Oskar Fischinger, Berlin; *Assistant:* Elfriede Fischinger; *Music:* Overture "Die lustigen Weiber von Windsor" (Merry Wives of Windsor) by Otto Nicolai; 4 min.—108 m

Krach im Päckchen (Uproar in a Package)

1942; *Animator:* Kurt Stordel; *Idea:* Dr. Willi Fischer; *Music:* Dr. Giuseppe Becce; Döring-Film-Werke G.m.b.H., Berlin; 3 min.— 80 m; Advertising film for Reichspost (Field Post)

Kraftfahrzeug im Mäusebauch

1942; Tiller-Film; 47 m; Puppet animation; Advertising film for client Sparkasse

Kreise (Circles)

Gasparcolor, 1933 and 1934; *Director/Animator:* Oskar Fischinger; *Music:* 1st part — Venusberg ballet music from Richard Wagner's Tannhauser; 2nd part — ending of Edvard Grieg's "Homage March" from Sigurd Jorsalfar; Ton-Lichtbild-Reklame A.G. (Tolirag), Berlin; 2 min.— 50 (44) m

Küchensinfonie (Kitchen Symphony)

1937; *Animator:* Georg Woetz; Commerz-Film; Advertising film for client Ata

...lau bis badewarm (...Lukewarm to Warm Water)

1942–43; *Director:* Wolfgang Kaskeline; Epoche-Color-Film A.G., Berlin; 58 m; Object animation; Advertising film for client Henkel (Dallita)

Leistungs-Sonder-Wettbewerb (Special Competition in Efficiency)

1937; *Animator:* Curt Schumann; Ufa Werbefilm (Universum-Film A.G.), Berlin; Advertising film for client shoe shop Böhmer

Die lieben Kinder (Dear Kids)

1938; *Animator:* Egon von Tresckow; Ufa Werbefilm (Universum-Film A.G.), Berlin

Das Lied von der Mühle (The Song of the Mill)

1934; *Animators:* Egon von Tresckow, Bernhard Huth, Wintzer; *Music:* Rudolf Perak; Ufa Werbefilm (Universum-Film A.G.), Berlin; 56 m; Advertising film for client BP Olex motor oil

Lufttoperdo-Schiesslehre (Air Torpedo Shooting Guide)

Mars-Film G.m.b.H., Berlin; Military training film

Die lustige Palette — Im Reiche der Micky Maus

Compilation of four Technicolor Silly Symphonies *and 2 black and white* Mickey Mouse *short films:* Der Rattenfänger von Hameln (The Pied Piper), Die Nacht vor dem Weihnachtsabend (The Night Before Christmas), Die mechanische Micky Maus (Mickey's Mechanical Man), Die drei kleinen Schweinchen (Three Little Pigs), Micky im Lande der Riesen (Giantland), Die Arche Noah (Father Noah's Ark); 1934; A United Artists Program distributed by Bayerische Film G.m.b.H. and premiered at Marmorhaus, Berlin

Ein lustiges Autorennen (A Funny Car Race)

1936; *Director/Animator:* Paul N. Peroff; Atelier Peroff, Berlin/ Kinagfa; 38 m; Released by KALLE on 16mm Ozaphan safety film stock

Die Macht der Liebe (The Power of Love)

1935; *Director/Animator:* Ferdinand Diehl; *Script:* Dr. Paul Diehl; *Puppets:* Hermann Diehl; *Camera:* Hans Asen; Gebrüder Diehl Filmproduktion, Munich; 21 min.; Puppet animation

Ein Märchen (A Fairy Tale) Purzel, Brumm und Quack

Gasparcolor, 1937–38; *Director/Animator:* Kurt Stordel; *Assistant:* Elli Stordel; *Camera:* Erwin Kramp; *Music:* Fritz Wenneis; Trickfilm-Atelier E. W. Stordel/Terra-Filmkunst A.-G., Berlin; c. 10 min.— 374 m

Kurt Stordel and composer Fritz Wenneis, 1938 (courtesy Thomas Stordel).

Märchen vom Orient (Arabian Fairy Tale)

Ufacolor, 1933–34; *Director/Supervising Animator:* Wolfgang Kaskeline; Ufa Kaskeline (Universum-Film A.G.), Berlin; 69 m; Advertising film for Gebrüder Schoeller, Düren (Anker Carpets)

Die Mäuse nagen alles (Mice Gnaw Everything)

1937; *Animator:* Curt Schumann; Ufa Werbefilm (Universum-Film A.G.), Berlin; Advertising film for Sparkasse (savings bank)

Max und Moritz (*sound version 1951:* Spuk mit Max und Moritz)

1940–41; *Director/Animator:* Ferdinand Diehl; *Script:* Dr. Paul Diehl adapted from Wilhelm Busch; *Puppets:* Hermann Diehl, Repsold; 15 min.—Gebrüder Diehl Filmproduktion, Munich, in cooperation with Geyer Laboratories (originally intended for 8mm home film distribution); Puppet animation

Meine Herren, ein Film für Sie! (Gentlemen, a Film for You!)

1936; *Director/Supervising Animator:* Wolfgang Kaskeline; Ufa Werbefilm (Universum-Film A.G.), Berlin; Advertising film for men's fashion

Meister Zwirn marschiert (Master Yarn Marches)

1938; *Director/Supervising Animator:* Wolfgang Kaskeline; Epoche Gasparcolor-Film A.G., Berlin; Advertising film for client fashion house Enders & Dyckhoff

Melodie des Südens (Melody of the South)

Color, 1942; *Music:* Rudolf Perak; Ufa Werbefilm (Universum-Film A.G.), Berlin; 83 m; Advertising film for client Cinzano

Der Mensch fliegt—Träume und Wirklichkeit (Man Flies: Dreams and Reality)

1933–34; Albert Roever Film G.m.b.H.; 585 m; Animation and Live Action

Miniatur-Kabarett (Miniature Cabaret)

1934; *Director/Animator:* Ferdinand Diehl; *Puppets:* Hermann Diehl; *Camera:* Hans Asen; *Musical Score:* Hans Hild; *Sound:* F. W. Dustmann; Gebrüder Diehl-Film, Munich; 501 m; Puppet animation

Mit dem D-Zug um die Wette (Racing Against an Express Train)

Ufacolor, 1938; *Director/Supervising Animator:* Dr. Werner Kruse; Ufa Werbefilm (Universum-Film A.G.), Berlin; 87 m; Advertising film for rail transport

Mit Musike (With Music)

Color, 1940; *Animator:* Egon von Tresckow; Ufa Werbefilm (Universum-Film A.G.), Berlin; 40 m; Advertising film for client Haus Bergmann (cigarettes)

Mitternacht (Midnight)

1933; *Director/Animation Supervisor:* Georg Pal; *Camera:* H(ugo) O(tto) Schulze; Levante-Film G.m.b.H., Cologne; Advertising film (stop-motion) for client Oberst Cigarettes, Cologne

Mode und Gesundheit (Fashion and Health)

1938; *Animator:* Curt Schumann; *Script:* Werbe-Klotz; Ufa Werbefilm (Universum-Film A.G.), Berlin; 50 (48) m; Advertising film for client Libelle-Laufmotor (shoes)

Die Morgenstunde (The Morning Hour)

Color, 1938; *Director/Supervising Animator:* Dr. Werner Kruse; Ufa Werbefilm (Universum-Film A.G.), Berlin; 60 m; Advertising film for client Odol (toothpaste and mouthwash)

Münchhausen (Munchausen)

Agfacolor, 1942–43; *Director:* Josef von Baky; *Production Group:* Eberhard Schmidt; *Screenplay:* Berthold Bürger (i.e., Erich Kästner); *Animation:* Hans Held (by arrangement with Bavaria-Filmkunst G.m.b.H.); *Special and Process Photography:* Konstantin Irmen-Tschet, Gerhard Huttula; Ufa Filmkunst, Ufastadt Babelsberg; (Expensive feature film with some brief animation scenes)

Muratti greift ein (Muratti Gets in the Act)

Gasparcolor, 1934; *Director:* Oskar Fischinger; *Assistants:* Elfriede Fischinger, Gertrude (Trudl) Gudjons; *Music:* Excerpts from Josef Bayer's ballet Die Puppenfee (The Doll-Fairy); Ton-Lichtbild-Reklame A.G. (Tolirag), Berlin; c. 2¾ min.—74 m

Muratti Privat (Muratti Private)

c. 1935; *Director/Animator:* Oskar Fischinger, Berlin; *Music:* Wolfgang Amadeus Mozart; 3 min.

Das musikalische Auto (The Musical Car)

1943–44; *Director:* Joop Geesink; *Story:* Horst von Möllendorff; *Music:* Hugo De Groot; *Production Manager:* Jan C. Bouman; Produced by Marten Toonder and Joop Geesink; Geesink-Toonder Productie Teekenfilm/Marten Toonder Studio's/Toonder-Bouman Film Producties, Amsterdam, for Ufa; 9 min.—239 m

Müssen Männer so sein? (Must Men Be Like That?)

1939; *Animator:* Curt Schumann; Ufa Werbefilm (Universum-Film A.G.), Berlin; Advertising film for client Immerglatt Insoles

Mutti, was ist denn? (What Is, Ma?)

1940; *Director:* Ernst Kochel; Ufa Werbefilm (Universum-Film A.G.), Berlin; Advertising film for client Volksfürsorge

Nachtasyl (Night Asylum)

1934; *Director/Animator:* Ferdinand Diehl; *Script:* Paul Diehl; *Puppets:* Hermann Diehl; *Camera:* Hans Asen; *Music:* Toni Thoms; *Sound:* F. W. Dustmann; *Editor:* Werner Leckebusch; Gebrüder Diehl Filmproduktion, Munich; 21 min.—545 m; Puppet animation

Nächtliches Abenteuer *see* Ski-Heil

Nach zwei Stunden (Two Hours Later)

1942–43; *Director:* Wolfgang Kaskeline; Epoche-Color-Film A.G., Berlin; 54 m; Object animation; Advertising film for client Henkel (Dallita)

Nautilus (Wupp-Nautilus)

1933; *Director/Animator:* Ferdinand Diehl; *Script:* Paul Diehl; *Puppets:* Hermann Diehl; *Camera:* Hans Asen; Gebrüder Diehl Filmproduktion, Munich; 10 min.; Puppet animation

Neue Begriffe (New Terms)

1936; *Directors:* Egon von Tresckow, Horst Tiller; Animation and live action; Advertising film for client Mobilöl-Vacuum (motor oil)

Neuzeitliche Weidewirtschaft (Modern Management of Pasture)

1936; *Animator:* Svend Noldan; I.G. Farbenindustrie A.G.; Industrial film with animated segments

Nichts für Mucker (Nothing for Yes-Men)

1940; *Director/Supervising Animator:* Wolfgang Kaskeline; Advertising film for client Henkell Champagne

Nikolaus in Sorgen (Santa Claus in Trouble)

1942; *Director:* Gerd (Gerhard) Krüger; Heinefilm; Advertising film for client Fahning

Noch ist Zeit (There Is Still Time)

1942–43; *Director:* Wolfgang Kaskeline; Ton-Lichtbild-Reklame A.G. (Tolirag), Berlin; 103 m; Object animation and live action; Advertising film for client Dr. Habermann's Biocitin

Der Notenhändler (Le Marchand de Notes)

Agfacolor, 1939; *Director:* Paul Grimault; Les Gemeaux, Paris.

Nr. 7 (No. 7)

1939; *Director:* Blachnitzky; Döring-Film-Werke, Berlin; Advertising film for client Sparkasse (savings bank)

Nur zum Einweichen (Only for Soak)

1942–43; *Director:* Wolfgang Kaskeline; Epoche-Color-Film A.G., Berlin; 45 m; Advertising film for client Henkel (Dallita)

Onkel Theodor amüsiert sich (Uncle Theodore Amuses Himself)

1934; *Animators:* Egon von Tresckow, Bernhard Huth; Ufa-Werbefilm (Universum-Film A.G.), Berlin; 123 m; Advertising film for client Kempinski (Haus Vaterland, Berlin)

Opta empfängt (Opta Radio Reception)

Gasparcolor, 1936; Gasparcolor Werbefilme G.m.b.H., Berlin; Advertising film for client Opta Radios

Ordnung schafft Brot (Order Provides Bread)

1942; *Animation:* Kurt Stordel; Foto-Vogt, Stettin; Short with animated parts

Orpheus in der Unterwelt (Orpheus in the Underworld)

1941 (?); *Producer:* Josef Pfister; AFIT, Prague

Palmenzauber (Palm Magic)

Ufacolor, 1933; *Director/Supervising Animator:* Wolfgang Kaskeline; Ufa Kaskeline (Universum-Film A.G.), Berlin; 102 m; Advertising film for client Palmin Pflanzenmargarine (margarine)

Panik durch Ping-Pong (Panic About Ping-Pong)

Color, 1938; *Supervising Animator:* Walter Born; *Animation:* Carla Stephanie Steuer; *Script:* Hans Thyssen; *Music:* Kurt Drabek; *Narrator:* Kurt Mühlhardt; Deutsche Film-Herstellungs- und Verwertungs G.m.b.H. (DFG); 120 m; Advertising film for front yards without metal fences

Parade

1941; *Producer:* Otto Waechter; Trickfilm-Atelier Waechter, Berlin; Advertising film for client Schuhhaus Ringia (shoes)

Parole!

1933; *Director/Chief Animator:* Egon von Tresckow; Ufa Werbefilm (Universum-Film A.G.), Berlin; Advertising film for client Melder's Coffee

Passen Sie, bitte, genau auf! (Attention, please!)

1939; *Director/Supervising Animator:* Wolfgang Kaskeline; Epoche Gasparcolor-Film A.G., Berlin; Advertising film for client Mädler Bags

Perlen (Pearls)

Color, 1940; *Director/Supervising Animator:* Wolfgang Kaskeline; Epoche Color-Film A.G., Berlin; 2 ¾ min.—75 m; Advertising film for client Henkell Champagne (Henkell Dry)

Peterle's Abenteuer (Peterle's Adventures)

1941–42; *Writer-Director:* Johann Weichberger; *Animation:* Johann Weichberger, Susi Weigel; Tobis-Degeto Kulturfilm G.m.b.H. (Tobis-Filmkunst G.m.b.H.), Berlin; 15 min.; Released in 16mm prints by Degeto Schmalfilmschrank; Peterle's Adventures were released as 4-episode home movie: Part 1: Die beiden Ausreisser (The Two Runaways); Part 2: Peterle im Zirkus (Peterle in the Circus); Part 3: Der kleine Jäger (The Little Hunter); Part 4: Ein guter Fang (A Good Catch)

Philips Werbefilm für Glühbirnen (Philips Commercial for Light Bulbs)

1935; *Director/Supervising Animator:* Hans Fischerkoesen; Advertising film for Philips light bulbs

Der praktische Geist (The Practical Spirit)

1938; *Director/Supervising Animator:* Wolfgang Kaskeline; Epoche Gasparcolor-Film A.G., Berlin; Advertising film for client Vobach-Schirka

Priembacke in Afrika; Priembacke und der Klabautermann; Priembacke und der Sägefisch

1933 (1930–32); I.G. Farbenindustrie A.G. (Agfa); *Director/Animator:* Svend Noldan; Released by KALLE on 16mm Ozaphan film stock

Prinzess Neugierde (Princess Nosiness)
1942; *Director:* Gerd (Gerhard) Krüger; Heinefilm

Das Publikum geht mit — und beobachtet (The Audience Goes Along — and Watches)
1933; *Producer:* Otto Waechter; Trickfilm-Atelier Waechter, Berlin; Advertising film for Department Store H. Joseph & Co., Berlin-Neukölln

Pulsschlag des Meeres (Pulse of the Sea)
1936–37; *Director:* Dr. Martin Rikli; *Camera:* Kurt Stanke; Ufa (Universum-Film A.G.), Berlin; 417 m; Animated segments

Punktgenau (Straight to the Point)
1940; *Producer:* Otto Waechter; Trickfilm-Atelier Waechter, Berlin; Advertising film for client Otto Schneider & Co., Ohlau

Purzel, der Zwerg, und der Riese vom Berg (Purzel the Dwarf and the Mountain Giant)
Gasparcolor, 1939; *Director/Animator:* Kurt Stordel; *Assistant:* Elli Stordel; *Camera:* Erwin Kramp; *Music:* Fritz Wenneis; Kurt Stordel Zeichentrick-Atelier/Terra-Filmkunst A.-G., Berlin; 9 min.

Purzelbaum ins Leben ***see*** **Schnuff, der Nieser**

Quadrate (Squares)
Color, 1934; *Director/Animator:* Oskar Fischinger, Berlin; Silent; 4 min.

Quellen-Wunder (Miracle of the Spring)
Ufacolor, 1935; *Director/Supervising Animator:* Wolfgang Kaskeline; Ufa Kaskeline (Universum-Film A.G.), Berlin; 57 m; Advertising film for client Bad Nauheim (health spa)

Quick macht Hochzeit (Quick Marries)
1941; *Director/Animator:* Kurt Stordel; *Animators:* Gerhard Fieber, Hildegard Greiser, Elisabeth Gröhn, Ursula Harms, Anna-Luise Subatzus, Annemarie Ullner, Ellen Brade, Sergei Sesin; *Backgrounds:* Kurt Bluemel; *Camera:* Erwin Kramp; Horst Kerutt production for Ufa (Universum-Film, A.G.), Berlin; Project was announced but not finished

Raum im kreisenden Licht (Room in Circling Light)
1936; *Director:* Dr. Carl Lamb; *Special Cinematography:* H(ugo) O(tto) Schulze; *Music:* Karl Höller, Walter Ulfig; *Narrator:* Bruno Fritz; Tobis-Melofilm G.m.b.H., Berlin; 17 min., 25 secs.; Animated camera movements follow the light streaming through the windows of a church.

Der rechte Weg (The Right Way)
Color, 1937; *Camera:* Piper; *Music:* Rudolf Perak; Döring-Film-Werke, Berlin; 70 m; Advertising film for client Sparkasse (savings bank)

Reineke Fuchs (Le Roman de Renard)

1929; German version released in 1937; *Director/Supervising Animator:* Ladislas Starevich; *Musical Score (German version):* Dr. Julius Kopsch; *Narration written by:* Wilhelm Krug; *Narrator:* Leo Peukert; 1719 m; German scored version produced and released by Ufa (Universum-Film A.G.), production group Erich Neusser

Reineke Fuchs: Der Zaubersee (Reynard the Fox: The Magic Lake)

1935; *Director/Animator:* Werner Drees; First part of proposed cartoon series

Ring frei (Clear the Ring)

1940

Das rollende Rad (The Rolling Wheel)

1935; *Director/Animator:* Ferdinand Diehl; *Puppets:* Hermann Diehl; Gebrüder Diehl Filmproduktion, Munich; Puppet animation

Roman de Renard, Le *see* Reineke Fuchs

Romanze (Romance)

1933; *Director/Animator:* Ferdinand Diehl; *Puppets:* Hermann Diehl; Gebrüder Diehl Filmproduktion, Munich for Bavaria-Film A.G., Munich; Puppet animation

Ruf der Pfennige (Call of the Pennies)

1940; Boehner-Film Fritz Boehner, Dresden; 56 m; Advertising film for Opekta

Eine rührende Geschichte (A Touching Story)

Color, 1941; *Animators:* Egon von Tresckow, Bernhard Huth; Ufa Werbefilm (Universum-Film A.G.), Berlin; 3½ min.—100 m; Advertising film for client Opekta

Der Sache auf den Grund gegangen (Going to the Bottom of Things)

1937; *Animators:* Egon von Tresckow, Bernhard Huth; Ufa Werbefilm (Universum-Film A.G.), Berlin; Advertising film for client Roeper Coffee

Saubere Arbeit (Clean Work)

Color, 1941; *Animators:* Egon von Tresckow, Bernhard Huth; 49 m; Advertising film for client Henkel (Imi washing powder)

Schall und Rauch (Noise and Smoke)

1933; *Director:* Hans Fischerkoesen; *Script:* Ernst von Wolzogen; Ufa Werbefilm (Universum-Film A.G.), Berlin; 2½ min.—60 m; Advertising film for client Ariston Cigarettes

Der scheintote Chinese (The Seemingly Dead Chinese)

1935; *Director/Animator:* Lotte Reiniger; I.G. Farbenindustrie A.G.; Silhouette animation

Scherben bringen Glück (Shards Bring Luck)

1940; Ufa Werbefilm (Universum-Film A.G.), Berlin; 26 m; Advertising film for Althoff (home appliances)

Scherzo *see* Verwitterte Melodie, Die

Schicksalswege (Paths of Destiny)

Color, 1939; *Producer:* Otto Waechter; Trickfilm-Atelier Waechter, Berlin; 68 m; Advertising film for client Deutsche Ring-Krankenversicherung (health insurance)

Die Schlacht um Miggershausen (The Battle for Miggershausen)

Color, 1937; *Director:* Georg Woelz; *Idea:* Paul Schwärzel; *Music:* Karl Sczuko; *Narrator:* Heinz Goedecke; Commerz-Film; 6:43 min. — 351 m; Propaganda for Volksempfänger (radio)

Der Schneemann (The Snowman)

Agfacolor, 1943–44; *Director/Supervising Animator:* Hans Fischerkoesen; *Story:* Horst von Möllendorff; *Animators:* Rudolf Bär, Leni Fischer, Egon von Tresckow, Susanne Birkner; *Dutch Animator:* Hill Beekman; *Camera:* Kurt Schleicher; *Music:* Rudolf Perak; Fischerkoesen Studio, Potsdam, for Deutsche Wochenschau G.m.b.H.; 13 min. — 354 m

Schnick und Schnorke

1934; *Director:* Friedrich Wollangk; Boehner-Film Fritz Boehner, Dresden; 65 m; Advertising film for client Volksfürsorge (insurance)

Schnuff, der Nieser (Schnuff the Sneezer)

Agfacolor, 1944–45; *Director/Supervising Animator/Character Design:* Gerhard Fieber; *Story:* Horst von Möllendorff, Gerhard Fieber; *Animation:* Stephanie Steuer, Jan Schadee, Sergei Sesin; *Camera:* Kurt Drews; *Music:* Friedrich Schröder; *Orchestra:* Deutsches Tanzorchester

Werner Drees: ***Reineke Fuchs.***

Schnuff der Nieser (1944).

Barnabas von Geczy; Deutsche Zeichenfilm G.m.b.H., Berlin-Dachau (supervisor Studio Dachau, H. Wöhrle); 9 min., 20 sec.—241 m; Finished by DEFA (Deutsche Film A.G.) and released as **Purzelbaum ins Leben** in 1946

Die Schönste von allen (The Most Beautiful of Them All)

1933; *Director:* Wolfgang Kaskeline; *Camera:* Conrad Wienecke; *Music:* Clemens Schmalstich; Ufa Kaskeline (Universum-Film A.G.), Berlin; 89 m; Advertising film for client Haus Bergmann (cigarettes: privat 2½); Object animation

Der Schwarzwald (The Black Forest)

1934; *Director/Chief Animator:* Wolfgang Kaskeline; Ufa Kaskeline (Universum-Film A.G.), Berlin; Advertising film for client Blaupunkt Radio

Jim + Plim in: Serenade

1933; *Director/Animator:* Alexander von Gontscharoff; Puppet animation

Sichtbare Gedanken (Visible Thoughts)

1934; *Director/Animator:* Hans Fischerkoesen; Ufa Werbefilm (Universum-Film A.G.), Berlin; 82 m; Advertising film for client Constantin 23 cigarettes

Die sieben Raben (The Seven Ravens)

1936–37; *Director/Animator:* Ferdinand Diehl; *Script:* Dr. Paul Diehl from a fairy tale by Wilhelm and Jacob Grimm; *Puppets:* Hermann Diehl; *Cinematography:* Alfons Lusteck; *Music:* Walter Pepper; Gebrüder Diehl Filmproduktion, Munich; 53 min.—1787 (1804) m; Puppet animation

Sieben wandern durch die Welt (Seven Wander Round the World)

Color, 1939; *Director/Supervising Animator:* Dr. Werner Kruse; Ufa Werbefilm (Universum-Film A.G.), Berlin; 109 m; Advertising film for client Esso-Club (motor oil)

Sieg (Victory)

1936; *Director/Chief Animator:* Wolfgang Kaskeline; Ufa Werbefilm (Universum-Film A.G.), Berlin; Advertising film for Bayer (Panflavin pastilles)

Sieg im Westen (Victory in the West)

1940–41; Svend Noldan (credited as Sven Nolan) co-directed with Fritz Brunsch and Werner Kortwich and provided all map animation; *Script:* Konrad Liss; Oberkommando der Wehrmacht (OKW)

Silah basina

1938; Döring-Film-Werke, Berlin; 122 m; Advertising film for client Aspirin

Ski Heil

1934; *Director/Animator:* Ferdinand Diehl; *Script:* Paul Diehl; *Puppets:* Hermann Diehl; *Camera:* Hans Asen; *Music:* Hans Hild; *Sound:* F. W. Dustmann; *Editor:* Werner Leckebusch; Gebrüder Diehl Filmproduktion, Munich; 19 min.—504 m; Puppet animation

...so appetitlich frisch (...So Deliciously Fresh)

1937; *Director/Supervising Animator:* Wolfgang Kaskeline; Ufa Kaskeline (Universum-Film A.G.), Berlin; 40 m; Advertising film for client Haus Bergmann (cigarettes)

Sonne, Erde und Mond (Sun, Earth and Moon)

1938; *Director:* Dr. Martin Rikli; *Animator:* Hans Neuberger; *Camera:* Kurt Stanke; *Music:* Fritz Steinmann; *Narrator:* Georg Heinrich Schnell; *Consultant:* Steindl; 448 m

Sonnenzauber (Sun Magic)

Ufacolor, 1937; *Animators:* Egon von Tresckow, Bernhard Huth; *Script:* E. Dahle; *Music:* Rudolf Perak; Ufa Werbefilm (Universum-Film A.G.), Berlin; 60 m; Advertising film for client Cinzano

Sonntagsabenteuer (Sunday Adventure) (after 1945: Der treulose Wecker)

Released in 1941; *Director/Animator:* Bernhard Klein; *Original Idea:* Bernhard Klein; *Lyrics:* Wilhelm Stöppler; *Music:* Emil Palm; *Vocals:* Die Metropol-Vokalisten; Distributed by Tobis-Filmkunst G.m.b.H., Berlin; 368 m

Sorgen, die keine sind (Tribulations Which Are Not)

1937; *Director/Supervising Animator:* Wolfgang Kaskeline; Ufa Werbefilm (Universum-Film A.G.), Berlin; Advertising film for apparel store Cords, Berlin

Der Sparstrumpf (The Money Sock)

Color, 1942; Commerz-Film; 56 m; Advertising film for client Raiffeisen-Genossenschaft

Ein Spiel in Farben (A Play in Colors) *also:* Studie Nr. 11 a (Study No. 11 a)

2-color process, 1934; *Animator:* Oskar Fischinger; Aafa-Film A.G., Berlin; 3 min.—53 m

Ein Sprichwort sagt... (A Proverb Says...)

1940; Boehner-Film Fritz Boehner, Dresden; 51 m; Advertising film for client Sparkasse (savings bank); Animated segment

Spuk bei Meister Hase (Spook at Master Rabbit's)

1938; Döring-Film-Werke, Berlin; 97 m; Advertising film for bank giro; Animated segment

Spuk im Walde (Spook in the Forest)

1937; *Animators:* Hans Fischerkoesen, Egon von Tresckow; Ufa Werbefilm (Universum-Film A.G.), Berlin; Advertising film for Stary-Wojak Liquor

Stadtgespräch (The Talk of the Town)

1938; *Animator:* Curt Schumann; Ufa (Universum-Film A.G.), Berlin; Advertising film for client City Breslau

Die Stadtmaus und die Feldmaus (The Town Mouse and the Country Mouse)

1939; *Director/Animator:* Ferdinand Diehl; *Script:* Paul Diehl; *Puppets:* Hermann Diehl; Gebrüder Diehl Filmproduktion, Munich; 12 min.; Live action and puppet animation

Sterntaler (Star Money)

1936–37; *Director/Animator:* Ferdinand Diehl; *Script:* Dr. Paul Diehl; *Puppets:* Hermann Diehl; Gebrüder Diehl Filmproduktion, Munich; Puppet animation; Finished but not released

Die Stichprobe (The Random Test)

1938; *Director/Chief Animator:* Hans Fischerkoesen; Ufa Werbefilm, Berlin; Avertising film for client Jenaer Glas

Stoffmärchen (Fabric Fairy Tale)

1935; *Director/Supervising Animator:* Wolfgang Kaskeline; Ufa Kaskeline (Universum-Film A.G.), Berlin

Der Störenfried (The Troublemaker)

Agfacolor/Gasparcolor, 1940; *Director/Supervising Animator:* Hans Held; *Music:* Leo Leux; *Production Manager:* Ernst Mosich; Bavaria Filmkunst G.m.b.H., Berlin/Munich; 12 min.—342 m

Sträfling Nr. 3 (Convict No. 3)

1934; *Director/Animator:* Ferdinand Diehl; *Script:* Dr. Paul Diehl; *Puppets:* Hermann Diehl; *Camera:* Hans Asen; *Scenario Consultant:* Walter Leckebusch; *Sound:* K. A. Keller; *Music:* Hilmar Georgi; Gebrüder Diehl Filmproduktion, Munich; 19 min.—522 m; Puppet animation

Die Streiche von Fritz und Franz (The Funny Pranks of Fritz and Franz)

1936 (1934?); *Director/Animator:* Paul N. Peroff; Atelier Peroff, Berlin/Kinagfa; 100 m; Released by KALLE on 16mm Ozaphan safety film stock as 5 episode home movie: Part 1: Das verbotene Bad (The Forbidden Bath); Part 2: Eine Apfelgeschichte (An Apple Story); Part 3: Winterfreuden

Hans Held: *Der Störenfried* (1940) (courtesy Erika Held).

(Winter Pleasures); Part 4: Fahrt ins Blaue (Trip into the Blue); Part 5: Das Nachtgespenst (The Night Ghost)

Strich-Punkt-Ballett (Line Dot Ballet)

Made without use of camera, 1943; *Director/Animator:* Herbert Seggelke, Munich

Studie Nr. 13 (Study No. 13)

1933–34; *Animator:* Oskar Fischinger, Berlin; 1 min.

Süsse Geheimnisse (Sweet Secrets)

Color, 1942; *Animators:* Egon von Tresckow, Bernhard Huth; Ufa Werbefilm (Universum-Film A.G.), Berlin; c. 3 min.—101 m; Advertising film for client Opekta

Die süsse Insel (Sweet Island)

1936–37; *Animators:* Heinz Tischmeyer, Ernst Joachim Schienke, Karl Sonntag; *Music:* Richard Ralf; *Narrator:* Kurt Mühlhardt; Atelier Tischmeyer for Stoecker-Film A. G., Berlin; Tobis-Klangfilm; 196 m; Advertising film for client Dr. August Oetker, Bielefeld

Taler, Taler, du musst wandern

1933; *Animator:* Hans Fischerkoesen; Pinschewer- Film A.G.; 77 (74) m; Advertising film for client Sparkasse

Tanz der Farben (Dance of the Colors)

Gasparcolor, 1939; *Director:* Hans Fischinger; *Music:* Petersburger Schlittenfahrt; 153 m

Das tapfere Schneiderlein (The Brave Little Tailor/The Valiant Little Tailor)

1944; *Director/Animator:* Ferdinand Diehl; *Script:* Paul Diehl from a fairy tale by the Brothers Grimm; *Puppets:* Hermann Diehl; Gebrüder Diehl Filmproduktion, Munich; Puppet animation; Finished but not released

Das tapfere Schneiderlein (The Brave Little Tailor/The Valiant Little Tailor)

194?; *Animators:* Schwab and Gerhardt; *Script:* adapted from a fairy tale by the Brothers Grimm

Die Tierwelt lacht (The Animal World Laughs)

Series; 1936; *Director/Animator:* Paul N. Peroff; Released by KALLE on 16mm Ozaphan film stock

Tischlein deck dich (The Wishing-Table)

1936; *Director/Animator:* Ferdinand Diehl; *Script:* Paul Diehl from a fairy tale by the Brothers Grimm; *Puppets:* Hermann Diehl; Gebrüder Diehl Filmproduktion, Munich, for RfdU; 32 min.—898 m; Puppet animation; Gold medal, World Expo 1937, Paris

Tobis Karikatur Nr. 1 (Tobis Caricature No. 1)

Color, 1940; *Animator:* Louis Seel; Tobis Filmkunst G.m.b.H., Berlin; 2 min.—44 m

Tom Puss — Das Geheimnis der Grotte (Tom Puss — The Secret of the Grotto) Episode 1: Der Zauberer; Episode 2: Der Raub im Schloss (Tom poes en het geheim van de grot)

1943; *Director:* Marten Toonder; Based on the first comic strips published in Dutch newspaper De Telegraaf; Geesink-Toonder Productie Teekenfilm/Tonder-Bouman Film Producties, Amsterdam, for Degeto Kulturfilm G.m.b.H.; 16mm — each part c. 36 m

Trari — Trara!

1938; *Director/Supervising Animator:* Wolfgang Kaskeline; Epoche Gasparcolor-Film A.G., Berlin; Advertising film for client Mouson Als Englisch

Der treue Kamerad (The Faithful Mate)

1934–35; Döring-Film-Werke, Berlin; 76 m; Advertising film for client Vivil

Trick-Werbefilm für Kartoffelmehl

Ton-Lichtbild-Reklame A.G. (Tolirag), Berlin; Advertising film for potato flour

Der U-Bahnschreck (The Tube Terror)

1946; *Director/Supervising Animator:* Gerhard Fieber; *Idea:* Kurt Drews; Deutsche Zeichentrick G.m.b.H. for DEFA-Wochenschau Der Augenzeuge (DEFA Newsreel The Eye witness) No. 1/1946 (February 1946); 1 min. — c. 23 m; Made after the war by the remaining personnel of Deutsche Zeichenfilm G.m.b.H.

Der Überfall (The Assault)

1937; *Director:* Piper; Döring-Film-Werke, Berlin; Advertising film for client Bayer (Panflavin mouthwash)

Überfall am Finkenhof

1937; *Director/Supervising Animator:* Hans Fischerkoesen; Ufa Werbefilm (Universum-Film A.G.), Berlin; 166 m; Advertising film for client P 3-Zinnfest-Bad (germless milk cans)

Überwinden von Minensperren (Break Through Mine Obstacles)

Mars-Film G.m.b.H., Berlin; Military training film

Gerhard Fieber: *Der U-Bahnschreck* (DEFA 1945).

Der Umzug (The Removal)

1933; *Producer:* Otto Waechter; Trickfilm-Atelier Waechter, Berlin; Advertising film

Unendlicher Weltenraum (Endless Space)

1936; *Producer/Director:* Dr. Martin Rikli; *Animator:* Curt Schumann; *Music:* Walter Gronostey; Trickatelier Schumann and Hans Neuberger; c. 28½ min.— 317 m; Short film with animated segments

Ungetrübter Genuss (Undiluted Pleasure)

1936; *Director/Supervising Animator:* Wolfgang Kaskeline; Ufa Werbefilm (Universum-Film A.G.), Berlin; Advertising film for client Melitta Coffee Filters

Unser gutes Recht (Our Good Right)

1938; *Animator:* Curt Schumann; Ufa Werbefilm (Universum-Film A.G.), Berlin; Advertising film for client Jenaer Glas

Der unsterbliche Wunsch (The Immortal Wish)

1941; *Director:* Ernst Kochel; Ufa Werbefilm (Universum-Film A.G.), Berlin; Advertising film for client Ellocar (cosmetics)

Unter der Haube (Under the Hood)

Ufacolor, 1938; *Director/Supervising Animator:* Hans Fischerkoesen; Ufa Werbefilm (Universum-Film A.G.), Berlin; 121 m; Advertising film for client Essolub motor oil

Van den Vos Reynaerde (About the Fox Reynard)

Agfacolor, 1942–43; *Director:* Egbert van Putten; *Script:* Henk Plaizier, based on Van den vos Reynaerde by Robert van Genechten, itself based on a medieval poem published in Nieuw-Nederland, a paper edited by the Dutch National Socialist movement; *Supervising Animator:* Hill Beekman; *Animators:* Jan Bouman, André C. J. Holla, Olga Tijssen, Jan van Hille; Netherland Film, The Hague for Departement van Volksvoerlichtung en Kunsten (DVK); 20 min. (only a 12-minute fragment survives today)

Vereint ist mehr (Together Is More)

Color, 1942; *Animator:* Curt Schumann; Ufa Werbefilm (Universum-Film A.G.), Berlin; 100 m; Advertising film for client Vim (cleaning compound)

Ein vergnügter Abend (A Jolly Evening)

Color, 1937; *Animator:* Curt Schumann; *Idea:* Horst Tiller; *Music:* Schütze; Ufa Werbefilm (Universum-Film A.G.), Berlin; 83 m; Advertising film for client Kempinski (Haus Vaterland, Berlin)

Vernunft und Lebensfreude (Reason and Joy of Life)

1938; *Director/Supervising Animator:* Wolfgang Kaskeline; Epoche Gasparcolor-Film A.G., Berlin; Advertising film for client Darboven (Coffee Haag)

Der versunkene Schatz (The Sunken Treasure)

1936; *Director/Animator:* Paul N. Peroff; Atelier Peroff, Berlin/Kinagfa; Released by KALLE on 16mm Ozaphan film stock

Vertrag mit der Hölle (Contract with Hell)

1935; *Director/Supervising Animator:* Hans Fischerkoesen; Ufa Werbefilm (Universum-Film A.G.), Berlin; Advertising film for client Union Briquettes

Verwitterte Melodie (Weather-Beaten Melody) (*working title:* Scherzo)

Agfacolor, 1943; *Director/Supervising Animator:* Hans Fischerkoesen; *Story:* Horst von Möllendorff; *Animators:* Rudolf Bär, Susanne Birkner, Leni Fischer, Egon von Tresckow; *Dutch Animator:* Hill Beekman; *Camera and Editor:* Kurt Schleicher; *Music:* Lothar Brühne; *Lyrics:* Bruno Balz; *Musical Director:* Willi Stech; *Singer:* Hertha Mayen; Fischerkoesen-Studio, Potsdam and The Hague, for Deutsche Wochenschau G.m.b.H.; 10 min.—266 m

Vielseitig und hilfsbereit (Versatile and Helpful)

1941; *Director:* Kurt Stefan; Ufa Werbefilm, Berlin; Advertising film for client Kaiser-Natron

Vier Asse (Four Aces)

Gasparcolor, 1934; *Director/Supervising Animator:* Georg Pál; 4 min.—102 m; Passed German Board of Censors on November 13, 1936; Excerpt from Der Zauberatlas; Advertising film for client Philips-Radio

Die 4 Frauen (The 4 Women)

1936; *Animation:* Kurt Stordel (?); Hansa-Film, Hamburg

Vier in der Waschküche (Four in the Washkitchen)

Color, 1937; *Camera:* Piper; *Music:* Rudolf Perak; Döring-Film-Werke, Berlin; 51 m; Advertising film for client Henkel (Imi washing powder)

Eine Viertelstunde Grossstadtstatistik (A Quarter Hour of City Statistics)

1933; Animation Sequences: Oskar Fischinger; *Assistant:* Peter Sachs; Cabinet Film Toni Attenberger, Munich

Die Vogelhochzeit (The Bird Marriage)

1944; *Director/Animator:* Kurt Stordel; Boehner-Film Fritz Boehner, Dresden; 78 m; Advertising film for client Sparkasse (savings bank), City of Dresden

Vom Bäumlein, das andere Blätter hat gewollt (About the Little Tree That Wanted Other Leaves)

Agfacolor, 1940; *Animation:* Heinz Tischmeyer; Illustration of a poem by Friedrich Rückert (1813); *Music:* Fritz Wenneis; Naturfilm Hubert Schonger, Berlin; 246 m

Vom Deutschtum im Ausland (About German Kind in Foreign Countries)

1935; *Animation:* Curt Schumann, Wolfgang Kaskeline; Ufa Kulturfilm, Berlin; Short with animated segments

Von einem, der auszog, das Gruseln zu lernen (The Story of the Youth Who Went Forth to Learn What Fear Was)

1935; *Director/Animator:* Ferdinand Diehl; *Script:* Paul Diehl from a fairy tale by the Brothers Grimm; *Puppets:* Hermann Diehl; Gebrüder Diehl Filmproduktion, Munich, for RfdU; 37 min.—958 (874) m; Puppet animation; Gold medal, World Expo 1937, Paris

Warmbad überall? (Warm Baths Everywhere?)

Color, 1935; Directors/*Animators:* Egon von Tresckow, Bernhard Huth; 62 m; Advertising film for client Junkers boilers

Das Waschgespenst (The Laundry Ghost)

Color, mid–1930s; 110 m; Advertising film for client Persil washing powder (Henkel)

Was die Eiche rauscht

1935; *Director:* Dr. Werner Kruse; Kruse Film-Produktion, Berlin; Advertising film for client Deutsche Reichsbahn

Was ist die Welt? (What Is the World?)

1933; *Director:* Svend Noldan; *Collaborator:* Walter Dillenberger; *Dubbing:* Dr. Konrad Paul Rohnstein; *Narrator:* Eugen Rex; *Choir:* Deutsche Arbeiter conducted by Georg Oskar Schuhmann; *Sound:* Emil Specht; *Sound Editor:* Erich Palme; Atelier Svend Noldan (Noldan, Brunsch, Noak, Friedrich, Fiedler, Born); 2245 m; Grand Prix, World Expo 1937, Paris; Animated segments

Was Kinder träumen (What Children Dream)

1935; *Director/Animator:* Ladislas Starevich; 350 m; Puppet animation

Was man liebt, das soll man schonen (What One Loves He Should Protect)

c. 1942; *Director:* Friedrich Wollangk; Boehner-Film Fritz Boehner, Dresden; 60 m; Advertising film for client Esders (department store), Dresden; Animated segment

Was Männer lieben (What Men Love)

1935; *Producer:* Otto Waechter; Trickfilm-Atelier Waechter, Berlin; Advertising film for client Carl Weber (stoves and ovens)

Was sich alle wünschen (What Everybody Wishes)

1935–36; Boehner-Film Fritz Boehner, Dresden; 75 m; Advertising film for client Volksfürsorge (insurance)

Was sich jeder merken muss (What Everybody Should Remember)

1942; *Director:* Gerd (Gerhard) Krüger; Heinefilm; Advertising film for gold and silver

Ufa Werbefilm (c. 1941): Ultraphan cel.

Der Weg ins Leben (Way into Life)

1938; *Director:* Hans Fischerkoesen; Ufa Werbefilm (Universum-Film A.G.), Berlin; Advertising film for client Typewriter Conti

Der Wegweiser (The Signpost)

1934; *Director/Supervising Animator:* Hans Fischerkoesen; Ufa Werbefilm (Universum-Film A.G.), Berlin; Advertising film for client C & A

Der Weihnachtsmann kommt (Santa Claus Comes)

1933; Gemeinnütziger Kulturfilm-Vertrieb (KFV); 16mm home movie

Weihnachtstraum (Vánocní sen) (The Christmas Dream)

1944 and 1946; *Directors:* Borivoj Zeman, Karel Zeman; *Animator:* Karel Zeman; *Camera:* P. Hrdlicka; *Music:* J. Sust; Puppet Studio B.M.S. Zlín; DESCHEG (Deutsche Schmalfilmvertriebs G.m.b.H.)/Degeto-Kulturfilm G.m.b.H., Berlin; c. 11 min.—301 m; Printed on 35mm film stock; Passed the Board of Censors on December 22, 1944, to be released theatrically

Weiss in Blau 1—3 Nivea

Gasparcolor, c. 1935–36; Ton-Lichtbild-Reklame A.G. (Tolirag), Berlin; Silhouette animation; Advertising films for client Nivea (lotion and tooth paste)

Wenn's brennt (In Case of Fire)

Color, c. 1938; *Director:* Walter Born; *Animator:* Stephanie Steuer; Atelier Walter Born, Berlin; 61 m; Advertising film for Minimax fire extinguisher

Wer will fleissige Handwerker sehen (Who Wants to See Busy Craftsmen)

1939; *Director/Animator:* Ferdinand Diehl; *Script:* Paul Diehl; *Puppets:* Elke Hecht, Hermann Diehl; Gebrüder Diehl Filmproduktion, Munich; Live action and puppet animation

Westfälische Landeszeitung

1938; *Directors:* Kurt Niele, Uwe Behrens; Gasparcolor Werbefilm G.m.b.H.; Advertising film for client Westfälische Landeszeitung (newspaper)

Der Wettlauf zwischen dem Hasen und dem Igel (The Race Between the Hare and the Hedgehog)

1938–39; *Director/Animator:* Ferdinand Diehl; *Script:* Paul Diehl; Adapted from a fairy tale by the Brothers Grimm; *Puppets:* Hermann Diehl; Gebrüder Diehl Filmproduktion, Munich, for RfdU; 12 min.—337 m (35mm), 127 m (16mm)

Die Wichtelmänner (The Elves)

1943–44; *Director/Animator:* Ferdinand Diehl; *Script:* Paul Diehl; *Puppets:* Hermann Diehl; Gebrüder Diehl Filmproduktion, Munich; Never finished; negative destroyed in air raid

Ein wichtiges Rätsel (An Important Riddle)

1935; *Director:* Friedrich Wollangk; Boehner-Film Fritz Boehner, Dresden; 85 m; Advertising film for client Versicherungsanstalt Ladol (insurance company)

Wie sag' ich's dem Berliner? (How Will I tell the Berlin People?)

1938; *Director/Chief Animator:* Wolfgang Kaskeline; Epoche Gasparcolor-Film A.G.; Advertising film for client Schuhhof (shoes)

Die Wiesenzwerge (The Grassland Dwarves)

Gasparcolor, 1940–41; *Director:* Gerhard Krüger; Based on a picture book by Ernst Kreidolf (published in 1902); *Music:* Richard Ralf; Naturfilm Hubert Schonger, Berlin; Distributed by Rolandfilm, Dusseldorf and Frankfurt am Main; 434 m; Passed the Board of Censors on February 10, 1941

Wilke-Hüte (Wilke Hats)

Gasparcolor, 1937; Gasparcolor Werbefilme G.m.b.H., Berlin; Advertising film for client Wilke Hats

Wintermärchen (Winter Fairy Tale)

1938; *Director/Supervising Animator:* Dr. Werner Kruse; Ufa Werbefilm (Universum-Film A.G.), Berlin; Advertising film for client Troll lignite briquettes

Wir rufen Dich! (We Call You!)

1936; *Director:* Richard Fischer; Reichspropagandaleitung der NSDAP

Die Wiesenzwerge (1941): Advertisement.

Wirtschaftseigenes Kraftfutter durch Silage (Concentrated Feed)

1936; *Animator:* Svend Noldan; I.G. Farbenindustrie A.G.; Industrial film with animated segments

Wohnung zu vermieten (Apartment for Rent)

1933; *Director/Supervising Animator:* Hans Fischerkoesen; Ufa Werbefilm (Universum-Film A.G.), Berlin; Advertising film for client Perwachs Floor Polish

Der Wolf und die sieben Geisslein (The Wolf and the Seven Little Goats/The Wolf and the Seven Little Kids)

1939; *Director/Animator:* Ferdinand Diehl; *Script:* Paul Diehl; *Puppets:* Hermann Diehl; *Camera:* Hans Schmid; Gebrüder Diehl Filmproduktion, Munich; 12 min.; Puppet animation

Der Wolf und die sieben jungen Geisslein (The Wolf and the Seven Little Goats/The Wolf and the Seven Little Kids)

1939; *Directors:* Kurt Niele, Hans Strohbach; *Music:* Fritz Wenneis; Naturfilm Hubert Schonger, Berlin; 309 m

Wort und Ton einst und jetzt (Word and Sound Then and Now)

1938; *Director:* Walter Born; Atelier Walter Born, Berlin; Advertising film for client Philips Weltempfänger (radio)

Wupp als Hochtourist (Wupp as Tourist in the Mountains)

1933; *Director/Animator:* Ferdinand Diehl; *Puppets:* Hermann Diehl; *Camera:* Hans Asen; Gebrüder Diehl Filmproduktion, Munich for I.G. Farbenindustrie A.G.; Puppet animation

Wupp filmt in Afrika (Wupp Films in Africa)

1933; *Director/Animator:* Ferdinand Diehl; *Script:* Paul Diehl; *Puppets:* Hermann Diehl; *Camera:* Hans Asen; Gebrüder Diehl Filmproduktion, Munich; 20 min.; Puppet animation

Zauber der Schönheit (Magic of Beauty)

1935; *Director/Supervising Animator:* Wolfgang Kaskeline; Ufa Kaskeline (Universum-Film A.G.), Berlin; Advertising film for client 4711

Zauberei und Wirklichkeit (Magic and Reality)

Gasparcolor, 1936; *Director:* Kurt Niele; *Animator:* Walter Born; *Production Manager:* Kurt Wolfes; Gasparcolor Werbefilm G.m.b.H., Berlin; 547 m

Der Zauberlehrling (The Sorcerer's Apprentice)

1943; *Director:* Dillenz; *Animators:* Louis Seel and others; *Producer:* Josef Pfister; AFIT, Prague

Der Zauberschrank (The Magic Wardrobe)

1941; *Director:* Gerhard Krüger; Heinefilm, Berlin; 46 m; Advertising film for women's clothing

Zum Neuen Jahr (To the New Year)

1941; *Director:* Gerd (Gerhard) Krüger; Heinefilm; Advertising film for client Herrmann (furniture)

Zu Wasser geworden (Becoming Water)

Color, 1942; Tiller-Film; 47 m; Puppet animation; Advertising film for client Sparkasse (savings bank)

Zwei Farben (Two Colors)

Color, 1933–34; *Director:* Wolfgang Kaskeline; *Assistant:* Gerhard Fieber; *Music:* "Feuerzauber" from Richard Wagner's The Ride of the Valkyries; Ufa Kaskeline (Universum-Film A.G.), Berlin; 70 m; Advertising film for client Muratti cigarettes

Zwei verregnete Jünglinge (Two Rain-Swept Lads)

1934; *Director/Animator:* Ferdinand Diehl; *Script:* Paul Diehl; *Puppets:* Hermann Diehl; Gebrüder Diehl Filmproduktion, Munich; 100 m; Puppet animation

Zwergenland in Not (The Country of the Dwarves in Need)

c. 1939; *Director/Supervising Animator:* Dr. Werner Kruse; Ufa Werbefilm (Universum-Film A.G.), Berlin; 144 m; Advertising film for client Kali fertilizer

Chapter Notes

Preface

1. Spitzy was repeatedly interviewed by Guido Knopp and editorial staff for ZDF documentaries (Zweites Deutsches Fernsehen, Mainz).

2. Hannah Arendt, *Eichmann in Jerusalem: A Report of the Banality of Evil* [1963]. Rev. ed. New York: Viking, 1968.

Chapter 2

1. In 1917 Pinschewer produced an animated anti–British propaganda film, *John Bull*, to promote the war effort and drum up the sales of war bonds.

2. William Moritz, *Optical Poetry: The Life and Work of Oskar Fischinger*. Bloomington and Indianapolis: Indiana University Press, 2004, p. 53.

3. "Bela and Imre Gaspar, Hungarian brothers, had invented a system which would allow three-color separation (yellow, cyan, magenta) images to be shot on three successive frames of a single black-and-white film-strip, then reconstituted on to a full-spectrum color release print which was actually coated on both sides with three separate emulsions, one for each of the component colors. Oskar [Fischinger] helped them by engineering the camera mechanism to take the three successive frames while the filters changed. Although the release prints projected a full spectrum of vivid true colors, the exposure time necessary, almost a half-minute for each color filter, precluded the use of GasparColor for live-action filming of fast moving objects, but worked well with animation." Moritz, *Optical Poetry*, p. 48.

4. Entry in 1933 *Universal Filmlexikon*.

5. After World War II, the mother-and-daughter team Otto would make *Pimpinella* (1948), *Die wandelnde Glocke* (1949–50), *Das Wunderfenster* (1951–52) and *Der kleine Däumling* (1952) for producer Hubert Schonger, who had moved his operation from Berlin to Bavaria. Both Gerda and Hedwig made the puppets, with Hedwig basically left to do the hands-on animation.

6. H.O. Schulze, interviewed by RG in 1984. Schulze might be mistaken about the production setup, however, as the cigarette short was made not by Pál and Wittke because they had split already, but under Pál's new studio label commissioned by Levante Film, a Cologne-based company. The groundbreaking short was thought lost but in spring 2011 resurfaced in the film vaults of Deutsche Kinemathek, alas, as totally washed-out nitrate print.

7. *Film-Kurier*, February 18, 1930.

8. *Kinematograph*, February 28, 1932.

Chapter 4

1. What the Disney brothers did, however, was to collect German art sources, illustrations as well as movies. And Heinz Kaskeline, the son of Wolfgang Kaskeline, claimed that Disney on one occasion tried to lure his father to Hollywood.

2. All correspondence from the files of Bundesarchiv. Brückner was Hitler's personal adjutant.

3. *Film-Kurier*, December 27, 1937.

4. When J.P. Storm learned about him via a TV documentary which contained an interview, Storm phoned Hitler's personal projectionist. The projectionist told him how happy the Führer was when he saw his favorite film, *Snow White*, and how much he would laugh about the antics of the dwarfs.
5. *Lichtbildbühne*, February 16, 1938.
6. *Lichtbildbühne*, August 26, 1938.
7. Ibid.
8. Anny Ondra was Schmeling's wife.
9. EG 6569 Deutscher Electrola/Columbia Hauptkatalog 1939/40.
10. *Film-Kurier*, January 28, 1939.
11. *Film-Kurier* refers to Chaplin's film *The Great Dictator*.
12. *Film-Kurier*, January 30, 1939.
13. *Film-Kurier*, December 16, 1941.

Chapter 5

1. January 1, 1937.

Chapter 6

1. Estate of Gerhard Fieber (in the collection of J.P. Storm).
2. The Reich Institute for Film and Image in Education and Science (RWU) in 1940 succeeded the Reichsstelle für den Unterricht (RFU), which was founded by Bernhard Rust, the Reich Minister for Education.
3. In *Film und Bild* 4/5, May 1, 1942, Paul Diehl published an article about the art of silhouette films: "Vom Wesen des Scherenschnitt-Films."
4. Franz Graf Pocci (1807–1876) wrote more than 40 marionette plays and was the creator of Kasperl Larifari, after World War II a puppet character animated by the Diehls. He was joined in puppetry by Josef Leonhard Schmid (1822–1912).
5. Rudolf Emil Pfenninger (1899–1976), who introduced *Tönende Handschrift*, was a forerunner of Norman McLaren.
6. Der Film, January 18, 1941: Gebr. Diehls eigenwillige Kunstschöpfung: Filmatelier für ... Puppen. Eine wohlorganisierte Märchenwelt, von der das Publikum wenig kennt.
7. "Märchenfilme bei den Soldaten," *Film und Bild*. Zeitschrift der Reichsanstalt für Film und Bild in Wissenschaft und Unterricht, 8. Jahrgang, Issue 4/5, 1 May 1942.
8. July 4, 1941, Deutscher Kulturdienst: "Knüppel aus dem Sack." School essay, recorded by Ferdinand Josef Holzer.
9. Hans Schumacher, "Starewitch in Berlin. Betrachtungen zu seiner Arbeit und zum absoluten Film," *Film-Kurier*, April 27, 1937.
10. Schumacher, "Starewitch in der Lessing-Hochschule," *Film-Kurier*, May 5, 1937.
11. Born in Moscow.
12. September 1938: Der deutsche Film "Poet am Tricktisch" Besuch bei Starewitsch.

Chapter 7

1. Gerhard Fieber interviewed by Gerd Gockell, 1997.
2. All following documents from Berlin Document Center file "Wolfgang Kaskeline."
3. Iron Cross 2nd Class.

Chapter 9

1. This brings to mind a recent remark by Daniel Kothenschulte, a film journalist working for *Frankfurter Rundschau*, who at a conference of Deutsche Kinemathek in Berlin claimed that dictators (with the exception of Mao Tse-Tung) loved animation because it was the utmost controlled movement: frame by frame.
2. *Film-Kurier*, July 24, 1940.
3. Conducted by J.P. Storm.
4. Maybe there is some kind of relationship between Heinz Benda and Berlin-born Dr. Ernst Benda who became minister of the interior in postwar Germany.

5. Held finally made a *Caliph Stork* cartoon in 1949 when he joined Hans Georg Dammann (Burg-Film) in Hamburg (*Der Spiegel* 1/1949).

6. September 19, 1941.

Chapter 10

1. *Film-Kurier*, November 27, 1935.
2. *Der Film*, December 10, 1938.
3. *Völkischer Beobachter*, Issue Munich, April 30, 1939.
4. "Konkurrenz für Micky Maus? Gespräch mit Kurt Stordel," 12 Uhr Blatt, December 22, 1938.
5. 20 000 Zeichnungen — ein Film. Interessante Versuche mit bunten deutschen Märchentrickfilmen. Hamburger Fremdenblatt, December 24, 1938.
6. Kameradschaft der deutschen Künstler.

Chapter 11

1. Frank Maraun *Der deutsche Film*, Special Issue 1940/41.
2. Estate of Stephanie Steuer (in the collection of J. P. Storm).
3. *How a Mosquito Operates* (1912) was done by McCay after introducing *Little Nemo* to animation in 1911.
4. *Film-Kurier*, October 1, 1940.

Chapter 12

1. According to Berlin Document Center file.
2. This and the following documents are from the files of Bundesarchiv and Berlin Document Center.
3. The Germans referred to this technique as *Kinoxen*.
4. Expensive anti–British propaganda film starring Emil Jannings.
5. This and all following Möllendorff quotes are from an interview conducted by J. P. Storm on July 30, 1988.
6. Cary Nathanson, *Fear of Flying: Education to Manhood in Nazi Film Comedies: Glückskinder and Quax, der Bruchpilot.* In: Robert C. Reimer, ed., *Cultural History Through a National Socialist Lens,* Rochester and Woodbridge, Suffolk: Camden House, 2000, p. 95.
7. Courtesy Gerhard Fieber.
8. According to our French correspondent, Sébastien Roffat, during occupation Feignoux volunteered to hide reels of film at the French Cinémathèque and even prepared a French dubbing of Disney's *Pinocchio*. See: *La Cinématographie française*, December 29, 1945.
9. One such paper was translated by Kruse himself: "Mickey-Maus zeigt..." von Walt Disney.
10. Berlin Document Center, file "Ingeburg Ammon."
11. *Sonntagsabenteuer*.
12. Addressed to a Mr. Rosen. (*The Stars Shine* was a popular song composed by Leo Leux.)

Chapter 13

1. Joseph Goebbels, *Tagebücher*, October 11, 1941.
2. "Gang durch ein Zeichenfilm-Atelier," *Film-Kurier*, January 7, 1944.
3. William Moritz, "Resistance and Subversion in Animated Films of the Nazi Era: The Case of Hans Fischerkoesen," *Animation Journal*, Fall 1992.
4. Interviewed by J. P. Storm on July 30, 1988.
5. William Moritz, ibid.
6. Radio broadcast, January 1944.
7. William Moritz, ibid.
8. *Film-Kurier* 7, 1944.

Chapter 14

1. Möllendorff interviewed by J. P. Storm on July 30, 1988.

Chapter 15

1. Estate of Horst von Möllendorff (in the collection of J.P. Storm).
2. Dr. Felix von Eckardt, who occasionally wrote screenplays, after the war, became the spokesman of the Adenauer government in West Germany.
3. According to French animation historian Sébastien Roffat, *Der Notenhändler* (original title: *Le Marchand de Notes*) made by Paul Grimault and Les Gemeaux in 1942 was not released for some reason at that time.

Chapter 16

1. Letter dated July 23, 1942.
2. In March 2009 conducted by RG.
3. Estate of Horst von Möllendorff (in the collection of J.P. Storm).

Chapter 17

1. Max Planck, "Svend Noldans 'Was ist die Welt?'" *Der Film heute und morgen*, Hamburg. Folge 31. December 17, 1939.
2. *Film-Kurier*, August 24, 1937.
3. Noldan.

Chapter 18

1. Major Steglich, "Der militärische Lehrfilm," *Film-Kurier*, September 5, 1944.

Bibliography

Print Material

Agde, Günther. *Flimmernde Versprechen. Geschichte des deutschen Werbefilms im Kino seit 1897.* Berlin: Verlag Das Neue Berlin, 1998.

Bock, Hans-Michael, ed. *CineGraph: Lexikon zum deutschsprachigen Film.* Munich: edition text + kritik, 1984.

Brandt, Hans-Jürgen. *Untersuchungen zum Dokumentarfilm des Dritten Reiches am Beispiel von drei Regisseuren: Hippler, Noldan und Junghans.* Dissertation. Frankfurt am Main: Johann Wolfgang von Goethe Universität, 1985.

Bundesarchiv/Filmarchiv. *Alles Trick. Deutscher Animationsfilm bis 1945.* Retrospektive des Internationalen Festivals für Dokumentar- und Animationsfilm. Leipzig/Berlin, 1998.

Bundesarchiv/Filmarchiv. *Bestandsnachweis: Deutsche Trickfilme (1909–1945).* Compiled by Manfred Lichtenstein. Edited by Doris Hackbarth. Berlin, 1998.

Deutscher Trickfilmverband. *Deutsches Trickfilmkaleidoskop.* Edited by Peter A. Hagemann and Herbert K. Schulz. Berlin: Deutsche Kinemathek, 1979.

Deutsches Filmmuseum. *Mecki, Märchen und Schnurren. Die Filme der Gebrüder Diehl.* Frankfurt am Main: Deutsches Filmmuseum, 1994.

Deutsches Filmmuseum. *Optische Poesie: Oskar Fischinger, Leben und Werk.* Frankfurt am Main: Deutsches Filmmuseum, 1993.

Dewald, Christian, Sabine Groschup, Mara Mattuschka, and Thomas Renoldner, eds. *Die Kunst des Einzelbilds: Animation in Österreich—1832 bis heute.* ASIFA Austria. Vienna: Verlag Filmarchiv Austria, 2010.

Diehl, Paul. *Der Puppenfilm als Kunstwerk.* In: Film und Bild in Wissenschaft, Erziehung und Volksbildung. No. 7, Berlin 1940, p. 118.

_____. *Werdegang der Firma Diehl-Film GmbH.* Unpublished typescript. Gräfelfing not dated (presumably after 1970).

Dütsch, Werner, ed. *Lotte Reiniger: Eine Dokumentation.* Berlin: Deutsche Kinemathek, 1969.

Filmblatt. Edited by CineGraph Babelsberg, Berlin-Brandenburgisches Centrum für Filmforschung e.V., 1996–.

Giesen, Rolf. *Drei Prinzessinnen aus Burbank: Europäische Märchen-Vorlagen in Disney-Filmen.* In Petra Josting and Klaus Maiwald, eds., *Verfilmte Kinderliteratur.* kjl&m 10.extra. Munich: Kopaed, 2010.

_____. *Lexikon des Trick- und Animationsfilms.* Berlin: Schwarzkopf & Schwarzkopf, 2003.

_____. *Nazi Propaganda Films: A History and Filmography.* Jefferson, NC: McFarland, 2003.

_____. *Special Effects Artists: A Worldwide Biographical Dictionary of the Pre-Digital Era with a Filmography.* Jefferson, NC: McFarland, 2008.

Girveau, Bruno, and Roger Diederen, eds. *Walt Disneys wunderbare Welt und ihre Wurzeln in der europäischen Kunst. [Il était une tois—Walt Disney. Aux sources de l'art des Studios Disney]. Munich: Hirmer Verlag, 2009.*

Gockell, Gerd, *Zwischen Abstraktion und Propaganda: Deutscher Animationsfilm vor 1945.* In Ralf Schenk and Sabine Scholz, eds., *Die Trick-Fabrik. DEFA-Animationsfilme 1955–1990. DIAF Deutsches Institut für Animationsfilm Dresden.* Berlin: Bertz, 2003.

Goergen, Jeanpaul: *Bibliografie zum deutschen Animationsfilm.* Edited in cooperation with DEFA-Stiftung Berlin. Filmblatt-Schriften: Beiträge zur Filmgeschichte, vol. I. Berlin: CineGraph Babelsberg, Berlin-Brandenburgisches Centrum für Filmforschung e.V., 2002.

Held, Erika, and Alfred Schubert. *Hans Held-Haid. Lebensmosaik eines Genies.* Munich: Verlag Wort-Bild-Technik, 2009.

Holtz, Reinhold Johann. *Die Phänomenologie und Psychologie des Trickfilms: Analytische Untersuchungen über die phänomenologischen, psychologischen und künstlerischen Strukturen der Trickfilmgruppe.* Dissertation. Hamburg: Philosophische Fakultät der Universität Hamburg, 1940.

Laqua, Carsten. *Wie Micky unter die Nazis fiel: Walt Disney und Deutschland.* Reinbek: Rowohlt, 1992.

Moritz, William. *Optical Poetry: The Life and Work of Oskar Fischinger.* Bloomington: Indiana University Press, 2004.

Moritz, William. "Resistance and Subversion in Animated Films of the Nazi Era: The Case of Hans Fischerkoesen," *Animation Journal 1,* Fall 1992.

Opfermann, H.C., and Georg Kramer. *Die neue Trickfilm-Schule: Ein Lehr- und Nachschlagebuch für Filmamateure, Film- und Fernsehfachleute und den filmtechnischen Nachwuchs.* Seebruck/Chiemsee: Heering Verlag, 1963.

Lotte Reiniger: Silhouettenfilm und Schattentheater. 2.6.-17.81979. Exhibition Puppentheatermuseum im Münchner Stadtmuseum. Catalogue by Margit Downar. Munich: Lipp, 1979.

Lotte Reiniger: Schattentheater—Schattenpuppen—Schattenfilm. Tübingen: Texte Verlag, 1981.

Optische Poesie: Oskar Fischinger. Leben und Werk. Exhibition 16.12.1993–3.4.1994. Edited by Herbert Gehr. Frankfurt am Main: Deutsches Filmmuseum, 1993.

Peters, Mette, and Egbert Barten. *Meestal in't verborgene. Animatiefilm in Nederland 1940–1945.* Nederlands Instituut voor Animatiefilm, 2000.

Roffat, Sébastien. *Animation et propaganda des dessins animés pendant la Seconde Guerre mondiale.* Paris: L'Harmattan, 2005.

Schoemann, Annika. *Der Deutsche Animationsfilm. Von den Anfängen bis zur Gegenwart 1909–2001.* Sankt Augustin: Gardez! Verlag, 2003.

Schummer, Rudolf J. *Bewegte Bilder: Deutsche Trickfilme der zwanziger Jahre. Filme im Schatten. Der Trickfilm im Dritten Reich.* Beiheft zu den Filmen 32 2856 + 32 2857. Munich: Institut für Bild und Film in Wissenschaft und Unterricht, 1977.

Sigl, Klaus, ed. *Von "A" bis "Zip/Zip": Trickfilme aus München 1918–1987.* Munich: Münchner Stadtbibliothek and Kulturreferat der Landeshauptstadt München, 1987.

Storm, J.P., and M. Dressler. *Im Reiche der Micky Maus. Walt Disney in Deutschland 1927–1945.* Exhibition at Filmmuseum Potsdam. Berlin: Hentschel Verlag GmbH, 1991.

TV and DVD

Dresler, Wolfgang. *Trickfilm-Fieber.* Cologne: Tacker Film.

Gockell, Gerd. *Muratti & Sarotti. Geschichte des deutschen Trickfilms 1920–1960.* Berlin: absolut Medien, *1999.*

Stoll, Ulrich. *Hitlers Traum von Micky Maus.* Cologne: De Campo Film for WDR and ARTE. 60 min. April 18, 1999.

Wegenast, Ulrich, curator. *Animation in der Nazizeit. Die Geschichte des deutschen Animationsfilms—DVD II.* Berlin: absolut-Medien, 2012.

Index